THE ECONOMIC CAUSES
OF IMPERIALISM

MAJOR ISSUES IN HISTORY

Editor
C. WARREN HOLLISTER
University of California, Santa Barbara

THE ECONOMIC CAUSES
OF IMPERIALISM

EDITED BY

Martin Wolfe

University of Pennsylvania

John Wiley & Sons, Inc.

New York • London • Sydney • Toronto

Library of Congress Catalogue Card Number: 77-38965

ISBN 0-471-95948-0 (cloth)
ISBN 0-471-95951-0 (paper)

Printed in the United States of America.

10 9 8 7 6 5 4 3 2 1

Library of Congress Cataloging in Publication Data

Wolfe, Martin, comp.
    The economic causes of imperialism.

    (Major issues in history)
    Bibliography: p.
    1. Economic history—Addresses, essays, lectures.
2. Imperialism—Addresses, essays, lectures.
I. Title.
HC51.W59   320.5   77-38965
ISBN 0-471-95948-0 (cloth)
ISBN 0-471-95951-0 (pbk.)

For Carolyn

SERIES PREFACE

The reading program in a history survey course traditionally has consisted of a large two-volume textbook and, perhaps, a book of readings. This simple reading program requires few decisions and little imagination on the instructor's part, and tends to encourage in the student the virtue of careful memorization. Such programs are by no means things of the past, but they certainly do not represent the wave of the future.

The reading program in survey courses at many colleges and universities today is far more complex. At the risk of oversimplification, and allowing for many exceptions and overlaps, it can be divided into four categories: (1) textbook, (2) original source readings, (3) specialized historical essays and interpretive studies, and (4) historical problems.

After obtaining an overview of the course subject matter (textbook), sampling the original sources, and being exposed to selective examples of excellent modern historical writing (historical essays), the student can turn to the crucial task of weighing various possible interpretations of major historical issues. It is at this point that memory gives way to creative critical thought. The "problems approach," in other words, is the intellectual climax of a thoughtfully conceived reading program and is, indeed, the most characteristic of all approaches to historical pedagogy among the newer generation of college and university teachers.

The historical problems books currently available are many and varied. Why add to this information explosion? Because the Wiley Major Issues Series constitutes an endeavor to produce something new that will respond to pedagogical needs thus far unmet. First, it is a series of individual volumes—one per problem. Many good teachers would much prefer to select their own historical issues rather than be tied to an inflexible sequence of issues imposed by a publisher and bound together between two covers. Second, the Wiley Major Issues Series is based on the idea of approaching the significant problems of history through a deft interweaving of primary sources and secondary analysis, fused together by the skill of a scholar-editor. It is felt that the essence of a historical issue cannot be satisfactorily probed either by placing a body of undigested source materials into the hands of inexperienced students or by limiting these students to the controversial literature of modern scholars who debate the meaning of sources the student never sees. This series approaches historical problems by exposing students to both the finest historical thinking on the issue and some of the evidence on which this thinking is based. This synthetic approach should prove far more fruitful than either the raw-source approach or the exclusively second-hand approach, for it combines the advantages— and avoids the serious disadvantage—of both.

Finally, the editors of the individual volumes in the Major Issues Series have been chosen from among the ablest scholars in their fields. Rather than faceless referees, they are historians who know their issues from the inside and, in most instances, have themselves contributed significantly to the relevant scholarly literature. It has been the editorial policy of this series to permit the editor-scholars of the individual volumes the widest possible latitude both in formulating their topics and in organizing their materials. Their scholarly competence has been unquestioningly respected; they have been encouraged to approach the problems as they see fit. The titles and themes of the series volumes have been suggested in nearly every case by the scholar-editors themselves. The criteria have been (1) that the issue be of relevance to undergraduate lecture courses in history, and (2) that it be an issue which the scholar-editor knows thoroughly and in which he has done creative work. And, in general, the second criterion has been given precedence over the first. In short, the question "What are the significant historical issues today?" has been answered not by general editors or sales departments but by the scholar-teachers who are responsible for these volumes.

University of California,   *C. Warren Hollister*
Santa Barbara

CONTENTS

INTRODUCTION

Is it mainly greed that drives men to build empires? This is a burning issue, and not only for scholars. The question was a polarizer of opinion even before the First World War; it provided a framework for countless debates in the League of Nations; during the 1950s it became an important weapon in the Cold War; and it remains today a reason for new (weak) countries to continue hating old (strong) countries. Several of the scholars represented by essays in the following readings argue that economic affairs are not the only important or even the primary motivation for imperialism. But the conviction remains among the rest of us that somehow man's implacable search for gain is at the bottom of it. Indeed, this is one reason the odor of imperialism is so rank. If the causes of imperialism are shameful, could the consequences be anything but bad? The concept of the economic causes of imperialism calls up images of cruel exploitation of one's fellow man, spoliation of natural resources, dollar diplomacy, and stupid rationalizations of racism—indecent features of the bad old days we are trying to leave behind us.

There has been published almost as much theorizing on the economic causes of imperialism as description of specific economic activities in empire-building. Today's student, faced by a need to know where he stands on neocolonialism at the same time that he becomes aware of a wilderness of tracts on imperialism's past and present, must become confused if he plunges in without a guide. This book aims to provide such a guide, by presenting and commenting on key statements by highly regarded analysts of imperialism.

Of course it is impossible for any one book to provide clarifi-

1

cation of all economic aspects of imperialism, let alone both economic and noneconomic aspects of imperialism. No work of modest dimensions can establish whether, even in individual cases of imperialism, we can actually measure whether economic affairs were more crucial than political, religious, diplomatic, or cultural factors. To solve this problem would be appallingly difficult; many historians would argue it is impossible. And little on the economic *effects* of imperialism can be attempted here. Demonstrating the economic effects of imperialism is as maddeningly complex a problem as that of weighing economic causes. This introduction is addressed, then, to a simpler task, but one quite necessary for clear thinking about imperialism. Its aim is to examine three overlapping but separable ways of looking at imperialism intermingled in the phrase "the economic causes of imperialism": (1) the stages thesis, which pivots on explaining the peculiar conjunction of factors at the time of the imperialist explosion of 1870–1900; (2) the neo-Leninist approach, which is directed at neocolonialism, that is, the persistence of imperialism since World War II, even in the absence of political subordination; and (3) the materialist interpretation, which sees all modern imperialism as primarily the result of national competition for the world's wealth or of individual drives for high profits and for loot.

Defining one's terms is an absolute requirement for any discussion of imperialism that attempts to generate light rather than heat. Outside the Communist world, "economic causes" and "imperialism" are each the subject of bitter debate. It is my belief that the only useful way to regard a given situation as imperialistic is to perceive in it an ongoing relation between two nations or nationalities in which the sovereignty of one is impaired in important ways by the other. (Nationalities—that is, peoples set apart by common languages or historical traditions—must be included as well as nations, since so much of what we regard as imperialism affects peoples not yet formally organized into nations or not as yet possessing a highly developed national consciousness.) By the impairment of sovereignty I mean evidence in the affairs of one people of certain marks of subordination, proofs that this people is not in control of its own activities. For example, if the people in country X are required to learn the language of country Y; and if a citizen of Y who resides in X commits a crime there but cannot be tried according to X's laws; and if the children in X are ordered to submit to being vaccinated for smallpox by Y's medical teams—even though this offends their parents' religious views; and if X is forced to buy aspirin from Y at two dollars the gross when the same goods are available from Z for one dollar, then we are entitled to assume an imperialistic relationship exists between X and Y. This definition allows us to see that imperialistic relationships can exist without a formal "occupation" or "protectorate." It also allows us to avoid the trap of thinking that any connections between a rich, powerful nation and a poor, weak one must necessarily be imperialistic.

"Imperialism" is a more complex term than "an imperialistic relationship." It can mean (again, outside the Communist world) either advocating imperialistic conquest ("ism" in the sense of ideology) or the existence of a set of widespread and well-established imperialistic relationships (as in the phrase "the orbit of French imperialism"). In this introduction "imperialism" will be limited to this second meaning.

The most thorny problem of definition involves that horribly misleading phrase, "economic imperialism." "Economic imperialism" can have four different meanings, and has become such a catch-all that we sometimes see it used two ways in the same paragraph. Does it mean (1) the push for imperialism that comes primarily from economic motives, (2) the economic activities by which imperialists clamp down their dominion over a territory, (3) the economic aspects of a total imperialistic relationship, (4) a partial imperialistic relationship which is limited to economic factors in the sense that there is no impairment of sovereignty in political, cultural, or other matters? This last situation is also labeled, by some writers, "informal empire," another imprecise and misleading term that contains a blatant contradiction. "Informal empire" makes about the same sort of sense as "informal pregnancy"; either there is impairment of a people's sovereignty or there is not.

"Colonialism" is another definitional headache. Most often it is used interchangeably with "imperialism" in the sense in which I define the term; it should be noted, however, that Marxists often use "colonialism" to designate what I call "imperialism"; "imperialism," for them, has a larger meaning which includes both their "colonialism" *and virtually all* relationships between strong capitalist and weak noncapitalist nations. There is also another, older use for "colonialism," that is, the transfer of nationals from the traditional area of a people into another area, especially into a vacant or thinly populated area. This still has some uses, for example in the distinction made by some writers when they call recent United States support of Israel a case of "imperialism," and the planting by Israel of additional agricultural communities on its borders as a case of "colonialism" or even "exclusionist colonialism."

W. K. Hancock, one of our foremost experts on the British Empire, once wearily concluded that "Imperialism is no word for scholars." This is unpardonable pessimism. It is difficult to see for whom the word imperialism exists, if not for scholars. Certainly the word is too ingrained in our language to be wiped out. On the other hand, there are two phrases I would gladly consign to the scholar's junk-heap: "informal empire" and "economic imperialism." To tolerate these is to open the door to other misbegotten concepts such as "financial imperialism," "cultural imperialism," and even "Coca-cola imperialism." How absurd this can become is shown by a recent work on the military-industrial complex in the United States which refers to the relations between our military-industrial élites and the rest of us as "inner imperialism."

• • •

It may seem strange that the term "economic causes" also is a matter of dispute. In simple terms, "economic causes" means those factors that are *not* political, cultural, and so on; it also is used at times as the equivalent of "materialistic causes," in the sense of the opposite of altruistic causes. A glance at the historiography of imperialism, however, will show that we cannot leave the matter there. For many of us in Western lands and in the Third World, as well as for most Communists, the phrase "economic causes of imperialism" refers to the nature of the capitalist system. It is part of the belief that "new imperialism" (the expansionist explosion of the era 1870–1900) was caused by structural changes in capitalism. This is the chief significance of the title of Lenin's work *Imperialism: The Highest Stage of Capitalism*. As we shall see, for Lenin "imperialism *is* the monopoly stage of capitalism."

Viewed this way, the economic causes of "new imperialism" are: (1) the shift in rich countries from a stage in which the business community is dominated by competitive manufacturers ("industrial capitalism") to one in which monopolies are increasingly important and which is controlled by bankers ("finance capitalism"); (2) the rapid shrinking of profits in these rich countries because of falling sales at home and the accompanying decline in the profitability of home investments; (3) the consequent need in these countries to send surplus goods and capital abroad, particularly to weak, underdeveloped territories. The causal sequence, according to this model, is completed when "the flag follows commerce," and formal political dominion is clamped down on these outlets for goods and investments. These are the essentials of the stages thesis of the economic causes of imperialism, often called the "Hobson-Lenin model."

The stages thesis was the work of some of the most brilliant and humane thinkers of the generation that came to maturity around 1900, dedicated social theorists, journalists, and political leaders who were pondering the significance of the misery and militarism they found all about them. This thesis spread so rapidly and has remained dominant for so long—among Marxists and non-Marxists alike—that it now constitutes the orthodox general interpretation of the "new imperialism." While many scholars (myself included) condemn the stages thesis as false and misleading, we must all admit that it contributed mightily to the progress of humanity. It convinced liberals and radicals they were right in taking a sharply hostile stance against imperialism, and therefore became a factor in causing the breakup of the older forms of imperialism in recent times.

Part of the explanation for the success of the stages thesis comes from the fact that its supporters wrongly assume that it is the only possible economic interpretation of imperialism. But more importantly, the stages thesis remains popular because it is appealingly simple, possessing (superficially) great explanatory power. Many historians agree, for example, that before 1870 there was a sort of "twilight era" in the history of imperialism, almost a century of slackening interest in expansion, during which imperialist relationships were weakened (some even were cancelled), and when politicians, industrialists, and intellectuals alike condemned colonies as "millstones around our necks."

Therefore the jingoist passion with which the great powers threw themselves into imperialist competition after 1870 represents one of the most violent shifts in foreign policy (and the public opinion supporting such policy) in recent history. Before this imperialist fervor was spent, no less than ten million square miles of additional lands of imperialist subordination were carved out, lands containing some 160 million people. Is it only a coincidence that this massive break in the history of imperialism came at the same time as the great change in the nature of capitalism?

Because it has remained in command so long, the stages thesis has become overlaid and intertwined with other explanatory factors drawn from the general as well as the economic history of the 1870–1900 era. The unification of Italy and Germany, coming as it did just on the eve of the "new imperialism," seems to support the stages thesis, since now the capitalists of two additional powers could turn from internal to colonial concerns. The stages thesis also seems to fit rather neatly another stage, in this case a stage in the history of nationalism. According to Carlton J. H. Hayes and other students of nationalism, the emotional commitment of Western peoples to their fatherlands began to show a basic change in the second half of the nineteenth century, a change that might be described as a shift from liberal and peaceful to highly intolerant or "integral" and militaristic nationalism.

The stages thesis also is intertwined with observations on the "Great Depression," a spectacular downturn in world prices and profits in the period 1873–1896; this depression, it has been argued, resulted in declining investment opportunities at home and therefore drove the capitalists to seek higher rates of return abroad, especially in backward and subordinate lands. Even the much-studied decline of free trade shows a timing that fits the stages thesis, since it is precisely during the "new imperialism" that we see protective tariff barriers going up once again, reversing the trend of the 1850s and 1860s, and causing traders— fearful of being locked out of African and Asian markets—to urge imperialism on their governments. The famous Anglo-German trade rivalry, beginning in the 1880s, also can be put in the picture, since it seems to show how economic pressures from the new nature of capitalism generated a shift in international economic relations. This shift can even be given part of the blame for the ominous consolidation of two rival diplomatic blocs, the Triple Alliance and the Triple Entente.

The Hobson-Lenin thesis has been attacked by a whole galaxy of learned opponents, and never more convincingly than in the essay by D. K. Fieldhouse reproduced here in Part One. Students should remark, however, on the contrast between the thoroughness with which Fieldhouse destroys the beast and his conviction that it will not stay dead—at least until an overwhelming mass of evidence piles up to demonstrate that each and every one of its propositions is a deception. The prospect does not seem bright.

The Hobson-Lenin model, it seems clear, depends completely on two explanatory concepts: "new imperialism" and "finance capitalism." Opponents of this model, then, are entitled to argue that it must stand or fall with each of these subsidiary concepts. We can add that even if both of these concepts prove valid, supporters of the stages thesis still would have to prove that convincing causal connections can be mapped between "new imperialism" and "finance capitalism." These are formidable requirements.

Two outstanding opponents of the standard "new imperialism" concept are John Gallagher and Ronald Robinson (see Part One). They hammer hard at the assumption by Hobson and Lenin that all one needs in order to posit "new imperialism" is to point to the increased pace of colonization after about 1870. Gallagher and Robinson deny a discontinuity here by showing how many important colonies were acquired during the preceding "twilight era" of imperialism. "New imperialism" also depends on proof that the causes of imperialism after 1870 were markedly different from those in the preceding era. But Gallagher and Robinson are able to show that in Britain, governmental decisions to acquire new colonies were roughly alike in the two periods; and they also prove that there is no good evidence that public opinion (at least, before about 1895) veered sharply from anti-imperialism to pro-imperialism. The relations between the causes of imperialism in the two eras, they claim, are marked not by a contrast but by a "fundamental continuity." Their position is strongly supported by other specialists in the history of imperialism.

"New imperialism," therefore, is best left in quotation marks.

While the concept is important, it has come under such heavy attack that its validity is dubious. This much is well known. It should also be established, however, that much the same can be said concerning "finance capitalism." Economic historians especially interested in entrepreneurial history agree that we are not at all sure there was such a thing, or even that there was a significant break in the history of enterprise around 1870. In fact the periodization of capitalism is an enormous task that has hardly begun.

The concept of finance capitalism was developed by Rudolf Hilferding, a brilliant economist and one of the leaders of the radical wing of the Social Democratic party. In his major work, *Das Finanzkapital* (1910), he examined monetary and credit institutions and explored the effects of the concentration of financial power on business competition, depressions, and foreign trade and investment. While he does have some important comments on imperialism in this work, these are incidental to his major interests. It was Lenin—building on the stinging attacks against bankers by Hobson and other reformers—who synthesized the concepts of "finance capitalism" and "new imperialism" into a cohesive model.

Recent work on the history of banking stresses the great importance of financiers during the 1840s, 1850s, and 1860s; so far as 1870–1900 is concerned, we may be witnessing the continuation into the era of "new imperialism" of a strongly established trend rather than a break with the past. This is true for Britain, France, the United States, Belgium, and Holland. In central Europe, it is true, the rise in the numbers and power of the financial community seems more marked. But our findings in the theory of economic development suggest that the great rise of banking in Germany, Italy, and Austria-Hungary comes from their attempts to exploit new credit mechanisms in their hurry to catch up with the leaders in industrialization in the West. That is, what we call "finance capitalism" in central Europe may be a specific reaction to the relative economic situation there rather than part of a development common to all capitalist nations.

• • •

By the late 1950s, spectators of "decolonization" began to

realize that they were witnessing a tragedy of gigantic proportions. Independence was not bringing rapid progress to the former colonies. This was one of the most shattering anticlimaxes
of modern times. Perhaps we had smiled a bit at naïve leaders of
colonial independence movements who seemed to feel that instant affluence was a birthright of freedom. But we, too, had
believed that subordination causes misery and that independence
would go far to end it. Instead we saw the gap in income between
ourselves and even the more fortunate new countries widening
at an alarming rate. As for the poorer new countries, massive
injections of loans and gifts were all that were keeping their
living standards from dropping below those of colonial days.
Thus in today's Africa, of some 48 countries only five or six have
enjoyed a steady increase in gross national product greater than
their increase in population. What now of the fair promises
made by fighters for independence? Are the conservatives who
had argued against the breakup of Western empires to have the
last laugh after all?

In the wake of this terrible disappointment, many of our older
notions on relations between rich and poor countries stand revealed as delusions. A jumble of new, contradictory, and imprecise hypotheses concerning these relations now struggle for
preeminence in the intellectual marketplace. Perhaps the most
challenging recent views are those concerning what we have
come to think of as "neocolonialism," views for the most part
emanating from angry "New Left" critics of modern capitalism.
These heated denunciations are represented by the essays in
Part Four. It is as yet impossible to obtain a consensus among
New Left intellectuals on the causes, the characteristics, and the
significance of neocolonialism. But it is important for students
of imperialism to wrestle with these new ideas. Neocolonialist
concepts aim not only at demonstrating that post–World War II
relations between rich and poor lands must be regarded as a
new form of imperialism, but they attempt also to shed light on
imperialism before 1939.

Perhaps the leading themes running through New Left dis-
cussions of neocolonialism are: 1) most of the former colonies
have been granted only sham independence, a façade behind
which the old imperialist subordination continues; and 2) the

reason for neocolonialism is that the very poverty of these former colonies affords opportunities for the rich of the world to
exploit them, opportunities that powerful capitalist nations cannot and will not relinquish. That is why, we are told, the poor
lands must put up with oppressive dictatorships, must refrain
from nationalizing foreign enterprises which enjoy shamefully
high "superprofits," and must stagger along under outmoded,
ineffective, and unfair social institutions. If the new lands were
to embark on aggressive reform programs and actually to achieve
modernization and industrialization, we are told, their under-
paid laborers, cheap raw materials, and hungry markets would
no longer be there for foreigners to exploit.

Another of the chief economic causes of neocolonialism, according to the New Left, is the nature and consequences of economic exploitation *during colonial days.* They mean by this
that when the flag of the "mother country" was hauled down, the
new countries—with pitifully inadequate transportation, education, communication, and bureacratic systems ("infrastructure")
—were left with very little to help them begin careers as self-
reliant nations. They mean also that where certain lands, before
being colonized, had been endowed with promising groups of
skilled craftsmen and other resources for small-scale industry,
these were snuffed out when the imperial network took over,
since the colonies could not compete with low manufacturing
costs in the advanced nations. Indeed, Michael B. Brown, in his
essay in Part Three, holds that this restriction of the spread of
industrialization in the colonies was a deliberate policy by the
great powers. Since foreign capitalists sought mainly agricultural
and mineral raw materials, the colonial economies suffered "agricultural involution," that is, they were actually forced back away
from industrialization, losing the distance they had travelled
before colonization. In Kwame Nkrumah's famous phrase, they
were condemned to remain "hewers of wood and drawers of
water." Such lands often became monocultures, one-resource
countries, at the mercy of foreign markets and under the thumb
of the foreign investors who ran their plantations and mines.

Anti-Marxists, on the other hand—many of whom prefer "neocolonialism" in quotation marks—are inclined to regard these
New Left arguments as in part a sort of ideological salvage operation. The Leninist stages thesis, which hardened into dogma

in the U.S.S.R. after 1917 and is still the foundation of most Marxian thinking on imperialism, received a severe challenge when the Western empires began to break up after World War II. Much in Lenin was anchored to the concept that imperialism is the highest (read: "last") stage of capitalism. Marxists therefore had as a fixed feature of their beliefs that without empires to exploit, capitalism would crumble or would at least suffer terrible dislocations. But during the late 1950s and the 1960s, just at the time "decolonization" of the French, British, Belgian, and Dutch empires was being completed, Western Europe was enjoying one of the best and longest-sustained economic booms in modern times. Japan, deprived of her empire in 1945, later experienced even more phenomenal economic growth.

The burden of proof, therefore, seems to rest squarely on Lenin's modern supporters. Their defence has been a counter-charge—that the reason capitalism still is thriving is that imperialist exploitation still is rampant, though operating in a new form. Even in 1948, Marshall Plan aid to Europe had been attacked as an attempt to turn Western Europe into American satellites. In the 1950s, with one colony after another being granted independence, the Marxists focused their attack on the grinding misery remaining in the Third World and linked this to holdovers of imperialism. The framework of their position is still the Leninist model—capitalism necessarily generates surplus funds and must invest them abroad especially in order to broaden markets for surplus manufactures. But in fitting this concept to the world of the 1960s, the New Left developed several important new points, as we see in the readings in Part Four. Therefore it is appropriate to call their position "neo-Leninist."

The notion that capitalism—including post-1945 capitalism—is necessarily expansionist has been given new life by the phenomenal increase in the number and wealth of international or "multinational" corporations in the wealthiest countries. Some of these changes in the international business world are spectacular enough to merit newspaper headlines; thus we learn (January 1970) that the International Business Machines Corporation controls 70 percent of the European computer market and that one-half the assets of the 400 largest Canadian enterprises are owned by United States firms. And we are all aware of the wealth and power of American and West European corporations operating in the Middle East and in Latin America. Less well known is the extensive penetration of new countries in Africa and Asia by international corporations.

As recently as 1961, Barbara Ward, a famous proponent of better treatment for the Third World, could state that imperialism on the part of the richer Western countries probably was a thing of the past. Her argument was that since all these powerful nations were rapidly becoming welfare states, the energies of their business leaders were increasingly channeled inwards, and their governments were not the sort to permit the establishment of potentially imperialist connections. Today the success of international corporations means we cannot be so sure that even the most progressive welfare states are not more or less willingly permitting some forms of neocolonialism.

Perhaps the real significance of neocolonialism is that it arises out of the failure of the nation state to function as a satisfactory mechanism for poor or recently consolidated countries intent on modernizing themselves. We who are products of Western culture long assumed that sovereign nations can, will, and must be equal as well as free. We also believed that patterns of economic relations (trade, investment, transfers of people and technology) are arranged among the free nations in a reciprocally beneficial manner according to their comparative advantages (location, resources, skills). But as H. W. Singer and Gunnar Myrdal show in their essays in Part Three, this is not necessarily so. Luck and power, it would seem, have a good deal to do with these international economic patterns. If a country has little to offer the world's markets, and if what she does possess commands low prices or goes mainly to enrich foreign investors, the acquisition of independence is far from enough to launch her down the road to economic progress. Today we are mulling over the various bitter truths in the observation in St. Matthew, that "For unto every one that hath shall be given, and he shall have abundance; but from him that hath not shall be taken away even that which he hath." Surely the devil must chuckle, for example, at the sight of a poor country finally managing to acquire Western-style banks, only to discover that these banks often make it all too easy for rich persons in that country to ship the nation's slender capital resources away to Europe or America.

Is poverty itself one of the chief economic causes of imperialism? Does the lack of wealth in one land tend to set off a train of events leading to impairment of its sovereignty by a richer and more powerful land? One of the clearest examples of links between poverty and imperialism is the need of poor countries for loans. This is the subject of the selection by Herbert Feis (Part Three) on Morocco during the first decade of the twentieth century. Such loans, whether used to prop up decaying despotisms or to construct desperately needed railways, soon became an object of tension between borrower and lender. Poor nations then as now have few facilities for repaying large loans. "Intervention" in the name of the owners of the money often followed. Another well-known link between poverty and imperialism was the existence of a highly prized, undeveloped resource (such as the rubber of the Malay peninsula) in a land where there was an overabundance of miserably poor persons who could be recruited for a labor force.

If there is some truth to the New Left charge that imperialism created conditions ensuring continued poverty in colonial lands, then we can imagine a vicious circle arising. As development of the colonial economy began, the number and variety of profit opportunities open to entrepreneurs of the imperialist country might well increase. New technological improvements arising out of the Western economies (the cable telegraph, the refrigerator steamer), as well as advances in medicine and hygiene (control of the tsetse fly), tightened the economic bonds between colony and "mother country" by multiplying the number of merchants and industrialists who felt their outlook would be improved by having their own colonial administrators and soldiers on the scene. This reinforced the circle from imperialism to poverty and back again.

• • •

Francis W. Hirst's famous sneer, "Every imperialist is at heart an emporialist," is false as well as unfair. No serious student of imperialism can deny that soldiers, statesmen, journalists, missionaries, rabid nationalists, and others motivated by humanitarian, political, or religious considerations tried their hand at empire building. What is the relative importance of such non-economic causes? Let us admit at once that historians and social

scientists are as yet far from being able to answer this vital
question. The motives behind even the most famous developments are still a matter of hot debate. One example is Bismarck's famous change of heart concerning the desirability of
African colonies—was he influenced primarily by a plan to increase German power in international relations or by the be-
lated realization that profits in imperial trade were becoming
crucial for the German economy? Another is the motives of the
French in finally deciding to establish a protectorate over all of
Indochina. For long we were told that national pride was behind the consolidation of France's empire. But recent study has
cast this all in doubt by demonstrating the strong interests of
France's silk manufacturers in the Indochina trade.

Even if we could establish what were the apparent or avowed
motives of the chief empire builders in specific episodes (for
their goals could change from one period of their lives to another), we still would suffer from doubts as to their "real"
motives. Was a complicated man such as Cecil Rhodes driven
primarily by racism, patriotism, or greed? Some students are
made uneasy by questions of basic personal motivations and
prefer to point to the "institutional framework" or to the "spirit
of the times" in which empire builders operated. This is certainly easier. But if what we want is the whole complicated truth
rather than a facile theory, we must realize that it was not social
structures or general trends that built empires, but men—men
with a great variety of compelling reasons for becoming involved
in new ventures in strange lands.

Both the stages thesis and the neo-Leninist approach distort
the history of imperialism. When we study the economic causes
of imperialism our subject matter is not blind forces but open-
eyed men hungry for profit. This is the advantage of the materialist interpretation of imperialism.

Imperialism for gain is a theme that runs through the history
of all modern Western imperialism. The famous question as to
whether the "old imperialism" of the sixteenth to eighteenth
century arose primarily from "gold, God, or glory" is unworthy
of close attention. The weight is all too obviously on the side
of gold. The "plantations," the trading bastions, and the looting
expeditions of early modern imperialism show that the search
for money is their least common denominator. Profit motives also

clearly dominated "free trade imperialism" of the first two-thirds of the nineteenth century. While nationalism and the "white man's burden" in the "new imperialism" of 1870–1900 have received more attention from historians, one cannot be sure these were *relatively* more important motives, since the tempo of imperial economic affairs also was increasing. Perhaps the drive for profits through imperialism did become less significant between the two World Wars; on the other hand, most of us would agree that profits and neocolonialism still seem to be connected today.

In the economic history of imperialism, a distinction between capitalists and capitalism is useful. During the 1950s, a good deal of controversy swirled around Joseph Schumpeter's remark that capitalism is anti-imperialist in its essence. (See Part Two.) Capitalism, according to Schumpeter, is essentially rational, constructive, peaceful. In this he was embracing the characterization of the "ethos," the legal nature, and other features of capitalism which had been worked out by the German historical school of economists.

It is far from established that Schumpeter's hypothesis concerning the relations between the capitalist system and imperialism is valid. But even if we grant that capitalism in essence is anti-imperialistic, we are not thereby entitled to imagine that "the system" stamped all or even most capitalists into the same mold. Capitalists, then as now—especially the entrepreneurs or true innovators—are a highly variegated, nonconformist, pushy group anxious to take advantage of any sort of monetary opportunity. It is true there are examples (in Colbert's France, Bismarck's Germany, and elsewhere) of business men who had to be picked up by the scruff of the neck and tossed into imperialist ventures. But there were others who risked their fortunes in daring undertakings on which they embarked without the approval of their fellows or their government. What percentage of the capitalists is needed to forge potentially imperialist bonds? Is it ten percent? One percent? But the fact is that only a handful of "non-Schumpeterian" capitalists is all that is required to begin turning an economic relationship into an imperialistic one.

More than an initial penetration by a few foreign merchants, of course, is needed to complete the establishment of an imperialistic relationship. This requires further action such as a powerful association of venturers (the British East Indies Company, for example) deciding it is necessary to safeguard its investments or the leaders of the imperialist nation deciding that crucial interests are at stake. In any case, a political change takes place that results in reducing the sovereignty of the (now) colony in favor of either the association of colonial venturers or the government of the imperialist power or both.

This distinction between mercantile incursions and impairment of sovereignty allows us to see that when we invoke "the economic causes of imperialism" we are dealing with causation on several levels. We also must recognize that these levels of causation need not be joined together in any uniform sequence, either in logic or in actual imperialist cases. It certainly is true that often "the flag followed commerce"; but there are instances of where the political decision came first, so that "commerce followed the flag," commerce that had not existed previously; and there are other cases too complicated to fit such simplified models, such as the support of the French East Indies Company by Louis XIV—partly because that monarch wanted to provide an economic and strategic base for the missionary operations of the Jesuits.

That statesmen combined economic with other goals in dealing with potential colonies is hardly surprising. From at least the seventeenth century, the connections between a nation's public power on the one hand and its private wealth on the other have been one of the primary concerns of those guiding the world's foreign relations. When creating "favorable conditions for our traders," or "pegging out claims for the future," or "turning natives from manslayers to productive labourers," the imperialist leaders, it is true, were making political decisions. But these were political decisions in the sense that unlike decisions of traders, they were binding on the whole community of the imperialist power. The goals of such decisions, and the methods by which they were implemented, often were quite as economic as those of individuals or associations. The statesmen who made them were not puppets responding to the pull of "underlying forces" they could but dimly perceive; rather, they were working quite consciously for specific improvements in their nation's wealth. This was still imperialism for gain, and therefore at least partly within the framework of the materialist interpretation. The same may be said for those imperialist impulses, described by Heinz Gollwitzer in his essay in Part Two, aimed at promoting social peace in the "mother country" by enlarging exports and so increasing employment. When statesmen supported imperialistic ventures in the hope of providing outlets for emigration, this too must be seen as partly an economic cause of imperialism.

Perhaps the most important lesson of the economic history of imperialism is that the establishment and strengthening of an imperialistic relationship did not require that *as a whole* this relationship had to be profitable for any given imperialist power. We have been badly misled here by wrong conclusions drawn from studies showing that "the balance sheet of imperialism" was sharply negative. The relevant question is not "Do colonies pay?" but rather "Cui bono?" As long ago as Karl Marx—who commented on this situation in India—we knew that in most cases the military, administrative, and other costs of imperialism can be expected to rise above the sum total of tax revenues drawn from the colonies plus private profits from colonial trade and investment.

Indeed, imperialism was (and is) "bad business for the nation." The fact that this was so obvious, however, does not mean that the rational entrepreneurs of the West recognized the situation and therefore to a man refused to have anything to do with imperialism. Neither does it mean that since the economic aspects were negative, *as a whole,* imperialism must have arisen from noneconomic motives. An imperialistic relationship required only that *some* business men—perhaps only a handful—in each case profited from a potential colony, expected these profits would continue or improve under imperialism, and succeeded in persuading their statesmen (either by direct pressure or through public opinion) that what was good for them was good for the nation.

"To whom the gain?" The materialist interpretation emphasizes that many others besides the obvious categories of merchants, manufacturers, and investors stood to profit from imperialism. The endless series of nasty little wars with "native rebels" enriched the military supply companies and the munitions manufacturers. Mine operators and plantation owners needed "law and order" to exploit their holdings to the limit. And we have the railroad builders, construction engineers, company agents, administrative officials, and army and navy officers who hoped for higher pay scales, faster promotions, and greater fringe benefits from colonial employment. We must not forget the Africans and Asians with a vested interest in originating, strengthening, and extending imperialism: "compradores," we call them, the middlemen who took up peripheral shopkeeping, warehousing, and transport businesses not profitable enough for citizens of the imperialist powers.

To point out errors in the stages thesis and the neo-Leninist approach, therefore, is *not* to rule out the importance of economic causes. There still remains the common-sense materialist interpretation, which does not require a characterization of the nature of an imperialist economy or indeed any elaborate socio-economic theory. The materialist interpretation never has enjoyed a large number of enthusiastic believers, perhaps because it has not yet had its Hobson, perhaps because the delicate task of disentangling economic from other motivations is still beyond our powers of historical analysis. But it deserves close attention.

The materialist interpretation of imperialism does not rely on impersonal forces or historical laws; rather it emphasizes another sort of historical explanation, the motives of individuals or groups. What do we find when we examine the evidence on the purposes of the relevant men, associations, or nations at the time these were forging imperialistic relationships? That on the whole they were primarily concerned with increasing their own wealth. To put it in a "counterfactual" manner: we can imagine modern imperialism developing more or less as it did in the absence of religious, humanitarian, or political causal factors. But imagine away the economic causes of Western imperialism and little is left.

PART ONE

Colonies and Capitalism

1   FROM   *J. A. Hobson*
The Economic and Financial Taproots
of Imperialism

John A. Hobson (1858–1940) was an English journalist with a keen interest in economics and one of the chief intellectual leaders of the Labour party in its formative years. In this selection he puts the blame for imperialism partly on "certain sectional interests" who stand to gain at the country's expense, partly on the inability of mature capitalism to consume all its output or find profitable domestic outlets for its huge mass of savings. In spite of the angry charges he levels at individuals and institutions, he was no revolutionary; his work essentially is an optimistic call to reform. Hobson's view is that while the economic system is diseased it is definitely curable, since higher wages and redistributive taxation can bring up the level of domestic purchasing power and thus induce exporters and financiers to forego colonial adventures. This is not a work of reflective scholarship but a brilliant, pioneering synthesis remarkable for the fact that in 1902 the processes Hobson was trying to analyze were still developing. Its continued appeal to anti-imperialists for almost three-quarters of a century makes this book the most influential attack against imperialism ever written.

SOURCE. J. A. Hobson, *Imperialism, A Study*, 3rd rev. ed. (London: George Allen & Unwin, Ltd., 1938; first published in 1902), pp. 28–38, 46–61, 71–86. Reprinted by permission of the publisher.

The absorption of so large a proportion of public interest, energy, blood and money in seeking to procure colonial possessions and foreign markets would seem to indicate that Great Britain obtained her chief livelihood by external trade. Now this was not the case. Large as was our foreign and colonial trade in volume and in value, essential as was much of it to our national well-being, nevertheless it furnished a small proportion of the total industry of the nation. . . .

This argument, of course, does not imply that Great Britain could dispense with her external markets, and be no great sufferer in trade and income. Some considerable foreign markets, as we know, are an economic necessity to her, in order that by her exports she may purchase foods and materials which she cannot produce, or can only produce at a great disadvantage.

This fact makes a considerable external market a matter of vital importance to us. But outside the limit of this practical necessity the value of our foreign markets must rightly be considered to be measured, not by the aggregate value of the goods we sell abroad, but by the superior gain from selling them abroad as compared with selling them (or corresponding quantities of other goods) at home. To assume that if these goods are not sold abroad, neither they nor their substitutes could be sold, even at lower prices, in the home market, is quite unwarranted. There is no natural and necessary limit to the proportion of the national product which can be sold and consumed at home. It is, of course, preferable to sell goods abroad where higher profit can be got by doing so, but the net gain to national industry and income must be measured not by the value of the trade done, but by its more profitable nature. . . .

Now the significance of these results for the study of modern Imperialism consists in the fact that the whole trend of this movement was directed to the acquisition of lands and populations belonging not to the self-governing order but to the "other possessions." Our expansion was almost wholly concerned with the acquisition of tropical and sub-tropical countries peopled by races to whom we have no serious intention of giving self-government. With the exception of the Transvaal and the Orange River Colony, none of our acquisitions since 1870 belonged, even prospectively, to the self-governing group, and even in the case of the two South African states, the prospective self-government was confined to a white minority of the population. The distinctive feature of modern Imperialism, from the commercial standpoint, is that it adds to our empire tropical and sub-tropical regions with which our trade is small, precarious and unprogressive. . . .

Seeing that the Imperialism of the last six decades is clearly condemned as a business policy, in that at enormous expense it has procured a small, bad, unsafe increase of markets, and has jeopardised the entire wealth of the nation in rousing the strong resentment of other nations, we may ask, "How is the British nation induced to embark upon such unsound business?" The only possible answer is that the business interests of the nation as a whole are subordinated to those of certain sectional interests that usurp control of the national resources and use them for their private gain. This is no strange or monstrous charge to bring; it is the commonest disease of all forms of government. The famous words of Sir Thomas More are as true now as when he wrote them: "Everywhere do I perceive a certain conspiracy of rich men seeking their own advantage under the name and pretext of the commonwealth."

Although the new Imperialism has been bad business for the nation, it has been good business for certain classes and certain trades within the nation. The vast expenditure on armaments, the costly wars, the grave risks and embarrassments of foreign policy, the checks upon political and social reforms within Great Britain, though fraught with great injury to the nation, have served well the present business interests of certain industries and professions. . . .

What is the direct economic outcome of Imperialism? A great expenditure of public money upon ships, guns, military and naval equipment and stores, growing and productive of enormous profits when a war, or an alarm of war, occurs; new public loans and important fluctuations in the home and foreign Bourses; more posts for soldiers and sailors and in the diplomatic and consular services; improvement of foreign investments by the substitution of the British flag for a foreign flag; acquisition of markets for certain classes of exports, and some protection and assistance for trades representing British houses in these manufactures; employment for engineers, missionaries, speculative miners, ranchers and other emigrants.

Certain definite business and professional interests feeding upon imperialistic expenditure, or upon the results of that expenditure, are thus set up in opposition to the common good, and, instinctively feeling their way to one another, are found united in strong sympathy to support every new imperialist exploit.

If the £60,000,000 which may now [1905] be taken as a minimum expenditure on armaments in time of peace were subject to a close analysis, most of it would be traced directly to the tills of certain big firms engaged in building warships and transports, equipping and coaling them, manufacturing guns, rifles, and ammunition, planes and motor vehicles of every kind, supplying horses, waggons, saddlery, food, clothing for the services, contracting for barracks, and for other large irregular needs. Through these main channels the millions flow to feed many subsidiary trades, most of which are quite aware that they are engaged in executing contracts for the services. Here we have an important nucleus of commercial Imperialism. Some of these trades, especially the shipbuilding, boiler-making, and gun and ammunition making trades, are conducted by large firms with immense capital, whose heads are well aware of the uses of political influence for trade purposes.

These men are Imperialists by conviction; a pushful policy is good for them.

With them stand the great manufacturers for export trade, who gain a living by supplying the real or artificial wants of the new countries we annex or open up. Manchester, Sheffield, Birmingham, to name three representative cases, are full of firms which compete in pushing textiles and hardware, engines, tools, machinery, spirits, guns, upon new markets. The public debts which ripen in our colonies, and in foreign countries that come under our protectorate or influence, are largely loaned in the shape of rails, engines, guns, and other materials of civilization made and sent out by British firms. The making of railways, canals, and other public works, the establishment of factories, the development of mines, the improvement of agriculture in new countries, stimulate a definite interest in important manufacturing industries which feeds a very firm imperialist faith in their owners.

The proportion which such trade bears to the total industry

of Great Britain is not great, but some of it is extremely influential and able to make a definite impression upon politics,
through chambers of commerce, Parliamentary representatives,
and semi-political, semi-commercial bodies like the Imperial
South African Association or the China Society.

The shipping trade has a very definite interest which makes
for Imperialism. This is well illustrated by the policy of State
subsidies now claimed by shipping firms as a retainer, and in
order to encourage British shipping for purposes of imperial
safety and defence.

The services are, of course, imperialist by conviction and by
professional interest, and every increase of the army, navy, and
air force enhances the political power they exert. The abolition
of purchase [of officers' commissions] in the army, by opening the
profession to the upper middle classes, greatly enlarged this most
direct feeder of imperial sentiment. The potency of this factor
is, of course, largely due to the itch for glory and adventure
among military officers upon disturbed or uncertain frontiers of
the Empire. This has been a most prolific source of expansion
in India. The direct professional influence of the services carries
with it a less organised but powerful sympathetic support on the
part of the aristocracy and the wealthy classes, who seek in the
services careers for their sons.

To the military services we may add the Indian Civil Service
and the numerous official and semi-official posts in our colonies
and protectorates. Every expansion of the Empire is also regarded
by these same classes as affording new openings for their sons
as ranchers, planters, engineers, or missionaries. This point of
view is aptly summarised by a high Indian official, Sir Charles
Crossthwaite, in discussing British relations with Siam. "The
real question was who was to get the trade with them, and how
we could make the most of them, so as to find fresh markets for
our goods and also employment for those superfluous articles
of the present day, our boys."

From this standpoint our colonies still remain what James
Mill cynically described them as being, "a vast system of outdoor
relief for the upper classes."

In all the professions, military and civil, the army, diplomacy,
the church, the bar, teaching and engineering, Greater Britain
serves for an overflow, relieving the congestion of the home mar-

ket and offering chances to more reckless or adventurous members, while it furnishes a convenient limbo for damaged characters and careers. The actual amount of profitable employment thus furnished by our recent acquisitions is inconsiderable, but it arouses that disproportionate interest which always attaches to the margin of employment. To extend this margin is a powerful motive in Imperialism.

These influences, primarily economic, though not unmixed with other sentimental motives, are particularly operative in military, clerical, academic, and Civil Service circles, and furnish an interested bias towards Imperialism throughout the educated classes.

By far the most important economic factor in Imperialism is the influence relating to investments. The growing cosmopolitanism of capital has been the greatest economic change of recent generations. Every advanced industrial nation has been tending to place a larger share of its capital outside the limits of its own political area, in foreign countries, or in colonies, and to draw a growing income from this course. . . .

Now . . . we cannot fail to recognise that in dealing with these foreign investments we are facing the most important factor in the economics of Imperialism. Whatever figures we take, two facts are evident. First, that the income derived as interest upon foreign investments enormously exceeds that derived as profits upon ordinary export and import trade. Secondly, that while our foreign and colonial trade, and presumably the income from it, were growing but slowly, the share of our import values representing income from foreign investments was growing very rapidly.

In a former chapter I pointed out how small a proportion of our national income appeared to be derived as profits from external trade. It seemed unintelligible that the enormous costs and risks of the new Imperialism should be undertaken for such small results in the shape of increase to external trade, especially when the size and character of the new markets acquired were taken into consideration. The statistics of foreign investments, however, shed clear light upon the economic forces which are dominating our policy. While the manufacturing and trading classes make little out of their new markets, paying, if they knew it, much more in taxation than they get out of them in trade, it is quite otherwise with the investor.

It is not too much to say that the modern foreign policy of Great Britain has been primarily a struggle for profitable markets of investment. To a larger extent every year Great Britain has been becoming a nation living upon tribute from abroad, and the classes who enjoy this tribute have had an ever-increasing incentive to employ the public policy, the public purse, and the public force to extend the field of their private investments, and to safeguard and improve their existing investments. This is, perhaps, the most important fact in modern politics, and the obscurity in which it is wrapped constitutes the gravest danger to our State. . . .

Aggressive Imperialism, which costs the tax-payer so dear, which is of so little value to the manufacturer and trader, which is fraught with such grave incalculable peril to the citizen, is a source of great gain to the investor who cannot find at home the profitable use he seeks for his capital, and insists that his Government should help him to profitable and secure investments abroad.

If, contemplating the enormous expenditure on armaments, the ruinous wars, the diplomatic audacity or knavery by which modern Governments seek to extend their territorial power, we put the plain, practical question, *Cui bono?* the first and most obvious answer is, the investor.

The annual income Great Britain derives from commissions on her whole foreign and colonial trade, import and export, is estimated by Sir R. Giffen at £18,000,000 for 1899, taken at 2½ per cent, upon a turnover of £800,000,000. This is the whole that we are entitled to regard as profits on external trade. Considerable as this sum is, it cannot serve to yield an economic motive-power adequate to explain the dominance which business considerations exercise over our imperial policy. Only when we set beside it some £90,000,000 or £100,000,000, representing pure profit upon investments, do we understand whence the economic impulse to Imperialism is derived.

Investors who have put their money in foreign lands, upon terms which take full account of risks connected with the political conditions of the country, desire to use the resources of their

Government to minimise these risks, and so to enhance the capital value and the interest of their private investments. The investing and speculative classes in general also desire that Great Britain should take other foreign areas under her flag in order to secure new areas for profitable investment and speculation.

If the special interest of the investor is liable to clash with the public interest and to induce a wrecking policy, still more dangerous is the special interest of the financier, the general dealer in investments. In large measure the rank and file of the investors are, both for business and for politics, the cat's-paws of the great financial houses, who use stocks and shares not so much as investments to yield them interest, but as material for speculation in the money market. In handling large masses of stocks and shares, in floating companies, in manipulating fluctuations of values, the magnates of the Bourse find their gain. These great businesses—banking, broking, bill discounting, loan floating, company promoting—form the central ganglion of international capitalism. United by the strongest bonds of organisation, always in closest and quickest touch with one another, situated in the very heart of the business capital of every State, controlled, so far as Europe is concerned, chiefly by men of a single and peculiar race, who have behind them many centuries of financial experience, they are in a unique position to control the policy of nations. [I.e., Jews.] No great quick direction of capital is possible save by their consent and through their agency. Does any one seriously suppose that a great war could be undertaken by any European State, or a great State loan subscribed, if the house of Rothschild and its connections set their face against it?. . .

In view of the part which the non-economic factors of patriotism, adventure, military enterprise, political ambition, and philanthropy play in imperial expansion, it may appear that to impute to financiers so much power is to take a too narrowly economic view of history. And it is true that the motor-power of Imperialism is not chiefly financial: finance is rather the governor of the imperial engine, directing the energy and determining its work: it does not constitute the fuel of the engine, nor does it directly generate the power. Finance manipulates the patriotic forces which politicians, soldiers, philanthropists, and traders generate; the enthusiasm for expansion which issues from these sources, though strong and genuine, is irregular and blind; the financial interest has those qualities of concentration and clear-sighted calculation which are needed to set Imperialism to work. An ambitious statesman, a frontier soldier, an over-zealous missionary, a pushing trader, may suggest or even initiate a step of imperial expansion, may assist in educating patriotic public opinion to the urgent need of some fresh advance, but the final determination rests with the financial power. The direct influence exercised by great financial houses in "high politics" is supported by the control which they exercise over the body of public opinion through the Press, which, in every "civilised" country, is becoming more and more their obedient instrument. While the specifically financial newspaper imposes "facts" and "opinions" on the business classes, the general body of the Press comes more and more under conscious or unconscious domination of financiers. The case of the South African Press, whose agents and correspondents fanned the martial flames in this country, was one of open ownership on the part of South African financiers, and this policy of owning newspapers for the sake of manufacturing public opinion is common in the great European cities. In Berlin, Vienna, and Paris many of the influential newspapers have been held by financial houses, which used them, not primarily to make direct profits out of them, but in order to put into the public mind beliefs and sentiments which would influence public policy and thus affect the money market. In Great Britain this policy has not gone so far, but the alliance with finance grows closer every year, either by financiers purchasing a controlling share of newspapers, or by newspaper proprietors being tempted into finance. Apart from the financial Press, and financial ownership of the general Press, the City has notoriously exercised a subtle and abiding influence upon leading London newspapers, and through them upon the body of the provincial Press, while the entire dependence of the Press for its business profits upon its advertising columns has involved a peculiar reluctance to oppose the organised financial classes with whom rests the control of so much advertising business. Add to this the natural sympathy with a sensational policy which a cheap Press always manifests, and it becomes evident that the Press is strongly biased towards Imperialism, and has lent itself with great facility to the suggestion of financial or political Imperialists who desire to work up patriotism for some new piece of expansion.

Such is the array of distinctively economic forces making for Imperialism, a large loose group of trades and professions seeking profitable business and lucrative employment from the expansion of military and civil services, and from the expenditure on military operations, the opening up of new tracts of territory and trade with the same, and the provision of new capital which these operations require, all these finding their central guiding and directing force in the power of the general financier.

The play of these forces does not openly appear. They are essentially parasites upon patriotism, and they adapt themselves to its protecting colours. In the mouths of their representatives are noble phrases, expressive of their desire to extend the area of civilisation, to establish good government, promote Christianity, extirpate slavery, and elevate the lower races. Some of the business men who hold such language may entertain a genuine, though usually a vague, desire to accomplish these ends, but they are primarily engaged in business, and they are not unaware of the utility of the more unselfish forces in furthering their ends. Their true attitude of mind is expressed by Mr. Rhodes in his famous description of "Her Majesty's Flag" as "the greatest commercial asset in the world.". . .

No mere array of facts and figures adduced to illustrate the economic nature of the new Imperialism will suffice to dispel the popular delusion that the use of national force to secure new markets by annexing fresh tracts of territory is a sound and a necessary policy for an advanced industrial country like Great Britain. It has indeed been proved that recent annexations of tropical countries, procured at great expense, have furnished poor and precarious markets, that our aggregate trade with our colonial possessions is virtually stationary, and that our most profitable and progressive trade is with rival industrial nations, whose territories we have no desire to annex, whose markets we cannot force, and whose active antagonism we are provoking by our expansive policy.

But these arguments are not conclusive. It is open to Imperialists to argue thus: "We must have markets for our growing manufactures, we must have new outlets for the investment of our surplus capital and for the energies of the adventurous surplus of our population: such expansion is a necessity of life to a nation with our great and growing powers of production. An ever larger share of our population is devoted to the manufactures and commerce of towns, and is thus dependent for life and work upon food and raw materials from foreign lands. In order to buy and pay for these things we must sell our goods abroad. During the first three-quarters of the century we could do so without difficulty by a natural expansion of commerce with continental nations and our colonies, all of which were far behind us in the main arts of manufacture and the carrying trades. So long as England held a virtual monopoly of the world markets for certain important classes of manufactured goods, Imperialism was unnecessary. After 1870 this manufacturing and trading supremacy was greatly impaired; other nations, especially Germany, the United States, and Belgium, advanced with great rapidity, and while they have not crushed or even stayed the increase of our external trade, their competition made it more and more difficult to dispose of the full surplus of our manufactures at a profit. . . . The value in 1905 of these [colonial] markets must not be taken as a final test of the economy of such a policy; the process of educating civilized needs which we can supply is of necessity a gradual one, and the cost of such Imperialism must be regarded as a capital outlay, the fruits of which posterity would reap. The new markets might not be large, but they formed serviceable outlets for the overflow of our great textile and metal industries, and, when the vast Asiatic and African populations of the interior were reached, a rapid expansion of trade might be expected to result.

". . . Large savings are made which cannot find any profitable investment in this country; they must find employment elsewhere; and it is to the advantage of the nation that they should be employed as largely as possible in lands where they can be utilized in opening up markets for British trade and employment for British enterprise.

"However costly, however perilous, this process of imperial expansion may be, it is necessary to the continued existence and progress of our nation; if we abandoned it we must be content to leave the development of the world to other nations, who will everywhere cut into our trade, and even impair our means of securing the food and raw materials we require to support our population. Imperialism is thus seen to be, not a choice, but a necessity."

The practical force of this economic argument in politics is strikingly illustrated by the later history of the United States. Here is a country which suddenly broke through a conservative policy, strongly held by both political parties, bound up with every popular instinct and tradition, and flung itself into a rapid imperial career for which it possessed neither the material nor the moral equipment, risking the principles and practices of liberty and equality by the establishment of militarism and the forcible subjugation of peoples which it cannot safely admit to the condition of American citizenship.

Was this a mere wild freak of spread-eaglism, a burst of political ambition on the part of a nation coming to a sudden realisation of its destiny? Not at all. The spirit of adventure, the American "mission of civilization," were as forces making for Imperialism, clearly subordinate to the driving force of the economic factor. . . .

Every improvement of methods of production, every concentration of ownership and control, seems to accentuate the tendency. As one nation after another enters the machine economy and adopts advanced industrial methods, it becomes more difficult for its manufacturers, merchants, and financiers to dispose profitably of their economic resources, and they are tempted more and more to use their Governments in order to secure for their particular use some distant undeveloped country by annexation and protection.

The process, we may be told, is inevitable, and so it seems upon a superficial inspection. Everywhere appear excessive powers of production, excessive capital in search of investment. It is admitted by all business men that the growth of the powers of production in their country exceeds the growth in consumption, that more goods can be produced than can be sold at a profit, and that more capital exists than can find remunerative investment.

It is this economic condition of affairs that forms the taproot of Imperialism. If the consuming public in this country raised its standard of consumption to keep pace with every rise of productive powers, there could be no excess of goods or capital clamorous to use Imperialism in order to find markets: foreign trade would indeed exist, but there would be no difficulty in exchanging a small surplus of our manufactures for the food and raw material we annually absorbed, and all the savings that we made could find employment, if we chose, in home industries.

There is nothing inherently irrational in such a supposition. Whatever is, or can be, produced, can be consumed, for a claim upon it, as rent, profit, or wages, forms part of the real income of some member of the community, and he can consume it, or else exchange it for some other consumable with some one else who will consume it. With everything that is produced a consuming power is born. If then there are goods which cannot get consumed, or which cannot even get produced because it is evident they cannot get consumed, and if there is a quantity of capital and labour which cannot get full employment because its products cannot get consumed, the only possible explanation of this paradox is the refusal of owners of consuming power to apply that power in effective demand for commodities. . . .

The fallacy of the supposed inevitability of imperial expansion as a necessary outlet for progressive industry is now manifest. It is not industrial progress that demands the opening up of new markets and areas of investment, but mal-distribution of consuming power which prevents the absorption of commodities and capital within the country. The over-saving which is the economic root of Imperialism is found by analysis to consist of rents, monopoly profits, and other unearned or excessive elements of income, which, not being earned by labour of head or hand, have no legitimate *raison d'être*. Having no natural relation to effort of production, they impel their recipients to no corresponding satisfaction of consumption: they form a surplus wealth, which, having no proper place in the normal economy of production and consumption, tends to accumulate as excessive savings. Let any turn in the tide of politico-economic forces divert from these owners their excess of income and make it flow, either to the workers in higher wages, or to the community in taxes, so that it will be spent instead of being saved, serving in either of these ways to swell the tide of consumption—there will be no need to fight for foreign markets or foreign areas of investment.

2 FROM   *V. I. Lenin*
The Stages Thesis Becomes Dogma

In 1916, during the last months of his exile in Switzerland, Lenin worked out an analysis of how socialists should interpret the First World War together with an explanation of how they could use the war to explain to their countrymen that the causes of this frightful calamity lay in the capitalist system itself. He needed such a statement not only because of the demands of the times but also to assert his leadership against socialists with different views in Russia and elsewhere. Much of his Imperialism, *therefore, is an attack against socialists who could not see that at "the highest stage of capitalism" a division of the less advanced lands of the world into colonies was inevitable, since, if the leaders of the powerful countries could do as Hobson urged, "capitalism would not be capitalism." Lenin declared that fighting over redivision of colonies and "semicolonies" was unavoidable and was in fact the chief explanation of world war. The selection from* Imperialism *that follows is a clever amalgam of theories from Hobson and Hilferding (to which Lenin added little), worked into an assertion that the end of capitalism is at hand. Lenin's statement quickly won recognition as the orthodox Communist interpretation of imperialism, and, with minor modifications, it remains so to this day.*

The fundamental and primary function of banks is to serve as an intermediary in the making of payments. In so doing the banks transform idle money capital into productive capital, that is, capital producing a profit; they collect all kinds of money incomes and place them at the disposal of the capitalist class.

In proportion as banking develops and becomes concentrated

SOURCE. V. I. Lenin, *Imperialism, The Highest Stage of Capitalism,* rev. translation (New York: International Publishers, 1933; first published in 1917), pp. 30–40, 54–62, 68–81. Reprinted by permission of International Publishers Co., Inc.

in a small number of institutions, the banks grow from modest intermediaries into all-powerful monopolists having at their command almost all the money capital of all the capitalists and small businessmen, as well as the greater part of the means of production and of the sources of raw materials of a given country or in a number of countries. This transformation of numerous small intermediaries into a handful of monopolists is one of the fundamental processes of the growing of capitalism into capitalist imperialism. . . .

. . . When carrying the current accounts of a few capitalists, the bank, as it were, transacts a purely technical and exclusively auxiliary operation. When, however, these operations grow to enormous dimensions we find that a handful of monopolists controls all the operations, both commercial and industrial, of capitalist society. They can, through their banking connections, through current accounts and other financial operations, first *exactly ascertain* the standing of the various capitalists, then *control* them, influence them by restricting or increasing, facilitating or hindering their credits, and finally they can *completely determine* their fate, determine their income, deprive them of capital, or enable them quickly to increase their capital rapidly and to enormous proportions, *etc*.

The close ties that exist between the banks and industry are the very things that bring out most strikingly the new rôle of the banks. When a bank discounts a bill for a certain businessman, opens an account for him, *etc.,* these operations, taken separately, do not in the least diminish the independence of that businessman, and the bank plays no other part than that of a modest intermediary. But when such operations are multiplied and become consolidated, when the bank "accumulates" in its own hands enormous sums of capital, when the keeping of an account for the firm in question enables the bank—and this is what happens—to become increasingly well and fully informed of the economic position of its client, then the result is that the industrial capitalist becomes more and more fully dependent on the bank.

Parallel with this there is being developed a personal connection between the banks and the biggest industrial and commercial enterprises, a fusion of one with another through shareholding, through the appointment of bank directors to the boards of directors of industrial and commercial enterprises, and *vice versa.* . . .

The "personal connection" between the banks and industry is completed by the "personal connection" between both of them and the government. . . .

While during periods of industrial boom, the profits of finance capital are disproportionately large, during periods of depression, small and unsound businesses go under, while the great banks "participate" by acquiring their shares for next to nothing, or through profitable "revivifications" and "reorganisations." In the "revivification" of undertakings which have been running at a loss, the share capital is written down, that is, profits are distributed on a smaller capital and for the future are calculated on this smaller basis. Or, if the income has fallen to zero, new capital is called in which, combined with the old and less remunerative capital, will bring in an adequate return. . . .

It is a peculiarity of capitalism in general that the ownership of capital is separate from the application of capital to production, money capital separate from industrial, or productive capital; the rentier, living solely on income from money capital, separate from the enterpreneur and from all those directly concerned in the management of capital. Imperialism, or the rule of finance capital, is that highest stage of capitalism in which this separation reaches vast proportions. The predominance of finance capital over all other forms of capital means the dominating position of the rentier and the financial oligarchy; it means the crystallisation of a small number of financially "powerful" states from among all the rest. . . .

Under the old capitalism, under which free competition prevailed, the export of *goods* was typical. Under the newest capitalism, when monopolies prevail, the export of *capital* has become typical.

Capitalism is commodity production at the highest stage of its development, when labour-power itself becomes a commodity. The growth of exchange within the country, and particularly of international exchange, is a characteristic feature of capitalism. Unevenness and irregularity in the development of individual enterprises, individual branches of industry, and individual countries, are inevitable under the capitalist system. England became a capitalist country before any other, and, in the middle of the nineteenth century, having introduced free trade, claimed to be the "workshop of the world," the great provider of manufactured goods for all other countries, which, in exchange, were to keep her supplied with raw materials. In the last quarter of the nineteenth century, *this* monopoly of England was already being undermined as other countries, protected by "protective" tariffs, grew into independent capitalist states. On the threshold of the twentieth century, we see a new type of monopoly being formed. First, monopolist combines of capitalists in all advanced capitalist countries; second, a few very rich countries, in which the accumulation of capital has reached gigantic proportions, occupy a monopolist position. An enormous "surplus of capital" accumulated in the advanced countries.

It goes without saying that if capitalism could develop agriculture, which to-day lags far behind industry everywhere, if it could raise the standard of living of the masses, which are still poverty-stricken and half-starved everywhere in spite of the amazing advance in technical knowledge, then there could be no talk of a surplus of capital. And the petty-bourgeois critics of capitalism advance this "argument" on every occasion. But then capitalism would not be capitalism; for unevenness of development and semi-starvation of the masses are fundamental, inevitable conditions and prerequisites of this method of production. As long as capitalism remains capitalism, surplus capital will never be used for the purpose of raising the standard of living of the masses, for this would mean a decrease in profits for the capitalists; instead it will be used to increase profits by exporting the capital abroad, to backward countries. In these backward countries profits are usually high, for capital is scarce, the price of land is relatively low, wages are low, raw materials are cheap. The possibility for exporting capital is created by the entry of a number of backward countries into international capitalist intercourse, the main railway lines have either been built or are being built there, the elementary conditions for industrial development have been assured, *etc.* The necessity for exporting capital arises from the fact that in a few countries capitalism has become "over-ripe," and, owing to the backward stage of agriculture and the impoverishment of the masses, capital lacks opportunities for "profitable" investment. . . .

The monopoly combines of the capitalists—cartels, syndicates, trusts—divide among themselves first of all the domestic market of a country, and more or less completely seize control of the country's production. But under capitalism the home market is inevitably bound up with the foreign market. Capitalism long ago created a world market. In proportion as the export of capital increased, and as all the foreign and colonial relations, the "spheres of influence" of the biggest monopolist combines, expanded, things tended "naturally" towards an international agreement among them, and towards the formation of international cartels.

This is a new stage of world concentration of capital and production, incomparably higher than the preceding stages. . . .

The capitalists partition the world, not out of personal malice, but because the degree of concentration which has been reached forces them to adopt this method in order to get profits. And they partition it "in proportion to capital," "in proportion to strength," for there cannot be any other method of division under the system of commodity production and capitalism. . . .

. . . As there are no unoccupied territories . . . we must say that the characteristic feature of this period is the final partition of the earth, final not in the sense that a *re-partition* would be impossible—on the contrary, re-partitions are possible and inevitable—but in the sense that the colonial policy of the capitalist countries *has completed* the seizure of unoccupied land on our planet. For the first time, the world is now divided up, so that in the future *only re-divisions* are possible; *i.e.*, a transfer from one "owner" to another, and not of unowned territory to an "owner."

We are therefore passing through a peculiar period of world colonial policy, which is very closely associated with the "latest stage in the development of capitalism," with finance capital. For this reason it is necessary to deal more in detail with the facts, in order to ascertain exactly what distinguishes this period from those preceding it, as well as the present situation. In the first place, two questions of fact arise here. Is an intensification of colonial policy, an intensification of the struggle for colonies, to be observed precisely in this period of finance capital? And just how, in this respect, is the world divided up at the present time? . . .

For Britain, the period of vast increase in colonial conquests falls between 1860 and 1880; and the last twenty years of the nineteenth century are also of great importance. For France and Germany it falls precisely during those last twenty years. We saw above that the apex of pre-monopoly capitalist development, of capitalism in which free competition was predominant, was reached in the period between 1860 and 1880. We now see that it is *precisely after that period* that the tremendous "boom" in colonial annexations begins, and that the struggle for a territorial division of the world becomes extraordinarily keen. It is beyond doubt, therefore, that the transition of capitalism to the stage of monopoly capitalism, to finance capital, is *connected* with the intensification of the struggle for the partition of the world.

Hobson, in his work on imperialism, marks the years 1884–1900 as being the period of intensified "expansion" of the chief European states. According to his estimate, England during these years acquired 3.7 million square miles of territory with a population of 57 million; France acquired 3.6 million square miles with a population of 36.5 million; Germany one million square miles with 16.7 million inhabitants; Belgium 900,000 square miles with 30 million inhabitants; Portugal 800,000 square miles with 9 million inhabitants. The quest for colonies by all the capitalist states at the end of the nineteenth century, and particularly since the 1880's, is a well-known fact in the history of diplomacy and of foreign policy.

Between 1840 and 1860, when free competition in England was at its height, the leading bourgeois politicians were *opposed* to the colonial policy, and were of the opinion that the liberation of the colonies and their complete separation from England was an inevitable and desirable thing. M. Beer in an article on modern British imperialism, published in 1898, shows that in 1852, Disraeli, a statesman generally inclined towards imperialism, declared: "The colonies are millstones round our necks." But by the end of the nineteenth century, the heroes of the hour were Cecil Rhodes and Joseph Chamberlain, the open advocates of imperialism and the most cynical exponents of imperialist policy!

It is not without interest to observe that already at that time the leading British bourgeois politicians fully appreciated the

connection between what might be called the purely economic
and the social-political roots of modern imperialism. Chamberlain preached imperialism as the "true, wise and economical policy," and he pointed particularly to the German, American and
Belgian competition which Great Britain to-day encounters on
the world market. Salvation lies in monopolies, said the capitalists, as they formed cartels, syndicates and trusts. Salvation lies
in monopolies, echoed the political leaders of the bourgeoisie,
hastening to seize the parts of the world not yet partitioned. . . .

Alongside the colonial possessions of the great powers, we
have placed the small colonies of the small states, which are, so
to speak, the nearest objects of a possible and probable new
colonial "redistribution." For the most part these small states
retain their colonies only because of conflicting interests, friction, *etc.,* among the great powers, which prevent them from
coming to an agreement in regard to the division of the spoils.
The "semi-colonial" states provide an example of those transi-
tional forms which are to be found in all domains of nature and
society. Finance capital is such a great, it may be said, such a
decisive force in all economic and international relations, that
it is capable of subordinating to itself, and actually does subordinate to itself, even states enjoying complete political independence. We shall shortly see examples of this. But, naturally,
finance capital finds it most "convenient," and is able to extract
the greatest profit from *such* a subordination as involves the loss
of the political independence of the subjected countries and
peoples. In this connection the semi-colonial countries are typical
of the "middle stage." It stands to reason that the struggle for
these semi-dependent countries should have become particularly
bitter during the period of finance capital, when the rest of the
world had already been divided up.

Colonial politics and imperialism existed even before the latest
stage of capitalism, and even before capitalism. Rome, founded
on slavery, carried out a colonial policy and was imperialistic.
But "general" arguments about imperialism, which ignore, or
put into the background the fundamental difference of social-
economic formations, inevitably degenerate into empty banali-
ties, or phrases such as the comparison of "greater Rome and
greater Britain." Even the colonial policy of capitalism in its

previous stages is essentially different from the colonial policy of finance capital.

The basic feature of the newest capitalism is the domination of monopolist combines of the biggest entrepreneurs. These monopolies are most durable when *all* the sources of raw materials are controlled by the one group. And we have seen with what zeal the international capitalist combines exert every effort to make it impossible for their rivals to compete with them; for example, by buying up mineral lands, oil fields, *etc.* Colonial possession alone gives a complete guarantee of success to the monopolies against all the risks of the struggle against competitors, including the possibility of the adversary's desire to defend himself by means of a law establishing a state monopoly. The more capitalism develops, the more the need for raw materials is felt; the more bitter competition becomes and the more feverish the hunt for sources of raw materials throughout the world, the more desperate the struggle for the acquisition of colonies becomes. . . .

We must now try to draw certain conclusions, to sum up what has been said above about imperialism. Imperialism emerged as a development and direct continuation of the fundamental properties of capitalism in general. But capitalism became capitalist imperialism only at a definite, very high stage of its development, when certain of its fundamental properties had begun to change into their opposites, when the features of a period of transition from capitalism to a higher socio-economic system had begun to take shape and reveal themselves all along the line. Economically fundamental in this process is the replacement of capitalist free competition by capitalist monopolies. Free competition is the fundamental property of capitalism and of commodity production generally. Monopoly is the direct opposite of free competition; but we have seen the latter being transformed into monopoly before our very eyes, creating large-scale production and squeezing out small-scale production, replacing large-scale by larger-scale production, finally leading to such a concentration of production and capital that monopoly has been and is the result: cartels, syndicates and trusts, and, merging with them, the capital of a dozen or so banks manipulating thousands of millions. And at the same time the monopolies,

which have sprung from free competition, do not eliminate it,
but exist alongside of it and over it, thereby giving rise to a
number of very acute and bitter antagonisms, points of friction,
and conflicts. Monopoly is the transition from capitalism to a
higher order.

If it were necessary to give the briefest possible definition of
imperialism, we should have to say that imperialism is the
monopoly stage of capitalism. Such a definition would include
the essential point, for, on the one hand, finance capital is bank
capital of the few biggest monopolist banks, merged with the
capital of the monopolist combines of industrialists; on the other
hand, the division of the world is the transition from a colonial
policy which has extended without hindrance to territories unoccupied by any capitalist power, to a colonial policy of monopolistic possession of the territories of the world, which has been
completely divided up.

But too brief definitions, although convenient, since they sum
up the main points, are nevertheless inadequate, because very
fundamental features of the phenomenon to be defined must still
be deduced. And so, without forgetting the conditional and relative value of all definitions, which can never include all the
connections of a fully developed phenomenon, we must give a
definition of imperialism that will include the following five
essential features:

1. The concentration of production and capital, developed to
such a high stage that it has created monopolies which play a
decisive rôle in economic life.

2. The merging of bank capital with industrial capital and
the creation, on the basis of this "finance capital," of a financial
oligarchy.

3. The export of capital, as distinguished from the export of
commodities, becomes of particularly great importance.

4. International monopoly combines of capitalists are formed
which divide up the world.

5. The territorial division of the world by the greatest capitalist powers is completed.

Imperialism is capitalism in that stage of development in
which the domination of monopolies and finance capital has
taken shape; in which the export of capital has acquired pro-

nounced importance; in which the division of the world by the international trusts has begun, and in which the partition of all the territory of the earth by the greatest capitalist countries has been completed.

3 FROM *D. K. Fieldhouse*
Dissecting the Hobson-Lenin Model

D. K. Fieldhouse teaches British Commonwealth history at Oxford University and is one of our foremost specialists in the history of imperialism. The following selection is his conclusions to a highly useful book of readings centering on what he calls "The Theory of Capitalist Imperialism." In this work he takes the position that Hobson's synthesis of 1902 depends at least in part on much earlier work by classical economists and by Marx. He is referring here to the concept, widely discussed by the 1860s, that under capitalism profits tend to decline and savings tend to accumulate into ever more concentrated masses. In the following selection he argues that economic theory, not to say simple logic, shows how wrong it is to claim that "new imperialism" arose from the need "to save capitalism from a moribund condition," and furthermore that the historical facts simply do not fit the Hobson-Lenin model.

The obvious conclusion is that the Theory of Capitalist Imperialism is of little value to the historian whose aim is simply to explain why the colonial empires expanded so widely and so fast in the period after about 1870. To support this statement let us recapitulate the Theory in its various forms and then survey its defects from the historian's point of view.

SOURCE. D. K. Fieldhouse, ed., *The Theory of Capitalist Imperialism* (London: Longmans, Green and Co. Ltd., 1967), pp. 187–192. Reprinted by permission of the publisher.

In every form in which the Theory is represented . . . its central
theme is that overseas colonies were acquired primarily because
of their relevance to the internal economic characteristics or
problems of European countries or of the United States. English
liberals such as Robertson, Hobson and Brailsford took the driving force to be "undercomsumption," by which they meant that
the unequal distribution of wealth in capitalist countries so
deprived the mass of workers of buying power that the capitalist
could not profitably invest his surplus capital in industry at
home. Hence his anxiety to acquire colonies as alternative fields
for profitable investment. The neo-Marxists had other arguments.
Rosa Luxemburg thought that capitalist countries depended on
trade with non-capitalist places at all stages of their development,
and that colonial acquisitions were primarily the result of a
shortage of such necessary extra-European commercial balancers.
By contrast, Hilferding, Bukharin and Lenin, followed thereafter
by most orthodox Marxists, thought imperialism was the product
of the special economic problems of capitalism in its last,
monopolistic, phase, when "finance capital" had absorbed competitive capital. Such differences of interpretation are important;
yet they do not destroy the essential unity of the Theory of
Capitalist Imperialism in its assumption that imperialism was the
product of factors within Europe and that colonies were acquired
primarily to save capitalism from a moribund condition in which
the further accumulation of capital within Europe was becoming
impossible.

Turning from the Theory to its critics . . . there are two main
ways in which to dissect and evaluate such concepts. First it is
possible to consider the basic premise that capitalist societies
have been forced by economic factors to invest abroad rather than
at home: that capital was forced out and had to find a home in
dependent territories or "semi-colonies." On purely theoretical
grounds this is highly dubious; and it is perfectly possible to construct a model for the economic development of modern Europe
on the assumption that the continent had no possibility of outside investment without necessarily accepting as a consequence
a stop to the process of investment or the accumulation of capital.
Economic development would certainly have been very different
and might have been slower; but it could still have taken place.
Conversely it is possible to explain the fact of capital exports

without accepting the premise that capital was forced out. It is equally arguable that capitalists merely chose to invest part of their capital overseas because at particular times such investment seemed more attractive than investment at home—that it was pulled out by higher interest or dividends, or to develop commodities needed in Europe. While such eclectic investment might well have led to colonial annexation, and so does not make it impossible that colonization might be economic in aim, it does emasculate the Theory of Capitalist Imperialism by making overseas investment a voluntary rather than a necessary phenomenon, and so eliminates the element of inevitability. At the same time such a modification leaves it open to the historian to decide whether, in particular cases, the attractive power of such overseas investment seems to have been the motive behind the process of colonial expansion.

A rather different approach to the Theory in its full form is to concede its economic premises, but to test its historical validity against facts and chronology. On this test also the critics have found it vulnerable. The key period for the establishment of the tropical colonial empires was during the 1880's and 1890's, when the partition of Africa and the east was virtually completed. If the main force behind imperialism was indeed the need of capitalism for new fields for investment, then this need must have been felt acutely during these twenty years. Yet the neo-Marxist argument based on finance capital simply does not fit this requirement. Lenin expressly dated the predominance of finance capital in Germany from about 1900. Germany was certainly more advanced along this line than any other great power, so that it would be unreasonable to look for similar conditions in, say, Britain or France, which were certainly not dominated by monopoly capitalism at any time before 1914. Hence it seems undeniable that the Lenin hypothesis, whatever its possible relevance to European attitudes to empire once the process of colonial expansion had taken place, cannot be used to explain the expansion itself.

If the neo-Marxist version of the Theory falls down most obviously on chronology, both this and the liberal Hobsonian version break on the test of geography. As most of the critics have indicated, the Theory can only be accepted as an historical explanation if it can be shown that there was in fact some direct connection between the desire of Europe to export capital and those parts of the world where capital was invested during the period of annexation or shortly after: which would suggest that the new colonies really did offer special attractions to the investor as against existing colonies or comparable independent states. In fact this was not so. The facts of European overseas investment, which were for the most part not available at the time when the Theory was being formulated, now make it clear that there was very little geographical correlation between capital export and the new colonies. In some places there was, of course, an apparent link. Europe had invested heavily in Tunis, Morocco, Egypt and the Transvaal before these were acquired by France and Britain respectively. In fact, these were the basic examples which convinced men like Hobson that their argument was demonstratively true. Moreover, in the years before 1914, significant amounts of capital were invested in new colonies, such as the Gold Coast, Malaya, the newly occupied parts of Indonesia and elsewhere. So far the Theory would seem correct. But in fact this is misleading. First, these places were not typical of the greater part of those areas acquired during the "imperialist" grab. They were the plums, the exceptionally favoured areas, which would almost certainly have attracted capital because of the opportunities they offered even if the possibility of political annexation had not existed. It was reasonable for the observer to assume that imperial control was imposed on these in order to safeguard or stimulate capital investment under the most favourable conditions: but what of the rest, which had previously attracted no keen attention from the investing capitalist and in fact never did so? Unless we accept the view that European capital was so desperate for future fields for investment that it was prepared to annex even the most unpromising regions of the world as a long-run precaution—a view which Lenin would have accepted, but which seems historically improbable—it is difficult to see the relevance of the Theory in explaining their annexation. In short, it is one major weakness of the Theory that capital exported on a large scale and tropical colonies annexed only rarely coincide.

Nevertheless, at first sight, the correlation of these two factors in certain of the new colonies would seem to give the Theory some historical basis. It is only when the historian investigates the evidence as to why obvious places like Egypt or the Transvaal were annexed that even this element of probability disappears. While few would deny that the fact of existing investment gave these regions heightened significance, it seems increasingly clear that "political" rather than economic considerations were decisive. Thus the British were more interested in the strategic relevance of Egypt to the security of India than in their holdings in the Canal Company; the Transvaal was annexed less to satisfy investors in the gold mines than to prevent the absorption of the Cape by an unfriendly Boer republic; France saw Tunisia in terms of the security of Algeria rather than as a place where French bankers had made large loans, and was determined to forestall an Italian takeover; and so on. In fact, although it would be out of place here to put forward alternative explanations of particular annexations, few historians would now concede that European motives, even in these apparently blatant examples of capitalist activity, were simply based on financial questions.

We are left, then, with clear evidence that the Theory has historical defects. Imperial expansion occurred too early to fit the chronology of the emergence of "finance capitalism"; many "imperialist" powers—notably Russia, Italy, Portugal and Spain —far from having an embarrassing surplus of capital, were net importers of capital and must have had other motives for making annexations. The greater proportion of capital exports after about 1870 did not go to the regions involved in the grab for new colonies, but either to existing European possessions— Canada, Australia, New Zealand, India—or to independent states, such as Russia, China, the Argentine or the United States. Capital went where it was most strongly attracted by economic conditions. There was no shortage of such places, and it is impossible to think that European capitalists were embarrassed by lack of fields for investment along traditional lines. Even where there does seem to be some correlation between capital export and the annexation of a new colony, as often as not there is inconvenient evidence that the statesmen of Europe had reasons for acting other than merely to further the interests of high finance.

But these conclusions leave us with a major historiographical problem. Why is it that the Theory of Capitalist Imperialism, despite the mauling it has received from critics, remains dogma in Marxist countries and influential amost everywhere? Although any answer must be speculative, it is important to provide one because this Theory is one of many quasi-historical concepts which have survived equally devastating analysis, often for analogous reasons. In this case there would appear to be two distinct explanations for its survival in different circumstances. The first is special to Marxists who accept the basic premises of Lenin's theory. If one accepts the hypothesis that capitalism at a certain stage in its development must either export capital or be strangled by lack of the opportunity to accumulate more capital, then the tests applied by the historian to see whether this need was the direct cause of colonial expansion become irrelevant. Once a capitalist country has become "imperialist" in Lenin's sense it is not only bound to export capital but also to protect that capital by political means. Whether these means include formal annexation or informal pressures is largely irrelevant, for imperialism is infinitely adaptable to changed conditions, preserving its essential control over its economically dependent territories even when these eventually become sovereign states after decolonization. In the face of such certainty historical quibbles over the exact chronology of partition or the precise motives of a few statesmen become irrelevant. The essential truth remains that the colonial empires were the product of the socio-economic condition of the imperialist states and were an inevitable outcome of their historical evolution. Hence any evidence to the contrary must be regarded as misleading.

But the Theory also won acceptance from many who were not Marxists, and we must therefore look for a more general explanation of its popularity. This is probably the simple fact that it provided a straightforward and apparently convincing explanation of what at first sight seemed an intractable question. Until the Theory is examined in detail it carries conviction. As has been seen . . . the classical economists and their successors postulated the need of all capitalist societies to export capital to preserve the rate of profit on investments. In the later nineteenth century and during the twentieth there was no doubt that Europe was exporting capital in very large amounts, some of it to the newly acquired colonies. Leading statesmen and enthusiasts for empire, such as Leopold II, Jules Ferry and Leroy-Beaulieu, supported by propagandists in many countries of Europe, deliberately justified colonization in economic terms. The rough chronology of colonization seemed to indicate that the rapid expansion after 1870 coincided with the unprecedented economic growth of Europe and North America. Some colonies, if not the majority, became important annexes of the European and American economies. On all counts the facts appeared to support the Theory, and it seemed pointless to look beyond it for an explanation of the modern colonial empires.

Thus the main reason for the general popularity of the Theory has been its sheer probability, coupled with its neatness and universality. Conversely, the difficulty of the critic has been that in rejecting or modifying it he seems to be merely captious. The onus is on him to show that the Theory is misleading, and he can do so only by a tedious examination of individual cases through which few are prepared to follow him. Yet by now the work done has largely demolished the foundations of the Theory. It remains possible still to say that imperialism might possibly have worked that way. Capital was being exported, colonies were being acquired, the two might well have been linked as cause and effect. Yet the evidence, perhaps surprisingly, points in the other direction. Despite the obvious explanation, colonization was more the product of political ambitions, international rivalries, and complex situations in the non-European world than of simple and universal economic forces. The Theory of Capitalist Imperialism might have been true, but in fact it was not. Sooner or later the sheer volume of the evidence and argument marshalled on the other side will convince the majority that imperialism was not the simple product of advanced capitalism.

4 FROM   *John Gallagher*
        and Ronald Robinson
  The Myth of a "Twilight Era" in the History
          of Imperialism

---

*Historians John A. Gallagher and Ronald Robinson (both
Cambridge University) launched, with this essay, one of the more
important salvos directed against the stages theory of imperialism. They attack a concept crucial to Hobson's, Hilferding's, and
Lenin's interpretation of imperialism: that the central question
to be answered is why there was an outburst of imperialist activity
after 1870 following the great decline in imperialism during the
previous generation. In this article Gallagher and Robinson deny
that such a question has any connection with historical reality.
If we grant that imperialism includes "informal empire," they
state, there is no tight connection whatsoever between "phases of
imperialism . . . [and] phases in the economic growth of the
metropolitan economy."*

It ought to be a commonplace that Great Britain during the
nineteenth century expanded overseas by means of "informal
empire" as much as by acquiring dominion in the strict constitutional sense. For purposes of economic analysis it would clearly
be unreal to define imperial history exclusively as the history of
those colonies coloured red on the map. Nevertheless, almost all
imperial history has been written on the assumption that the
empire of formal dominion is historically comprehensible in itself
and can be cut out of its context in British expansion and world
politics. The conventional interpretation of the nineteenth-century empire continues to rest upon study of the formal empire
alone, which is rather like judging the size and character of ice-
bergs from the parts above the water-line. . . .

SOURCE. John Gallagher and Ronald Robinson, "The Imperialism of Free
Trade," *The Economic History Review*, 2nd ser., VI, no. 1 (1953), pp. 1–15.
Reprinted by permission of The Economic History Society.

In the last quarter of the century, Professor [William L.] Langer finds that "there was an obvious danger that the British (export) market would be steadily restricted. Hence the emergence and sudden flowering of the movement for expansion. . . . Manchester doctrine had been belied by the facts. It was an outworn theory to be thrown into the discard." [This] argument may be summarized in this way: the mid-Victorian formal empire did not expand, indeed it seemed to be disintegrating, therefore the period was anti-imperialist; the later-Victorian formal empire expanded rapidly, therefore this was an era of imperialism; the change was caused by the obsolescence of free trade.

The trouble with this argument is that it leaves out too many of the facts which it claims to explain. Consider the results of a decade of "indifference" to empire. Between 1841 and 1851 Great Britain occupied or annexed New Zealand, the Gold Coast, Labuan, Natal, the Punjab, Sind and Hong Kong. In the next twenty years British control was asserted over Berar, Oudh, Lower Burma and Kowloon, over Lagos and the neighbourhood of Sierra Leone, over Basutoland, Gruiqualand and the Transvaal; and new colonies were established in Queensland and British Columbia. Unless this expansion can be explained by "fits of absence of mind," we are faced with the paradox that it occurred despite the determination of the imperial authorities to avoid extending their rule. . . .

. . . If we refuse to narrow our view to that of formal empire, we can see how steadily and successfully the main imperial interest was pursued by maintaining supremacy over the whole region, and that it was pursued as steadily throughout the so-called anti-imperialist era as in the late-Victorian period. But it was done by shutting in the Boer Republics from the Indian Ocean: by the annexation of Natal in 1843, by keeping the Boers out of Delagoa Bay in 1860 and 1868, out of St. Lucia Bay in 1861 and 1866, and by British intervention to block the union of the two Republics under Pretorius in 1860. . . .

Are these the actions of ministers anxious to preside over the liquidation of the British Empire? Do they look like "indifference" to an empire rendered superfluous by free trade? On the contrary, here is a continuity of policy which the conventional interpretation misses because it takes account only of formal methods of control. It also misses the continuous grasp of the

West African coast and of the South Pacific which British sea-power was able to maintain. Refusals to annex are no proof of reluctance to control. . . .

Nor can the obvious continuity of imperial constitutional policy throughout the mid- and late-Victorian years be explained on the orthodox hypothesis. If the granting of responsible government to colonies was due to the mid-Victorian "indifference" to empire and even a desire to be rid of it, then why was this policy continued in the late-Victorian period when Britain was interested above all in preserving imperial unity? The common assumption that British governments in the free-trade era considered empire superfluous arises from over-estimating the significance of changes in legalistic forms. In fact, throughout the Victorian period responsible government was withheld from colonies if it involved sacrificing or endangering British paramountcy or interests. Wherever there was fear of a foreign challenge to British supremacy in the continent or sub-continent concerned, wherever the colony could not provide financially for its own internal security, the imperial authorities retained full responsibility, or, if they had already devolved it, intervened directly to secure their interests once more. In other words, responsible government, far from being a separatist device, was simply a change from direct to indirect methods of maintaining British interests. By slackening the formal political bond at the appropriate time, it was possible to rely on economic dependence and mutual good-feeling to keep the colonies bound to Britain while still using them as agents for further British expansion. . . .

Moreover, in this supposedly *laissez-faire* period India, far from being evacuated, was subjected to intensive development as an economic colony along the best mercantilist lines. In India it was possible, throughout most of the period of the British Raj, to use the governing power to extort in the form of taxes and monopolies such valuable primary products as opium and salt. Furthermore, the characteristics of so-called imperialist expansion at the end of the nineteenth century developed in India long before the date (1880) when Lenin believed the age of economic imperialism opened. Direct government promotion of products required by British industry, government manipulation of tariffs to help British exports, railway construction at high and guaranteed rates of interest to open the continental interior—all of these techniques of direct political control were employed in ways which seem alien to the so-called age of *laissez-faire*. . . .

The hypothesis which is needed must include informal as well as formal expansion, and must allow for the continuity of the process. The most striking fact about British history in the nineteenth century . . . is that it is the history of an expanding society. The exports of capital and manufactures, the migration of citizens, the dissemination of the English language, ideas and constitutional forms, were all of them radiations of the social energies of the British peoples. Between 1812 and 1914 over twenty million persons emigrated from the British Isles, and nearly 70 per cent of them went outside the Empire. Between 1815 and 1880, it is estimated, £1,187,000,000 in credit had accumulated abroad, but no more than one-sixth was placed in the formal empire. Even by 1913, something less than half of the £3,975,-000,000 of foreign investment lay inside the Empire. Similarly, in no year of the century did the Empire buy much more than one-third of Britain's exports. The basic fact is that British industrialization caused an ever-extending and intensifying development of overseas regions. Whether they were formally British or not, was a secondary consideration.

Imperialism, perhaps, may be defined as a sufficient political function of this process of integrating new regions into the expanding economy; its character is largely decided by the various and changing relationships between the political and economic elements of expansion in any particular region and time. Two qualifications must be made. First, imperialism may be only indirectly connected with economic integration in that it sometimes extends beyond areas of economic development, but acts for their strategic protection. Secondly, although imperialism is a function of economic expansion, it is not a necessary function. Whether imperialist phenomena show themselves or not, is determined not only by the factors of economic expansion, but equally by the political and social organization of the regions brought into the orbit of the expansive society, and also by the world situation in general.

It is only when the polities of these new regions fail to provide satisfactory conditions for commercial or strategic integration and when their relative weakness allows, that power is used imperialistically to adjust those conditions. Economic expansion,

it is true, will tend to flow into the regions of maximum opportunity, but maximum opportunity depends as much upon
political considerations of security as upon questions of profit.
Consequently, in any particular region, if economic opportunity
seems large but political security small, then full absorption into
the extending economy tends to be frustrated until power is
exerted upon the state in question. Conversely, in proportion as
satisfactory political frameworks are brought into being in this
way, the frequency of imperialist intervention lessens and imperialist control is correspondingly relaxed. It may be suggested
that this willingness to limit the use of paramount power to
establishing security for trade is the distinctive feature of the
British imperialism of free trade in the nineteenth century, in
contrast to the mercantilist use of power to obtain commercial
supremacy and monopoly through political possession.

On this hypothesis the phasing of British expansion or imperialism is not likely to be chronological. Not all regions will
reach the same level of economic integration at any one time;
neither will all regions need the same type of political control at
any one time. As the British industrial revolution grew, so new
markets and sources of supply were linked to it at different times,
and the degree of imperialist action accompanying that process
varied accordingly. Thus mercantilist techniques of formal empire were being employed to develop India in the mid-Victorian
age at the same time as informal techniques of free trade were
being used in Latin America for the same purpose. It is for this
reason that attempts to make phases of imperialism correspond
directly to phases in the economic growth of the metropolitan
economy are likely to prove in vain. The fundamental continuity
of British expansion is only obscured by arguing that changes
in the terms of trade or in the character of British exports neces-
sitated a sharp change in the process. . . .

The economic importance—even the pre-eminence—of informal empire in this period has been stressed often enough.
What was overlooked was the inter-relation of its economic and
political arms; how political action aided the growth of commercial supremacy, and how this supremacy in turn strengthened
political influence. In other words, it is the politics as well as the
economics of the informal empire which we have to include in

the account. Historically, the relationship between these two factors has been both subtle and complex. It has been by no means a simple case of the use of gunboats to demolish a recalcitrant state in the cause of British trade. The type of political lien between the expanding economy and its formal or informal dependencies, as might be expected, has been flexible. In practice it has tended to vary with the economic value of the territory, the strength of its political structure, the readiness of its rulers to collaborate with British commercial or strategic purposes, the ability of the native society to undergo economic change without external control, the extent to which domestic and foreign political situations permitted British intervention, and, finally, how far European rivals allowed British policy a free hand. . . .

In both the formal and informal dependencies in the mid-Victorian age there was much effort to open the continental interiors and to extend the British influence inland from the ports and to develop the hinterlands. The general strategy of this development was to convert these areas into complementary satellite economies, which would provide raw materials and food for Great Britain, and also provide widening markets for its manufactures. This was the period, the orthodox interpretation would have us believe, in which the political arm of expansion was dormant or even withered. In fact, that alleged inactivity is seen to be a delusion if we take into account the development in the informal aspect. Once entry had been forced into Latin America, China and the Balkans, the task was to encourage stable governments as good investment risks, just as in weaker or unsatisfactory states it was considered necessary to coerce them into more co-operative attitudes. . . .

The types of informal empire and the situations it attempted to exploit were as various as the success which it achieved. Although commercial and capital penetration tended to lead to political co-operation and hegemony, there are striking exceptions. In the United States, for example, British business turned the cotton South into a colonial economy, and the British investor hoped to do the same with the Mid-West. But the political strength of the country stood in his way. It was impossible to stop American industrialization, and the industrialized sections successfully campaigned for tariffs, despite the opposition of those sections which depended on the British trade connexion. In the same way, American political strength thwarted British attempts to establish Texas, Mexico and Central America as informal dependencies. . . .

The simple recital of these cases of economic expansion, aided and abetted by political action in one form or other, is enough to expose the inadequacy of the conventional theory that free trade could dispense with empire. We have seen that it did not do so. Economic expansion in the mid-Victorian age was matched by a corresponding political expansion which has been overlooked because it could not be seen by that study of maps which, it has been said, drives sane men mad. It is absurd to deduce from the harmony between London and the colonies of white settlement in the mid-Victorian age any British reluctance to intervene in the fields of British interests. The warships at Canton are as much a part of the period as responsible government for Canada; the battlefields of the Punjab are as real as the abolition of suttee.

Far from being an era of "indifference," the mid-Victorian years were the decisive stage in the history of British expansion overseas, in that the combination of commercial penetration and political influence allowed the United Kingdom to command those economies which could be made to fit best into her own. A variety of techniques adapted to diverse conditions and beginning at different dates were employed to effect this domination. A paramountcy was set up in Malaya centred on Singapore; a suzerainty over much of West Africa reached out from the port of Lagos and was backed up by the African squadron. On the east coast of Africa British influence at Zanzibar, dominant thanks to the exertions of Consul Kirk, placed the heritage of Arab command on the mainland at British disposal.

But perhaps the most common political technique of British expansion was the treaty of free trade and friendship made with or imposed upon a weaker state. The treaties with Persia of 1836 and 1857, and Turkish treaties of 1838 and 1861, the Japanese treaty of 1858, the favours extracted from Zanzibar, Siam and Morocco, the hundreds of anti-slavery treaties signed with crosses by African chiefs—all these treaties enabled the British government to carry forward trade with these regions. . . .

. . . Throughout, British governments worked to establish and maintain British paramountcy by whatever means best suited to circumstances of their diverse regions of interest. The aims of the mid-Victorians were no more "anti-imperialist" than their successors', though they were more often able to achieve them informally; and the late Victorians were no more "imperialist" than their predecessors, even though they were driven to annex more often. British policy followed the principle of extending control informally if possible and formally if necessary. To label the one method "anti-imperialist" and the other "imperialist," is to ignore the fact that whatever the method British interests were steadily safeguarded and extended. The usual summing up of the policy of the free trade empire as "trade not rule" should read "trade with informal control if possible; trade with rule when necessary." This statement of the continuity of policy disposes of the over-simplified explanation of involuntary expansion inherent in the orthodox interpretation based on the discontinuity between the two periods. . . .

Thus the mid-Victorian period now appears as an era of large-scale expansion, and the late-Victorian age does not seem to introduce any significant novelty into that process of expansion. The annexations of vast undeveloped territories, which have been taken as proof that this period alone was the great age of expansion, now pale in significance, at least if our analysis is anywhere near the truth. That the area of direct imperial rule was extended is true, but is it the most important or characteristic development of expansion during this period? The simple historical fact that Africa was the last field of European penetration is not to say that it was the most important; this would be a truism were it not that the main case of the Hobson school is founded on African examples. On the other hand, it is our main contention that the process of expansion had reached its most valuable targets long before the exploitation of so peripheral and marginal a field as tropical Africa. Consequently arguments, founded on the technique adopted in scrambling for Africa, would seem to be of secondary importance.

Therefore, the historian who is seeking to find the deepest meaning of the expansion at the end of the nineteenth century should look not at the mere pegging out of the claims in African jungles and bush, but at the successful exploitation of the empire, both formal and informal, which was then coming to fruition in India, in Latin America, in Canada and elsewhere.

The main work of imperialism in the so-called expansionist era was in the more intensive development of areas already linked with the world economy, rather than in the extensive annexations of the remaining marginal regions of Africa. The best finds and prizes had already been made; in tropical Africa the imperialists were merely scraping the bottom of the barrel.

5 FROM   *H. S. Ferns*
Was "Informal Empire" Imperialism?

H. S. Ferns teaches political science at the University of Birmingham. His detailed study of Anglo-Argentine relationships, of which the following selection forms the conclusions, shows that "informal empire" can be a thoroughly misleading concept. One cannot assume that wherever a great country enjoyed a preponderance of the foreign trade of another country, there must have existed an imperialist situation. Ferns' work weakens somewhat the attack by Gallagher and Robinson against the stages thesis of imperialism in their 1953 article. It also can be interpreted as contradicting the neo-Leninist argument that today's heavy investments by rich countries in Latin America proves the existence of neocolonialism.

Speculation on the subject of British enterprise in Argentina carries us to the heart of Anglo-Argentine relationship both as it has existed historically and as it exists at the present time. The term "imperialism" is widely used in Argentina and elsewhere in discussing the connexion between the two countries. Argentina never belonged to the British Empire, of course; but Argentina is, or was, part of Britain's informal empire. Argentina is within a British sphere of influence. Britain exercises great influence in

SOURCE. H. S. Ferns, *Britain and Argentina in the Nineteenth Century* (Oxford: The Clarendon Press, 1960), pp. 487–491. Reprinted by permission of the publisher.

Argentina. Britain exploits Argentina. So the argument runs, and the argument is widely believed, and attitudes affecting action derive from it.

There is a case for the large British investment in Argentina, and there is a case against it. The evidence suggests, however, that neither case has been sufficiently related to the facts.

Can the term imperialism be applied to the Anglo-Argentine relations? If we accept the proposition that imperialism embraces the fact of control through the use of political power, then the verdict for Britain is unquestionably "Not Guilty." The only complete attempt made by Britain to establish political power in the River Plate failed [1806–1807], and out of that failure developed a policy which specifically recognized that political power exercised in and over Argentina or any other country in South America was an ineffective means of achieving the British objective of a beneficial commercial and financial relationship. The Anglo-Argentine political equation, which recognized Britain and Argentina as independent variables, was not derived from the liberal idealism of Canning, but from the material facts learned on the field of battle and discernible to anyone familiar with the character of the terrain and people of Argentina. During the nineteenth century there was no alteration in the Anglo-Argentine equation, and there is no reason for supposing it is any different today than it was a century and a half ago.

This political equation is the equation from which all equations in the sphere of economics have been derived. The Argentine Government has always possessed the power to forbid, to encourage, or to shape the economic relations of Argentina with other communities including the British community. The British Government has never had the power to oblige Argentina to pay a debt, to pay a dividend, or to export or import any commodity whatever. The only occasion when the British Government went beyond talk in dealing with Argentina, during the troubled time of General Rosas, they were defeated and they formally admitted that they were defeated [1845–1847]. When powerful financial interests urged the use of political power to influence Argentine economic policy in 1891 [during the thundering crisis involving the great banking house of Baring Brothers], the British Foreign Secretary privately and publicly repudiated such a suggestion. Every crisis in the economic and financial relations of Britain and Argentina has been resolved in economic and financial terms—by a weighing of advantages and disadvantages by both parties—and not by the intrusion of political power. Of course, British commercial and financial interests have exercised great influence in Argentina; but so have Argentine interests exercised great influence in Britain. Any agricultural landlord or farmer in Britain between the years 1890 and 1939 could argue that Argentina was a factor in their fate, and a very adverse one. Derelict fields in Cambridgeshire existed in part because fields in the Argentine Republic were heavy with cheap cereals, and Argentine *estancieros* have wintered on the Riviera while herdsmen in Shropshire went bankrupt. These are facts which make nonsense of myths about British imperialism and Argentina as a semi-colony of a great and powerful state.

One may deplore the consequences for Argentina, and likewise the consequences for Britain, of the kind of relationship worked out by the Argentine landed and commercial interest in conjunction with the financial, industrial, and commercial interests of Great Britain, but when one starts deploring let no one blame an abstraction called Britain or another one called Argentina. If, over a long span of time, Argentina has possessed a weak and narrowly based industrial structure compared with that of the United States or even Canada, this has been due to the concentration of effort in Argentina upon agricultural and pastoral enterprise and upon the production of pastoral and agricultural commodities. Political power and/or decisive influence upon policy in Argentina has belonged until recent times to the interests with most to gain by such a concentration.

The dominant interests in Argentina sought out the foreign capitalists in the first instance; the foreign capitalists did not invade Argentina, and in the beginning and for many years after the investment process commenced European investors were reluctant to supply Argentina with as much purchasing power as the Argentine Government required. That the European investors invested anything depended partly upon the guarantees given by the Argentine authorities, partly upon the direct responsibility for payment undertaken by the state, and partly upon the existence in Argentina of a British business community capable of organizing in a practical way enterprises like railways and meat-freezing plants. Contrary to common belief the British investor received help and protection from the Argentine Government not the British Government. When the British Government finally felt obliged to assist British investors in Argentina, it did so not by sending an expeditionary force to the River Plate, but by underwriting the Bank of England, which in turn underwrote the private and joint-stock banks, which in their turn underwrote the firm of Baring Brothers.

There is still much work to be done before any convincing answer can be given to the question: who benefited most from economic development in Argentina? The evidence in hand, however, suggests some tentative answers. Some foreign interests benefited greatly; for example, the shareholders of some of the banks; some railway shareholders and investors in meat-processing and cold-storage enterprises and some mercantile establishments. But the overall profits of British investors were sufficiently low to prompt the hypothesis that the great interests of Argentina did not dominate the fields occupied so largely by British enterprise because the returns were greater in the fields dominated by Argentinos. The appreciation of land values and the profits of pastoral enterprise, commercial agriculture, and share-cropping seem to have been the best sources of wealth in the years from 1860 to 1914. The political power, the social knowledge, the entrenched position of native Argentinos gave them a tremendous advantage in this field. The system of education, handicapped in its scope by niggardly state expenditure and in its content by the influence of the Roman Catholic Church, further ordained that native Argentinos were ill equipped to take control of enterprises requiring great technical knowledge and habits of exact application to managerial responsibilities. Thus foreigners, and particularly the British, dominated in the less rewarding and more demanding fields of endeavour.

There seems to be considerable evidence during the period [of the nineteenth century] that the permanent wage worker both urban and rural benefited least . . . If this is so, why was immigration so abundant? Economic opportunities not wage rates seem to be the predominant inducement to immigrants. Argentine wages in the long run seem to have been rather better than wages in Italy and Spain, from whence the majority of immigrants came, but much inferior to wage rates in the United States, Canada, or Australia. But economic opportunities seem

to have been roughly alike. Indeed, in Argentina the prizes
open to people possessed of peasant shrewdness in buying and
selling were, perhaps, greater than elsewhere. For a man with
only a strong back and a willingness to work, Argentina was,
perhaps, a slight improvement on his homeland, but not a place
of rich rewards.

Among the beneficiaries of Argentine expansion before 1914
we must not neglect mention of the English wage working class.
Some benefited from employment opportunities created by manufacturing for the Argentine market. A much wider mass benefited
as consumers from the cheap food products flowing in increasing
flood from the River Plate. If the Englishman of that age was
the biggest meat eater in Europe it was partly due to the fact
that Argentina was the cheapest producer of beef in the world.

The Anglo-Argentine connexion, with the benefits and disadvantages which we have described as they existed in the years
between the Boer War and World War I, was a phase in the
life of growing communities and not a system which can be
recreated. The passage of time and the changing social composition of the Argentine community revealed weaknesses and
altered the objectives of economic activity. One of the leading
staples of Argentine international trade—cereals—was marketed
under conditions of nearly perfect competition. So long as the
overall factors in the world market kept up cereal prices in relation to the prices of manufactured goods, the Argentine economy
functioned without crippling frustrations. When the overall
factors in the world market began to alter this relationship
between cereal prices and the prices of manufactured goods,
Argentina began to discover the limitations and defects of concentration on food production.

Changes in world-market conditions ran parallel after World
War I with changes in the social composition of the Argentine
community. So long as Argentina possessed an open frontier
where new land was continuously being brought into production, the flow of immigrants and the growth of great commercial
metropolises like Buenos Aires and Rosario did not seriously
disturb the rural-urban balance either in politics or policy making. When the land frontier closed, as it did in the golden age
at the beginning of this century, the urban masses began to
assert themselves, and the better educated began to question the

wisdom of placing all Argentina's eggs in the well-worn basket of agricultural and pastoral production. Why not make more jobs and more opportunities for native Argentinos? The popular pressure for industrialization began to develop even before World War I. Perhaps rich land is Argentina's best resource, but Argentina is also a people, and a growing number of them after World War I began rightly to doubt whether the life of a farm labourer, a cold-storage worker, or a grain clerk was good enough. When the Great Depression of 1928 struck down cereal and meat prices, the bell began to toll for the old Anglo-Argentine relationship. . .

PART TWO

Economic and Other Causes

6 FROM Carlton J. H. Hayes
New Imperialism—New Nationalism

Carlton Hayes (1882–1964) was America's most outstanding student of the history of nationalism. His many and immensely successful textbooks on European history and his long and prestigious career at Columbia University firmly implanted in the scholarly world his ideas on the nationalistic bases of imperialism. As we can see in the following selection, Hayes (along with many other historians) failed to distinguish between a general materialist interpretation of imperialism and the Hobson-Lenin model.

A favorite explanation of why European imperialism turned abruptly within a decade from nadir to apogee, has been the economic. It was advanced originally by publicists and statesmen to win the support of business interests for imperialistic policies, and it received classical treatment, at the time of the Boer War, by John A. Hobson. Latterly it has been taken up by Marxian writers and integrated with their dogma of materialistic determinism. . .

Doubtless large-scale mechanized industry, with accompanying

SOURCE. Carlton J. H. Hayes, *A Generation of Materialism, 1871–1900,* pp. 217–229. Copyright 1941 by Harper & Row, Publishers, Inc.; renewed 1969 by Evelyn Hayes. Reprinted by permission of Harper & Row, Publishers, Inc.

improvement of transportation facilities, did immensely stimulate an ever-widening quest for markets where surplus manufactures might be disposed of, necessary raw materials procured, and lucrative investments made. Nor can there be any doubt that by the 1870's, when industrialization on the Continent was beginning seriously to vie with England's, the quest was being as eagerly pursued by commercial and banking houses of Hamburg and Bremen, Marseilles and Paris, as by those of London and Liverpool. . . .

But commercial expansion into the tropics was a novelty of degree rather than of kind and hardly suffices to explain the political imperialism of the '70's and '80's. This was inaugurated prior to any general resort to tariff protectionism in Europe, and prior also to any universal export of capital. Neither Russia nor Italy had surplus manufactures to dispose of or surplus wealth to invest; yet both engaged in the scramble for imperial dominion, the one with striking success and the other not. Germany exported little capital until after she had acquired an extensive colonial empire, and France secured a far more extensive one while her industrial development lagged behind Germany's. Great Britain had long had all the supposed economic motives for imperialism—export of manufactured goods, demand for raw materials, supply of surplus capital—and yet these did not move her in the '60's as much as they did in the '70's. On the other hand, Norway, whose ocean-borne commerce was exceeded only by Great Britain's and Germany's, remained consistently aloof from overseas imperialism.

Apparently the flag of a European nation did not have to follow its trade—or its financial investments. But once flag raising became common and competitive in Africa and on the Pacific, economic considerations undoubtedly spurred most of the European participants to greater efforts and keener competition in those regions. Then the tariff protectionism of Continental nations was applied, in one form or another, to their respective colonies, and the more colonies each one had the greater were its opportunities for favorable trade and investment and the closer it approached to the ideal of all-around self-sufficiency. And to prevent too much of the world from being thus monopolized by France, Germany, Italy, or any other protectionist power, Great Britain moved mightily to gather the lion's share into her own free-trade empire. In other words, neo-mercantilism, once established, had very important imperialistic consequences.

The fact remains, nevertheless, that the founding of new colonial empires and the fortifying of old ones antedated the establishment of neo-mercantilism, and that the economic arguments adduced in support of imperialism seem to have been a rationalization *ex post facto*. In the main, it was not Liberal parties, with their superabundance of industrialists and bankers, who sponsored the outward imperialistic thrusts of the '70's and early '80's. Instead, it was Conservative parties, with a preponderantly agricultural clientele notoriously suspicious of money-lenders and big business, and, above all, it was patriotic professors and publicists regardless of political affiliation and unmindful of personal economic interest. These put forth the economic arguments which eventually drew bankers and traders and industrialists into the imperialist camp.

Basically the new imperialism was a nationalistic phenomenon. It followed hard upon the national wars which created an all-powerful Germany and a united Italy, which carried Russia within sight of Constantinople, and which left England fearful and France eclipsed. It expressed a resulting psychological reaction, an ardent desire to maintain or recover national prestige. France sought compensation for European loss in oversea gain. England would offset her European isolation by enlarging and glorifying the British Empire. Russia, halted in the Balkans, would turn anew to Asia, and before long Germany and Italy would show the world that the prestige they had won by might inside Europe they were entitled to enhance by imperial exploits outside. The lesser powers, with no great prestige at stake, managed to get on without any new imperialism, though Portugal and Holland displayed a revived pride in the empires they already possessed and the latter's was administered with renewed vigor.

Public agitation for extending overseas the political dominion of European national states certainly began with patriotic intellectuals. As early as 1867 Lothar Bucher, one of Bismarck's associates in the Prussian foreign office, published in the influential *Norddeutsche Allgemeine Zeitung* a series of articles endorsing and advertising the hitherto neglected counsels of

Friedrich List: "Companies should be founded in the German seaports to buy lands in foreign countries and settle them with German colonies; also companies for commerce and navigation whose object would be to open new markets abroad for German manufacturers and to establish steamship lines. . . . Colonies are the best means of developing manufactures, export and import trade, and finally a respectable navy."

The next year Otto Kersten, traveler and explorer, founded at Berlin a "Central Society for Commercial Geography and German Interests Abroad," with an official journal, *Der Export*. Simultaneously the "Royal Colonial Institute" was founded at London; and a brilliant young English gentleman, Sir Charles Dilke, returning from a trip around the world, published his patriotic and immensely popular *Greater Britain*. Two years later, in the midst of the Franco-Prussian War, the redoubtable Froude scored his fellow Englishmen in the pages of *Fraser's Magazine* for their blindness to imperial glories. In 1872 Disraeli practically committed the Conservative party in Britain to a program of imperialism, and in 1874 Paul Leroy-Beaulieu, dean of political economists in France and implacable foe of tariff protection, plumped for French imperialism in a "scientific" treatise, *De la Colonisation chez les peuples modernes*.

These were foretastes. Heartier fare was served immediately after the Russo-Turkish War and the Congress of Berlin. In 1879 Friedrich Fabri, a pious promoter of Christian foreign missions, asked rhetorically "Does Germany need Colonies?" and answered with a resounding "Yes!" Germany's surplus population, he argued, should have places where it could go and still buy German goods and share in the other blessings of German *Kultur*. Fabri was eloquently seconded in 1881 by Hübbe-Schleiden, a lawyer and sometime explorer in equatorial Africa, who now insisted that through imperialistic endeavors "a country exhibits before the world its strength or weakness as a nation." In like vein the historian Treitschke edified his student audiences at the University of Berlin with the moral that "every virile people has established colonial power."

In 1882 a frankly propagandist "Colonial Society" was formed in Germany through the joint efforts of a naturalist, a geographer, and a politician, while in France Professor Leroy-Beaulieu brought out a new edition of his classic with the dogmatic addendum that "colonization is for France a question of life and death: either France will become a great African power, or in a century or two she will be no more than a secondary European power; she will count for about as much in the world as Greece and Rumania in Europe." The following year Professor John Seeley published his celebrated Cambridge lectures on the *Expansion of England*. The book took the British public by storm. It sold 80,000 copies within a brief time and won for its author the warm discipleship of Lord Rosebery and a knighthood.

In 1883 the stridently imperialistic "Primrose League" was launched by Tory Democrats, and soon afterwards the more sedate "Imperial Federation League" by nationalistic Liberals. In 1883, also, was founded a "Society for German Colonization." And capping the academic contributions to the imperialist cause, Froude published *Oceana* in 1885, while Alfred Rambaud, historian of Russia and first occupant of the chair in contemporary history at the Sorbonne, edited in 1886 a co-operative work on *La France coloniale*.

Already, statesmen were following the professors and proclaiming that commerce and investments should follow the flag. If Gladstone hesitated, Disraeli and Salisbury did not; nor did such "new" Liberals as Rosebery, Chamberlain, and Grey. Jules Ferry surely did not hesitate. Replying to parliamentary critics of his aggressive policy in Tunis and Tonkin, he marshaled in speeches from 1881 to 1885 all the professorial arguments: that superior races have a civilizing mission to inferior races; that an industrial nation needs colonial markets; that coaling stations are requisite for navy and mercantile marine; and that if France refrained from imperialism, she would "descend from the first rank to the third or fourth." Bismarck seemed to hesitate more than he actually did. He privately expressed sympathy with imperialist ambitions in 1876 and publicly backed them, at least in the case of Samoa, in 1879. By 1884–85 he was persuading the Reichstag that colonies were vital to national economy. "Colonies would mean the winning of new markets for German industries, the expansion of trade, and a new field for German activity, civilization and capital."

Most simply, the sequence of imperialism after 1870 appears to have been, first, pleas for colonies on the ground of national prestige; second, getting them; third, disarming critics by economic argument; and fourth, carrying this into effect and relating the results to the neo-mercantilism of tariff protection and social legislation at home.

There were, of course, complexities in the imperialistic movement. In so far as it was economic, it did not affect the "capitalist class" as a whole, but only particular business interests: exporters and manufacturers of certain commodities such as calico and cheap alcoholic beverages; importers of rubber, raw cotton, coffee, copra, etc.; shipping magnates; some bankers, though a very small percentage of all; and those "parasites of imperialism," the makers of arms and uniforms, the producers of telegraph and railway material, etc. But these last did not "cause" imperialism; they merely throve on it.

Christian missions provided an important adjunct to imperialism. They spread and multiplied in the second half of the nineteenth century as never before, in part as a reaction, we have suggested elsewhere, to the prevalent materialism in Europe, and in larger part because of the immensely improved means of travel and communication throughout the world. A missionary might have gone his way, like a merchant, the one conveying spiritual and the other material goods to heathen peoples, without any thought of raising a national flag over them or subjecting them to European rule. Actually, however, missionaries like merchants lived in a nationalistic age, and many of them were quite willing, on occasion, to invoke the naval or military protection of their respective national states. Not a few of Europe's footholds in other Continents were obtained as penalties for the persecution of Christian missionaries. Even where missionaries did not directly prompt the extension of European dominion, they frequently paved the way for adventurers who did; and stories published back home by them or about them stimulated popular interest in, and support of, imperial undertakings. About David Livingstone, for example, something like a cult grew up in England, so that when he died in the wilds of Africa on May Day, 1873, his body was borne with hierophantic solemnity all the way to Zanzibar and thence under naval escort to England, where finally it was deposited amid Britain's national heroes in Westminster Abbey on April 18, 1874. The year was that of Disraeli's accession to the premiership, and for the popular favor accorded his subsequent imperial activities, he should have thanked the dead Livingstone more than any live merchant or banker. . . .

In many instances European flags were hoisted as a sport—a competitive sport—with about the same indifference to economic motives as characterized the later planting of American and other flags on cakes of ice around the North or South Pole. As one reads of successive French flag raisings in oases of the Sahara and on coral reefs of the Pacific, one gets a lively impression that it was all *pour le sport.*

Some capitalists undoubtedly promoted imperialism, and more profited by it. But in the last analysis it was the nationalistic masses who made it possible and who most vociferously applauded and most constantly backed it. Disraeli and Joseph Chamberlain were good politicians as well as patriots, and with a clairvoyance greater than Gladstone's they perceived that in a country where the masses were patriotic, literate, and in possession of the ballot, a political party which frankly espoused imperialism would have magnetic attraction for them. So it proved. An unwonted popularity attended the Conservative parties of Britain and Germany during the '80's and '90's. The masses, of course, had no immediate economic interest in the matter, and it would have required an extraordinary act of faith on their part to believe the predictions of imperialistic intellectuals that somehow, sometime, everybody would be enriched from the Congo or the Niger or Tahiti. Rather, the masses were thrilled and stirred by front-page news in the popular press of far-off things and battles still to come. They devoured the yarns of a Rider Haggard—he had been secretary to the governor of Natal in the '70's and he *knew* his Africa. They learned by heart the vulgar verses of a Rudyard Kipling—he had lived in India and been a chum of doughty, swearing British soldiers. And the sporting impulse, which drew crowds to prize fights and to football and cricket matches, evoked a whole nation's lusty cheers for its "team" in the mammoth competitive game of imperialism.

Into the imperial-mindedness of the masses, scarcely less than into that of Rhodes or Peters, Ferry or Chamberlain, fitted neatly the preaching of Darwinian sociology, that human progress depends upon struggle between races and nations and survival of the fittest. Obviously most eligible for the "fittest" were the white peoples of Europe, who therefore owed it to science as well as to civilization (and religion) to establish their supremacy over inferior populations in all other continents. Which of them would ultimately be adjudged the absolutely fittest would depend on the outcome of conflict among themselves as well as with lesser breeds. This preaching justified competitive imperialism and cloaked attendant ruthlessness in the mantle of idealistic devotion to duty.

7   FROM   *Joseph A. Schumpeter*
       Aristocratic Values and Bourgeois Aggression

Joseph A. Schumpeter (1883–1950) was an Austrian social scientist who left Europe in 1932 to take up a second brilliant career at Harvard University. His essay on imperialism, first published in 1919, was conceived as an attack against the apparently triumphant Leninist dictum that "capitalism is imperialism." In spite of its obvious weaknesses, this synthesis of economics, sociology, and history remains the most all-encompassing interpretation we have of "new imperialism." Although this essay was written when he was a relatively young man, Schumpeter did not change his ideas on the subject later in life. In his History of Economic Analysis, *published in 1954 from the unfinished manuscript on which he was working at the time of his death, he states that "the imperialist urge is a stark reality that roots in other soil than that of the economic self-interest of the individual." To think otherwise, Schumpeter says, would be "bad sociology." Schumpeter's demonstration that today's policies are often based on yesterday's social structures and values is a lesson for our times as well as for his.*

SOURCE. Joseph A. Schumpeter, *Imperialism and Social Classes* (New York: Augustus M. Kelley, Inc.), reprinted by permission of the owners from pp. 5–7, 74–75, 76–77, 78, 83–87, 89–91, 120–121, 121–122, 123–124, 127–130. Copyright 1951 by Elizabeth Boody Schumpeter.

No one calls it imperialism when a state, no matter how brutally and vigorously, pursues concrete interests of its own; and when it can be expected to abandon its aggressive attitude as soon as it has attained what it was after. The word "imperialism" has been abused as a slogan to the point where it threatens to lose all meaning, but up to this point our definition is quite in keeping with common usage, even in the press. For whenever the word imperialism is used, there is always the implication—whether sincere or not—of an aggressiveness, the true reasons for which do not lie in the aims which are temporarily being pursued; of an aggressiveness that is only kindled anew by each success; of an aggressiveness for its own sake, as reflected in such terms as "hegemony," "world dominion," and so forth. And history, in truth, shows us nations and classes—most nations furnish an example at some time or other—that seek expansion for the sake of expanding, war for the sake of fighting, victory for the sake of winning, dominion for the sake of ruling. This determination cannot be explained by any of the pretexts that bring it into action, by any of the aims for which it seems to be struggling at the time. It confronts us, independent of all concrete purpose or occasion, as an enduring disposition, seizing upon one opportunity as eagerly as the next. It shines through all the arguments put forward on behalf of present aims. It values conquest not so much on account of the immediate advantages —advantages that more often than not are more than dubious, or that are heedlessly cast away with the same frequency—as because it *is* conquest, success, action. Here the theory of concrete interest in our sense fails. What needs to be explained is how the will to victory itself came into being.

Expansion for its own sake always requires, among other things, concrete objects if it is to reach the action stage and maintain itself, but this does not constitute its meaning. Such expansion is in a sense its own "object," and the truth is that it has no adequate object beyond itself. Let us therefore, in the absence of a better term, call it "objectless." It follows for that very reason that, just as such expansion cannot be explained by concrete interest, so too it is never satisfied by the fulfillment of a concrete interest, as would be the case if fulfillment were the motive, and the struggle for it merely a necessary evil—a counterargument, in fact. Hence the tendency of such expansion to transcend all bounds and tangible limits, to the point of utter exhaustion. This, then, is our definition: imperialism is the objectless disposition on the part of the state to unlimited forcible expansion. . . .

[Louis XIV of France] was carefully intent on remaining the leader of the aristocracy. Hence he drew its members to his court, rewarded those that came, sought to injure and discredit those that did not. He endeavored successfully to have only those play a part who had entered into relations with him and to foster the view, within the aristocracy, that only the *gens de la cour*—court society—could be considered to have full and authoritative standing. Viewed in this light, those aspects that historians customarily dispose of as court extravagance and arbitrary and avoidable mismanagement take on an altogether different meaning. It was a class rather than an individual that was actually master of the state. That class needed a brilliant center, and the court had to be such a center—otherwise it might all too readily have become a parliament. . . .

. . . There they were at Versailles, all these artistocrats—socially interned, consigned to amuse themselves under the monarch's gracious smile. There was absolutely nothing to do but to engage in flirtation, sports, and court festivities. These are fine pastimes, but they are life-filling only for relatively rare connoisseurs. Unless the nobles were to be allowed to revolt, they had to be kept busy. Now all the noble families whose members were amusing themselves at Versailles could look back on a warlike past, martial ideas and phrases, bellicose instincts. To ninety-nine out of a hundred of them, "action" meant military action. If civil war was to be avoided, then external wars were required. Foreign campaigns preoccupied and satisfied the nobility. From the viewpoint of the crown they were harmless and even advantageous. As it was, the crown was in control of the military machine, which must not be allowed to rust or languish. Tradition—as always surviving its usefulness—favored war as the natural pursuit of kings. And finally, the monarchy needed outward successes to maintain its position at home—how much it needed them was later shown when the pendulum swung to the other extreme, under Louis XV and Louis XVI. Small wonder that France took the field on every possible occasion, with an excess of enthusiasm that becomes wholly understandable from its position and that left it quite indifferent to the actual nature of the occasion. Any war would do. If only there was war, the details of foreign policy were gladly left to the king.

Thus the belligerence and war policy of the autocratic state are explained from the necessities of its social structure, from the inherited dispositions of its ruling class, rather than from the immediate advantages to be derived by conquest. In calculating these advantages it is necessary to realize that possible gains to the bourgeoisie were not necessarily valid motives. For the king was in control of foreign policy, and bourgeois interests, on the whole rather impotent, weighted in the balance only when the king stood to gain by them. Certainly he stood to gain tax revenues when he promoted trade and commerce. But even then wars had already grown so costly that they might be doubtful risks to the king, even though they offered indubitable advantages to business. Moreover, from the contemporary economic perspective—which is the one that must be adopted—by no means all the undertakings of Louis XIV were calculated to promote commercial interests. On the contrary, he showed little discrimination, eagerly seizing both on plans asserted, sometimes falsely, to be commercially advantageous (such as the subjugation of the Netherlands), and on those for which no one put forward any such claim (such as the plan of the "reunions"). Indeed, the king actually showed a certain indifference toward commercial and colonial undertakings, seeming to prefer small and fruitless undertakings in near-by Europe that appeared easy and promised success. . . . The monarchs may have been avaricious, but they were far too remote from commercial considerations to be governed by them. Even colonial questions impinged only slightly on the European policies of the great powers. Settlers and adventurers were often allowed to fight out such problems on the spot, and little attention was paid to them. That the basic theory of mercantilism was quite adequate to justify violent measures against foreign powers, and that in every war economic interests, as conceived by mercantilism, were safeguarded whenever possible—these facts tend to exaggerate the mercantilist element. Certainly it made a contribution. But industry was the servant of state policy to a greater degree than state policy served industry. . . .

Our analysis of the historical evidence has shown, first, the unquestionable fact that "objectless" tendencies toward forcible expansion, without definite, utilitarian limits—that is, non-rational and irrational, purely instinctual inclinations toward war and conquest—play a very large role in the history of mankind. It may sound paradoxical, but numberless wars—perhaps the majority of all wars—have been waged without adequate "reason"—not so much from the moral viewpoint as from that of reasoned and reasonable interest. The most herculean efforts of the nations, in other words, have faded into the empty air. Our analysis, in the second place, provides an explanation for this drive to action, this will to war—a theory by no means exhausted by mere references to an "urge" or an "instinct." The explanation lies, instead, in the vital needs of situations that molded peoples and classes into warriors—if they wanted to avoid extinction—and in the fact that psychological dispositions and social structures acquired in the dim past in such situations, once firmly established, tend to maintain themselves and to continue in effect long after they have lost their meaning and their life-preserving function. Our analysis, in the third place, has shown the existence of subsidiary factors that facilitate the survival of such dispositions and structures—factors that may be divided into two groups. The orientation toward war is mainly fostered by the domestic interests of ruling classes, but also by the influence of all those who stand to gain individually from a war policy, whether economically or socially. Both groups of factors are generally overgrown by elements of an altogether different character, not only in terms of political phraseology, but also of psychological motivation. Imperialisms differ greatly in detail, but they all have at least these traits in common, turning them into a single phenomenon in the field of sociology, as we noted in the introduction.

Imperialism thus is atavistic in character. It falls into that group of surviving features from earlier ages that play such an important part in every concrete social situation. In other words, it is an element that stems from the living conditions, not of the present, but of the past—or, put in terms of the economic interpretation of history, from past rather than present relations of production. It is an atavism in the social structure, in individual, psychological habits of emotional reaction. Since the vital needs that created it have passed away for good, it too must gradually disappear, even though every warlike involvement, no matter how non-imperialist in character, tends to revive it. It tends to disappear as a structural element because the structure that brought it to the fore goes into a decline, giving way, in the course of social development, to other structures that have no room for it and eliminate the power factors that supported it. It tends to disappear as an element of habitual emotional reaction, because of the progressive rationalization of life and mind, a process in which old functional needs are absorbed by new tasks, in which heretofore military energies are functionally modified. If our theory is correct cases of imperialism should decline in intensity the later they occur in the history of a people and of a culture. Our most recent examples of unmistakable, clear-cut imperialism are the absolute monarchies of the eighteenth century. They are unmistakably "more civilized" than their predecessors.

It is from absolute autocracy that the present age has taken over what imperialist tendencies it displays. And the imperialism of absolute autocracy flourished before the Industrial Revolution that created the modern world, or rather, before the consequences of that revolution began to be felt in all their aspects. These two statements are primarily meant in a historical sense, and as such they are no more than self-evident. We shall nevertheless try, within the framework of our theory, to define the significance of capitalism for our phenomenon and to examine the relationship between present-day imperialist tendencies and the autocratic imperialism of the eighteenth century.

The floodtide that burst the dams in the Industrial Revolution had its sources, of course, back in the Middle Ages. But capitalism began to shape society and impress its stamp on every page of social history only with the second half of the eighteenth century. Before that time there had been only islands of capitalist economy imbedded in an ocean of village and urban economy. True, certain political influences emanated from these islands, but they were able to assert themselves only indirectly. Not until the process we term the Industrial Revolution did the working masses, led by the entrepreneur, overcome the bonds of older life-forms—the environment of peasantry, guild, and aristocracy. The causal connection was this: A transformation in the basic economic factors (which need not detain us here) created the objective opportunity for the production of commodities, for large-scale industry, working for a market of customers whose individual identities were unknown, operating solely with a view to maximum financial profit. It was this opportunity that created an economically oriented leadership—personalities whose field of achievement was the organization of such commodity production in the form of capitalist enterprise. Successful enterprises in large numbers represented something new in the economic and social sense. They fought for and won freedom of action. They compelled state policy to adapt itself to their needs. More and more they attracted the most vigorous leaders from other spheres, as well as the manpower of those spheres, causing them and the social strata they represented to languish. Capitalist entrepreneurs fought the former ruling circles for a share in state control, for leadership in the state. The very fact of their success, their position, their resources, their power, raised them in the political and social scale. Their mode of life, their cast of mind became increasingly important elements on the social scene. . . .

These are things that are well known today, recognized in their full significance—indeed, often exaggerated. Their application to our subject is plain. Everything that is purely instinctual, everything insofar as it is purely instinctual, is driven into the background by this development. It creates a social and psychological atmosphere in keeping with modern economic forms, where traditional habits, merely because they were traditional, could no more survive than obsolete economic forms. Just as the latter can survive only if they are continually "adapted," so instinctual tendencies can survive only when the conditions that gave rise to them continue to apply, or when the "instinct" in question derives a new purpose from new conditions. The "instinct" that is *only* "instinct," that has lost its purpose, languishes relatively quickly in the capitalist world, just as does an inefficient economic practice. We see this process of rationalization at work even in the case of the strongest impulses. We observe it, for example, in the facts of procreation. We must therefore anticipate finding it in the case of the imperialist impulse as well; we must expect to see this impulse, which rests on the primitive contingencies of physical combat, gradually disappear, washed away by new exigencies of daily life. There is another factor too. The competitive system absorbs the full energies of most of the people at all economic levels. Constant application, attention, and concentration of energy are the conditions of survival within it, primarily in the specifically economic professions, but also in other activities organized on their model. There is much less excess energy to be vented in war and conquest than in any precapitalist society. What excess energy there is flows largely into industry itself, accounts for its shining figures—the type of the captain of industry—and for the rest is applied to art, science, and the social struggle. In a purely capitalist world, what was once energy for war becomes simply energy for labor of every kind. Wars of conquest and adventurism in foreign policy in general are bound to be regarded as troublesome distractions, destructive of life's meaning, a diversion from the accustomed and therefore "true" task.

A purely capitalist world therefore can offer no fertile soil to imperialist impulses. That does not mean that it cannot still maintain an interest in imperialist expansion. We shall discuss this immediately. The point is that its people are likely to be essentially of an unwarlike disposition. Hence we must expect that anti-imperialist tendencies will show themselves wherever capitalism penetrates the economy and, through the economy, the mind of modern nations—most strongly, of course, where capitalism itself is strongest, where it has advanced furthest, encountered the least resistance, and preeminently where its types and hence democracy—in the "bourgeois" sense—come closest to political domination. . . .

Trade and industry of the early capitalist period . . . remained strongly pervaded with precapitalist methods, bore the stamp of autocracy, and served its interests, either willingly or by force. With its traditional habits of feeling, thinking, and acting molded along such lines, the bourgeoisie entered the Industrial Revolution. It was shaped, in other words, by the needs and interests of an environment that was essentially noncapitalist, or at least precapitalist—needs stemming not from the nature of the capitalist economy as such but from the fact of the coexistence of early capitalism with another and at first overwhelmingly powerful mode of life and business. . . . Capitalism did bring about many changes on the land, springing in part from its automatic mechanisms, in part from the political trends it engendered—abolition of serfdom, freeing the soil from feudal entanglements, and so on—but initially it did not alter the basic outlines of the social structure of the people, and least of all their political goals. This explains why the features and trends of autocracy—including imperialism—proved so resistant, why they exerted such a powerful influence on capitalist development, why the old export monopolism [the push by monopolies for domination over foreign and colonial markets] could live on and merge into the new.

These are facts of fundamental significance to an understanding of the soul of modern Europe. Had the ruling class of the Middle Ages—the war-oriented nobility—changed its profession and function and become the ruling class of the capitalist world; or had developing capitalism swept it away, put it out of business, instead of merely clashing head-on with it in the agrarian sphere—then much would have been different in the life of modern peoples. . . . The bourgeoisie did not simply supplant the sovereign, nor did it make him its leader, as did the nobility. It merely wrested a portion of his power from him and for the rest submitted to him. It did not take over from the sovereign the state as an abstract form of organization. The state remained a special social power, confronting the bourgeoisie. In some countries it has continued to play that role to the present day. It is in the *state* that the bourgeoisie with its interests seeks refuge, protection against external and even domestic enemies. The bourgeoisie seeks to win over the state for itself, and in return serves the state and state interests that are different from its own. Imbued with the spirit of the old autocracy, trained by it, the bourgeoisie often takes over its ideology, even where, as in France, the sovereign is eliminated and the official power of the nobility has been broken. . . .

Just as we once found a dichotomy in the social pyramid, so now we find everywhere, in every aspect of the bourgeois portion of the modern world, a dichotomy of attitudes and interests. Our examples also show in what way the two components work together. Nationalism and militarism, while not creatures of capitalism, become "capitalized" and in the end draw their best energies from capitalism. Capitalism involves them in its workings and thereby keeps them alive, politically as well as economically. And they, in turn, affect capitalism, cause it to deviate from the course it might have followed alone, support many of its interests.

Here we find that we have penetrated to the historical as well as the sociological sources of modern imperialism. It does not *coincide* with nationalism and militarism, though it *fuses* with them by supporting them as it is supported by them. It too is—not only historically, but also sociologically—a heritage of the autocratic state, of its structural elements, organizational forms, interest alignments, and human attitudes, the outcome of precapitalist forces which the autocratic state has reorganized, in part by the methods of early capitalism. It would never have been evolved by the "inner logic" of capitalism itself. This is true even of mere export monopolism. It too has its sources in absolutist policy and the action habits of an essentially precapitalist environment. That it was able to develop to its present dimensions is owing to the momentum of a situation once created, which continued to engender ever new "artificial" economic structures, that is, those which maintain themselves by political power alone. In most of the countries addicted to export monopolism it is also owing to the fact that the old autocratic state and the old attitude of the bourgeoisie toward it were so vigorously maintained. But export monopolism, to go a step further, is not yet imperialism. And even if it had been able to arise without protective tariffs, it would never have developed into imperialism in the hands of an unwarlike bourgeoisie. If this did happen, it was only because the heritage included the war machine, together with its socio-psychological aura and aggressive bent, and because a class oriented toward war maintained itself in a ruling position. This class clung to its domestic interest in war, and the pro-military interests among the bourgeoisie were able to ally themselves with it. This alliance kept alive war instincts and ideas of overlordship, male supremacy, and triumphant glory—ideas that would have otherwise long since died. It led to social conditions that, while they ultimately stem from the conditions of production, cannot be explained from capitalist production methods alone. And it often impresses its mark on present-day politics, threatening Europe with the constant danger of war.

This diagnosis also bears the prognosis of imperialism. The precapitalist elements in our social life may still have great vi-

tality; special circumstances in national life may revive them
from time to time; but in the end the climate of the modern
world must destroy them. This is all the more certain since
their props in the modern capitalist world are not of the most
durable material. Whatever opinion is held concerning the vi-
tality of capitalism itself, whatever the life span predicted for
it, it is bound to withstand the onslaughts of its enemies and its
own irrationality much longer than essentially untenable export
monopolism—untenable even from the capitalist point of view.
Export monopolism may perish in revolution, or it may be peace-
fully relinquished; this may happen soon, or it may take some
time and require desperate struggle; but one thing is certain—
it *will* happen. This will immediately dispose of neither warlike
instincts nor structural elements and organizational forms oriented toward war—and it is to their dispositions and domestic
interests that, in my opinion, much more weight must be given
in every concrete case of imperialism than to export monopolist
interests, which furnish the financial "outpost skirmishes"—a
most appropriate term—in many wars. But such factors will be
politically overcome in time, no matter what they do to maintain among the people a sense of constant danger of war, with
the war machine forever primed for action. And with them, imperialisms will wither and die.

It is not within the scope of this study to offer an ethical, es-
thetic, cultural, or political evaluation of this process. Whether
it heals sores or extinguishes suns is a matter of utter indifference
from the viewpoint of this study. It is not the concern of science
to judge that. The only point at issue here was to demonstrate,
by means of an important example, the ancient truth that the
dead always rule the living.

8 FROM   *Ronald Robinson*
       and John Gallagher, with Alice Denny
  An Alternative Model for the Scramble for Africa

Ronald Robinson and John Gallagher here sum up their famous views on the scramble for Africa. Britain abandoned "informal empire" in favor of colonies neither because of a basic change in her economy [the Hobson-Lenin model] nor because of a new and more aggressive sort of nationalism [the approach of Carlton Hayes]. This great change in the history of imperialism, rather, they see linked to the threatening changes in international relations, that is, to Britain's increasingly precarious position in Europe and especially to her fears for the security of her "cardinal interest," her routes to India.

Did new, sustained or compelling impulses towards African empire arise in British politics or business during the Eighteen eighties? The evidence seems unconvincing. The late-Victorians seem to have been no keener to rule and develop Africa than their fathers. The business man saw no greater future there, except in the south; the politician was as reluctant to expand and administer a tropical African empire as the mid-Victorians had been; and plainly Parliament was no more eager to pay for it. British opinion restrained rather than prompted ministers to act in Africa. Hence they had to rely on private companies or colonial governments to act for them. It is true that African lobbies and a minority of imperialists did what they could to persuade government to advance. Yet they were usually too weak to be decisive. Measured by the yardstick of official thinking, there was no strong political or commercial movement in Britain in favour of African acquisitions.

SOURCE. Ronald Robinson and John Gallagher, with Alice Denny, *Africa and the Victorians: The Climax of Imperialism in the Dark Continent* (New York: St. Martin's Press, Inc.; London: Macmillan & Co., 1961), pp. 462–472. Reprinted by permission of St. Martin's Press, Inc., The Macmillan Company of Canada and Macmillan London and Basingstoke.

The priorities of policy in tropical Africa confirm this impression. West Africa seemed to offer better prospects of markets and raw materials than east Africa and the Upper Nile; yet it was upon these poorer countries that the British government concentrated its efforts. These regions of Africa which interested the British investor and merchant least, concerned ministers the most. No expansion of commerce prompted the territorial claims to Uganda, the east coast and the Nile Valley. As Mackinnon's failure [the collapse of the British East Africa Company, 1892] showed, private enterprise was not moving in to develop them; and they were no more useful or necessary to the British industrial economy between 1880 and 1900 than they had been earlier in the century. Territorial claims here reached out far in advance of the expanding economy. Notions of pegging out colonial estates for posterity hardly entered into British calculations until the late Eighteen nineties, when it was almost too late to affect the outcome. Nor were ministers gulled by the romantic glories of ruling desert and bush. Imperialism in the wide sense of empire for empire's sake was not their motive. Their territorial claims were not made for the sake of African empire or commerce as such. They were little more than by-products of an enforced search for better security in the Mediterranean and the East. It was not the pomps or profits of governing Africa which moved the ruling *élite,* but the cold rules for national safety handed on from Pitt, Palmerston and Disraeli. . . .

It is the private calculations and actions of ministers far more than their speeches which reveal the primary motives behind their advances. For all the different situations in which territory was claimed, and all the different reasons which were given to justify it, one consideration, and one alone entered into all the major decisions. In all regions north of Rhodesia, the broad imperative which decided which territory to reserve and which to renounce, was the safety of the routes to the East. It did not, of course, prompt the claiming of Nyassaland or the lower Niger. Here a reluctant government acted to protect existing fields of trading and missionary enterprise from foreign annexations. In southern Africa the extension of empire seems to have been dictated by a somewhat different imperative. Here the London government felt bound as a rule to satisfy the demands for more territory which their self-governing colonials pressed on them.

Ministers did this in the hope of conserving imperial influence. Nevertheless, the safety of the routes to India also figured prominently in the decision to uphold British supremacy in south Africa. It was the same imperative which after impelling the occupation of Egypt, prolonged it, and forced Britain to go into east Africa and the Upper Nile, while yielding in most of west Africa. As soon as territory anywhere in Africa became involved, however indirectly, in this cardinal interest, ministries passed swiftly from inaction to intervention. If the papers left by the policy-makers are to be believed, they moved into Africa, not to build a new African empire, but to protect the old empire in India. What decided when and where they would go forward was their traditional conception of world strategy. . . .

An essentially negative objective, it had been attained hitherto without large African possessions. Mere influence and cooperation with other Powers had been enough to safeguard strategic points in north Africa; while in south Africa control of coastal regions had sufficed. The ambition of late-Victorian ministers reached no higher than to uphold these mid-Victorian systems of security in Egypt and south Africa. They were distinguished from their predecessors only in this: that their security by influence was breaking down. In attempting to restore it by intervention and diplomacy, they incidentally marked out the ground on which a vastly extended African empire was later to arise. Nearly all the interventions appear to have been consequences, direct or indirect, of internal Egyptian or south African crises which endangered British influence and security in the world. . . .

Hence the question of motive should be formulated afresh. It is no longer the winning of a new empire in Africa which has to be explained. The question is simpler: Why could the late-Victorians after 1880 no longer rely upon influence to protect traditional interests? What forced them in the end into imperial solutions? The answer is to be found first in the nationalist crises in Africa itself, which were the work of intensifying European influences during previous decades; and only secondarily in the interlocking of these crises in Africa with rivalries in Europe. Together the two drove Britain step by step to regain by territorial claims and occupation that security which could no longer be had by influence alone. The compelling conditions for British advances in tropical Africa were first called into being,

not by the German victory of 1871, nor by Leopold's interest in
the Congo, nor by the petty rivalry of missionaries and merchants, nor by a rising imperialist spirit, nor even by the French
occupation of Tunis in 1881—but by the collapse of the Khe-
divial *régime* in Egypt.

From start to finish the partition of tropical Africa was driven
by the persistent crisis in Egypt. When the British entered Egypt
on their own, the Scramble began; and as long as they stayed in
Cairo, it continued until there was no more of Africa left to
divide. . . .

. . . There were structural changes taking place in European
industry cutting down Britain's lead in commerce. The European balance of power was altering. Not only the emergence of
Germany, but the alignment of France with Russia, the century-
old opponent of British expansion, lessened the margins of imperial safety. National and racial feelings in Europe, in Egypt
and south Africa were becoming more heated, and liberalism
everywhere was on the decline. All these movements played some
part in the African drama. But it seems that they were only
brought to the point of imperialist action by the idiosyncratic
reactions of British statesmen to internal crises in Africa. Along
the Mediterranean shores, Muslim states were breaking down
under European penetration. In the south, economic growth and
colonial expansion were escaping from imperial control. These
processes of growth or decay were moving on time scales different
from that of European expansion which was bringing them
about.

By 1882 the Egyptian Khedivate had corroded and cracked
after decades of European paramountcy. But economic expansion
was certainly not the sufficient cause of the occupation. Hitherto,
commerce and investment had gone on without the help of out-
right political control. The thrusts of the industrial economy
into Egypt had come to a stop with Ismail's bankruptcy, and
little new enterprise was to accompany British control. Although
the expanding economy had helped to make a revolutionary
situation in Egypt, it was not the moving interest behind the
British invasion. Nor does it seem that Anglo-French rivalry or
the state of the European balance precipitated the invasion. It
was rather the internal nationalist reaction against a decaying
government which split Britain from France and switched European rivalries into Africa.

But the cast of official thinking profoundly influenced the outcome of the emergency. Moving instinctively to protect the Canal, the Liberals intended a Palmerstonian blow to liberate the progressives and chasten the disruptive elements in Egyptian politics. But instead of restoring their influence and then getting out, the need to bottle up anarchy and stave off the French forced them to stay on. This failure to work the mid-Victorian techniques, by coming to terms with the nationalists and finding Egyptian collaborators, meant that Indian solutions had to be applied to Egypt as well. The disenchantment of the "Guardians" was replacing the liberal faith in voluntary cooperation; and Gladstone's sympathy with oppressed nationalities was hardening into Cromer's distrust of subject races. For similar reasons, official pessimism deepened about the reliability of the Turkish bastion in the Mediterranean; and as the balance tilted against Britain in the inland sea, her rulers realised that they were in Egypt to stay. Weighing the risks of Ottoman decay and the shifts in the European balance, remembering Indian experience and distrusting Egyptian "fanatics," England's rulers pessimistically extended the search for security up the Nile to Fashoda, and from the Indian Ocean to Uganda and the Bahr-el-Ghazal.

The causes of imperial expansion in southern Africa were altogether different. It was essentially unconnected with the contemporary crisis in Egypt and its consequences in tropical Africa; it moved on a different time-scale, and the impulses behind it were separate. Unlike Egypt and tropical Africa, south Africa was to a great extent insulated from the rivalries of European Powers. Unlike them also, it was being rapidly developed by British commercial interests. The crisis which faced British governments was produced by colonial growth, and not by the decay of a native government. It arose from internal conflicts among the colonists, rather than from rivalries among the Powers. But the south African and Egyptian crises were alike in this: neither was precipitated by drastic changes in the local purposes of British expansion; but in both, the late-Victorians strained to keep up their supreme influence against a nationalist threat, and they were drawn at last into reconquering paramountcy by occupation. . . .

There are many evidences that towards the end of the century the wearing out of well-tried devices and the emergence of so many intractable problems shocked ministers out of their self-confidence and turned them to desperate expedients. The beliefs which had inspired earlier expansion were failing. Palmerston's axioms were giving way to Salisbury's re-appraisals. Liberal values could not be exported to all with cases of Birmingham hardware. Self-government would not always travel. Some nationalisms could not be killed with kindness. The growth of communities into harmonious commercial and political partnership with Britain was not after all a law of nature. The technique of collaborating classes had not worked everywhere. And as difficulties and doubts mounted, the men presiding over the destinies of the British Empire found themselves surrounded by the Eumenides.

Why were these catastrophes overtaking them? All the processes of British expansion were reaching their peak. The metropolitan society was putting forth its strongest energies. It was at this climactic point that the social changes in its satellites were quickest and most violent. Hence it was at this time that their relations with the metropolis tended to move into crisis. The colonial communities were breaking off toward full independence; while anti-western nationalism and social upheaval were estranging the non-European partners of British interests. The effects of growth were also coming back to roost at Home. England's rulers were alarmed by the symptoms of distintegration, the demand for collectivism, the decay of the landed interest and the running sore of Ireland. The late-Victorians were confronted with nationalist upsurges in Ireland, Egypt and south Africa, and with their beginnings in India. They were losing the faith of their fathers in the power of trade and anglicisation to turn nationalists into friends and partners. They were no longer so sure as they had been that revolutionary change worked naturally and inevitably to advance British interests. And so they ceased to foster and encourage change and tended to be content to preserve the *status quo*. They became less concerned to liberate social energies abroad and concentrated on preserving authority instead.

Canning and Palmerston had known that the liberals of the world were on their side. But the late-Victorians had to find their allies more and more among Indian princes, Egyptian pashas or African paramount chiefs. Finding themselves less successful in assimilating nationalists to British purposes, their distrust of them grew. And becoming uncertain of the reliability of mere influence, they turned more often from the technique of informal control to the orthodoxies of the Indian *raj* for dealing with political anomalies and for securing their interests. They were ceasing to be a dynamic force and becoming a static power. They were more and more preoccupied throughout the world to guard what they had won; and they became less able to promote progress, as they lapsed into the cares of consolidation. . . .

The notion that world strategy alone was the sole determinant of British advances is superficial. For strategy is not merely a reflection of the interests which it purports to defend, it is even more the register of the hopes, the memories and neuroses which inform the strategists' picture of the world. This it is which largely decides a government's view about who may be trusted and who must be feared; whether an empire assumes an optimistic or pessimistic posture; and whether the forces of change abroad are to be fostered or opposed. Indeed any theory of imperialism grounded on the notion of a single decisive cause is too simple for the complicated historical reality of the African partition. No purely economic interpretation is wide enough, because it does not allow for the independent importance of subjective factors. Explanations based entirely on the swings of the European balance are bound to remain incomplete without reference to changes outside Europe.

Both the crises of expansion and the official mind which attempted to control them had their origins in an historical process which had begun to unfold long before the partition of Africa began. That movement was not the manifestation of some revolutionary urge to empire. Its deeper causes do not lie in the last two decades of the century. The British advance at least, was not an isolated African episode. It was the climax of a longer process of growth and decay in Africa. The new African empire was improvised by the official mind, as events made nonsense of its old historiography and hustled government into strange deviations from old lines of policy. In the widest sense, it was an off-shoot of the total processes of British expansion throughout the world and throughout the century.

How large then does the new African empire bulk in this setting? There are good reasons for regarding the mid-Victorian period as the golden age of British expansion, and the late-Victorian period as an age which saw the beginnings of contraction and decline. The Palmerstonians were no more "anti-imperialist" than their successors, though they were more often able to achieve their purposes informally; and the late-Victorians were no more "imperialist" than their predecessors, though they were driven to extend imperial claims more often. To label them thus is to ignore the fact that whatever their method, they were both of set purpose engineering the expansion of Britain. Both preferred to promote trade and security without the expense of empire; but neither shrank from forward policies wherever they seemed necessary.

But their circumstances were very different. During the first three-quarters of the century, Britain enjoyed an almost effortless supremacy in the world outside Europe, thanks to her sea power and her industrial strength, and because she had little foreign rivalry to face. Thus Canning and Palmerston had a very wide freedom of action. On the one hand, they had little need to bring economically valueless regions such as tropical Africa into their formal empire for the sake of strategic security; and on the other, they were free to extend their influence and power to develop those regions best suited to contribute to Britain's strength. Until the Eighteen eighties, British political expansion had been positive, in the sense that it went on bringing valuable areas into her orbit. That of the late-Victorians in the so-called "Age of Imperialism" was by comparison negative, both in purpose and achievement. It was largely concerned with defending the maturing inheritance of the mid-Victorian imperialism of free trade, not with opening fresh fields of substantial importance to the economy. Whereas the earlier Victorians could afford to concentrate on the extension of free trade, their successors were compelled to look above all to the preservation of what they held, since they were coming to suspect that Britain's power was not what it once had been. The early Victorians had been playing from strength. The supremacy they had built in the world had been the work of confidence and faith in the future. The African empire of their successors was the product of fear lest this great heritage should be lost in the time of troubles ahead.

Because it went far ahead of commercial expansion and imperial ambition, because its aims were essentially defensive and strategic, the movement into Africa remained superficial. The partition of tropical Africa might seem impressive on the wall maps of the Foreign Office. Yet it was at the time an empty and theoretical expansion. That British governments before 1900 did very little to pacify, administer and develop their spheres of influence and protectorates, shows once again the weakness of any commercial and imperial motives for claiming them. The partition did not accompany, it preceded the invasion of tropical Africa by the trader, the planter and the official. It was the prelude to European occupation; it was not that occupation itself. The sequence illuminates the true nature of the British movement into tropical Africa. So far from commercial expansion requiring the extension of territorial claims, it was the extension of territorial claims which in time required commercial expansion. The arguments of the so-called new imperialism were *ex post facto* justifications of advances, they were not the original reasons for making them. Ministers had publicly justified their improvisations in tropical Africa with appeals to imperial sentiment and promises of African progress. After 1900, something had to be done to fulfill these aspirations, when the spheres allotted on the map had to be made good on the ground. The same fabulous artificers who had galvanised America, Australia and Asia, had come to the last continent.

9   FROM   *A. G. Hopkins*
Economic Motives in the British Acquisition of Lagos

A. G. Hopkins is an economic historian who teaches at the Centre of West African Studies of the University of Birmingham. In this selection we change the focus from sweeping generalizations about whole continents and entire economic systems to a specific case of a small land that was swept up in the scramble

SOURCE. A. G. Hopkins, "Economic Imperialism in West Africa: Lagos, 1880–92," *Economic History Review,* 2nd ser., XXI, no. 3 (1968), pp. 580–606. Reprinted by permission of the Economic History Society and the author.

for Africa. Hopkins shows that the initiative for consolidating
control over the tribes in the Lagos hinterland came not from
the government in London but from merchants involved in the
Lagos trade, who were doing their best to avoid being ruined by
a disastrous fall in the prices of their products. This is a direct
challenge to the thesis of Robinson and Gallagher.

Brave hunters have pursued, cornered, and now claim to have
slain "the decrepit, mythological beast of economic imperialism." [The phrase is Ronald Robinson's.] The undertakers have
prepared the corpse; the funeral oration has been written:

"The British colonies and protectorates in tropical Africa had
not been claimed originally because they were needed as colonial
estates. Rather, they had been claimed for strategic reasons, and
they had to be developed as colonial estates to pay the costs of
their administration. Their economic development was more a
consequence than a motive of the 'scramble.' As an explanation of
European rule in tropical Africa, the theory of economic imperialism puts the trade before the flag, the capital before the
conquest, the cart before the horse." [From Robinson and Gallagher, *Africa and the Victorians.*]

It might be thought premature to suggest that the economics of
imperialism now require reconsideration. But in attacking the
conventional concept of economic imperialism the critics have
tended to underrate all other economic motives. The purpose of
the present investigation is to explore some neglected economic
aspects of the partition of West Africa with special reference to
the case of Lagos, and to put forward for future use some propositions which take account of the economic elements in the
scramble for tropical Africa. . . .

Lagos was originally a small fishing village which became one
of the most important slave-trading centres on the west coast in
the first half of the nineteenth century. The demand for slaves
generated a new export sector. It called into being a new group
of entrepreneurs, new trade routes, new consumer goods, and
new political systems in the interior dominated largely by military leaders. In 1851 the British occupied Lagos, and ten years

later they formally annexed the port and made it a colony. The purpose of these moves was to suppress the slave trade and to encourage instead the rise of "legitimate" commerce, that is, trade in commodities other than slaves. The era of legitimate commerce is usually treated simply as another phase in the long history of Afro-European trading relations; that it was also a period of crisis and change in export production has been recognized less clearly.

The transition to legitimate commerce appeared at first to be relatively smooth. The new export trade was based almost entirely on palm-oil and palm-kernels, products of the palm-tree which grew in abundance in the immediate hinterland of Lagos. The palm-tree was indigenous to West Africa, and it had been exploited for domestic purposes long before the end of the Atlantic slave trade. . . . The transition to legitimate commerce was also consistent with a marked degree of continuity in the organization of west-coast trade. The Europeans remained on the coast, as they had done for centuries; they still exchanged much the same consumer goods as during the time of the Atlantic slave trade; they still employed African traders as intermediaries; they still transacted business by barter and by offering certain "primitive" currencies, such as cowrie shells, in exchange for the new export crop; and, to begin with, they still used sailing ships on the route between Europe and Africa. These merchants were the original "palm-oil ruffians," a tough and pretty unscrupulous bunch of men, who in certain cases were not averse to making money on the side by dealing in slaves where an opportunity offered itself. . . .

In the early days of legitimate commerce events appeared to justify the view that the transition from the slave trade could be made without dislocating the economy of the west coast. Demand for vegetable oils in the industrial and urban centres of Europe was rising, and high prices were paid to west-coast merchants and producers. . . . In these circumstances, the European merchants were content to stay on the coast, and operate in a small market which offered generous profit margins. Consequently, the political arm of legitimate commerce, as represented by the administrator and his small staff, was used with restraint. Few doubted that the task of safeguarding trade could be carried out simply by working to maintain the status quo. Superficially, there was no reason why a greater Britain could not be maintained in West Africa by informal rather than by formal means.

During the last quarter of the nineteenth century legitimate commerce passed through a period of crisis, as the prosperity of West African trade was undermined by acute market problems in Europe, where changing conditions of supply and demand had a profound effect on exports from the west coast. The discovery and exploitation of petroleum resources, and the entry of Indian, Australian, and Russian products into the market led to a great increase in the supply of oils and fats, and weakened the competitive position of palm-oil. Some compensation was provided by the development of the market for palm-kernels, but the full utilization of this product did not take place until shortly after the turn of the century. This increase in the supply of oils and fats was not matched by a corresponding expansion in demand. In England the financial crisis of 1873 signalled the advent of the so-called Great Depression, a period when wholesale prices of raw materials in general, and of palm produce in particular, tended to fall. . . . When it is realized that palm-oil and palm-kernels together averaged 82.5 per cent of the annual value of all exports from Lagos in the years between 1880 and 1892, it becomes clear that the fall in price was a serious matter for all those whose fortunes were tied to legitimate commerce Contemporaries had no doubt that this adverse trend constituted the greatest commercial crisis that West Africa had known since the abolition of the slave trade. As the 1880's drew to a close, newspaper comment began to read more and more like obituary notices of legitimate commerce. . . .

There were only about a dozen European firms in Lagos at any one time in the 1880's, but between them they handled the greater part of the import and export trade. It was their contribution to the rise of legitimate commerce that the Governor was required to protect, and their contribution to the revenue of the colony that enabled him to carry out his task. The immediate effect of the depression was to squeeze the profit margins of those luckless firms which found themselves shipping produce to a falling market. In 1890 the difference between the average price realized in England and the average purchasing price in Lagos was £4 0s. 2d. per ton for palm-kernels and £6 18s. 9d. per ton for oil, yet a careful estimate concluded that the shipper needed a margin of £4 14s. 0d. per ton on palm-kernels in order to break even, and the corresponding figure for palm-oil must have been greater because exporting costs were higher for this product. Some relief was obtained from the modest increase in the volume of produce exported, but this was barely sufficient to keep gross returns at the level they had been at the beginning of the decade, especially since there was an increase in the number of firms competing for produce. Net returns must undoubtedly have dropped, for the merchant's total operating costs had risen as a result of the need to handle a greater volume of produce. By the end of the decade margins had narrowed to the point of invisibility, and losses on shipments were common. . . .

The outcome of the crisis of the 1880's was a trade war in which the European merchants fought not only among themselves but also with the African traders and producers in an attempt to pass on as much of their losses as they possibly could. In the export trade the expatriate firms sought to cut the buying price of produce by purchasing direct from traders instead of from the African brokers who had supplied them previously. However, this change did not bring about any significant economies because the brokers had always worked on very small margins, and their ability to judge the quality of palm produce made them valuable agents. The merchants also attempted to reduce the prices they paid for produce, and in this they appear to have achieved some success. But this move aroused the opposition of the Lagos traders, who retaliated by trying to prevent rival traders in the interior from bringing produce across the lagoon to Lagos, and by adulterating the produce that they themselves sold to the European firms. In the import trade growing competition in the 1880's led to a period of price-cutting, with the result that the selling prices of consumer goods in Lagos declined at the same time that produce prices in Europe were falling. As there was no hope of increasing the retail prices of manufactures, more devious means of preserving profit margins were adopted. As early as 1872 a European firm began to sell short-folded cloth, and this practice was soon copied and became widespread in the 1880's. The quality also declined, and the weight and appearance of inferior cotton goods were maintained by adding china clay, an expedient which could be detected only after the cloth had been washed, when it assumed for its astonished owner a new and threadbare form. Short-folding was a specialty of the merchants, but the traders played a similar game by diluting imported spirits with water, so that by the time liquor reached the consumer its strength had been greatly reduced. Commerce in West Africa had never ranked as one of the most honorable occupations, and these fraudulent innovations lowered its reputation still further. . . .

While economic conditions were favorable, a combination of *laissez-faire* and informal rule in West Africa met the needs of both merchants and statesmen. But the limitations of this policy were revealed in the 1880's, as the economic crisis reduced the profits and undermined the principles of legitimate commerce. The mechanism of trade no longer adjusted itself, in Smithian fashion, to suit the needs of the merchants, and by the end of the decade their own attempts to regulate its movements had proved unsuccessful. As a last and most drastic alternative, they turned to the government for assistance. In this way the economic problems of the 1880's led to political intervention in the 1890's.

The British government did not expect that the growth of legitimate commerce would lead to any additional political commitments in West Africa. Abroad as well as at home the aim was minimum government at minimum expense, and in this context the acquisition of Lagos was seen as an end rather than as a beginning. While free trade and private enterprise appeared to guarantee both progress and profits, there was little incentive for colonial adventures, which besides being costly could also have unwelcome diplomatic repercussions. The discreet influence of a few representatives on the west coast was considered sufficient to maintain the conditions necessary for satisfactory trading relations. Consequently, the Colonial Office sought to curb any expansionist tendencies which it detected in the actions of its officials on the west coast. No matter that the policy had ceased to fit the changing facts of West African affairs; Britain did not intend to precipitate a scramble for this part of Africa. . . .

Nevertheless, some expansion of British rule took place in the Lagos area, mainly through the initiative of local officials, and the Colonial Office found itself gradually accumulating commitments which were largely unplanned and certainly unwanted. This paradox arose out of a conflict between the aims of policy and the means allowed for their realization. To protect the trade of Lagos a skeleton administration had been provided on the understanding that it should not extend its power into the hinterland, and that it should pay for itself. But a foothold on the coast proved insufficient for these purposes. In the first place, the affairs of the interior could not be controlled by a mixture of bribes and threats from Lagos, particularly at a time when the growth of legitimate commerce had itself caused widespread economic and social upheaval. Secondly, the colony depended for its upkeep on the revenue from customs duties, which in turn rested on the prosperity of trade and on the ability of the administration to tax the mercantile community. As both trade and traders tended to gravitate to areas where tariffs were either low or non-existent, the officials felt the need to extend the boundaries of the colony in order to preserve their revenue. Instead of supporting a policy of non-intervention, as directed by the Colonial Office, the local administration became identified with groups which favored expansion, and the officials in London had a constant struggle to restrain this "creeping imperialism" which surreptitiously edged the traders' frontier towards the interior.

The merchants had to weigh their need for protection against their unwillingness to pay for a larger administration and to conform to the regulations which it would inevitably impose. They were not prepared to organize a sustained campaign for government action while business was prosperous, and until the late 1870's they favored non-intervention, fearing that a forward policy would provoke retaliation and harm trade. But the economic crisis of the 1880's led to a realization that a more vigorous policy was required, and the merchants began to mobilize their forces. In Lagos, the English firms, supported by the greater part of the mercantile community, led the way in 1888 in founding the Lagos Chamber of Commerce, which was designed to act as a pressure group for local commercial interests. In England, the chambers of commerce with important African connections also began to organize. In 1884 the African Trade Section of the London Chamber of Commerce was formed. . . . Early in 1892 about 100 manufacturing and trading firms petitioned the directors of the Chamber for greater representation of African business connections. As a result, two men with extensive com-

mercial ties with Africa were appointed to the Board of the
Chamber. Outside of the Chambers of Commerce the appearance
of a number of new organizations indicated that an influential
section of public opinion was also becoming anxious for the
British government to take a more positive line on imperial affairs. Two events, the Great Depression and the growth of new
competitors in America and Europe, gave rise in the 1880's
to the Fair Trade movement, which aimed at promoting free
trade within the empire and protection against the rest of the
world. This program first found expression in the National Fair
Trade League, which was formed in 1881, and subsequently in
the United Empire Trade League, which superseded it ten years
later with the more general aim of encouraging closer economic
and political ties with the empire. At the same time, the ideas
of social imperialism were being canvassed by a number of influential writers and politicians, including Joseph Chamberlain.
By the 1890's interest in the possibilities of an imperial solution
to pressing domestic problems had greatly increased, and the
clamor which arose in England helped to amplify the small voice
which sounded in Lagos.

The merchants . . . wanted law and order brought to the
interior; they wanted the political power of the middlemen abol-
ished, together with all internal tolls; they wanted a railway system which would develop West Africa in the same way as it had
opened up the rest of the world; and they wanted a free-trading
area marked out and preserved against the protectionist en-
croachments of the Continental powers. The nature of these
demands was very largely responsible for determining the shape
of the colonial economies which were created in British West
Africa shortly after the turn of the century.

By the close of the 1880's all the motives for intervention were
present. The precise timing of the final crisis leading to British
expansion into the interior was determined by two events—the
increasing tempo of French activity west of Lagos, and the total
failure of informal means of dealing with the independent and
uncooperative Yoruba states. . . .

Political actions [in the partition of West Africa] did not
spring, in mechanistic fashion, from problems of surplus capital,
but they did arise in part from a threat to existing investments,
which had increased considerably since the abolition of the At-

lantic slave trade. Not all the European firms wanted to move into the interior, but the majority came to realize that radical changes were needed in their relations with the hinterland peoples. This shift in attitude occurred for a variety of reasons, ranging from deep fears of foreign competition to grand illusions about the wealth of the interior. But to a large extent expansion inland was the result of a growing conviction that the existing socio-political order was no longer equipped to deal efficiently with problems of production and exchange in the era of legitimate commerce. . . .

To deny the rigid application of Hobson-Leninism is neither to destroy the economic basis of the process of empire-building in West Africa nor to reject the overall, global economic interests of Great Britain in the formulation of policy. In the last analysis, the partition of West Africa may be thought of as a political act carried out to resolve the economic conflicts which had arisen as a result of the meeting of two disparate societies, one developing, the other underdeveloped. Seen in these terms, economic imperialism was not a mythical beast, a paper tiger, but a real, live creature after all.

10   FROM   *Heinz Gollwitzer*
      Social Imperialism: An Alternative to
                Class Warfare

Heinz Gollwitzer is professor of political and social history at the Westphalia Wilhelms University in Münster. His book from which this selection is taken treats a subject too often neglected in studies of imperialism, that is, the social and cultural changes that took place in Europe during the era of "new imperialism," and that help explain the causes of imperialism. He shows here that the conviction "imperialism is a matter of bread and

SOURCE. Heinz Gollwitzer, *Europe in the Age of Imperialism*, pp. 133–140, © copyright 1969 by Heinz Gollwitzer and Thames & Hudson, Ltd. Reprinted by permission of Harcourt Brace Jovanovich, Inc.

butter" (for the lower classes) was shared by radicals and liberals as well as conservatives. This suggests that we have to separate the questions of whether economic drives were in fact requiring Europe to undertake imperialism and whether contemporary makers of public opinion believed this to be the case.

"Democracy wants two things," said Austen Chamberlain: "imperialism and social reform." But does a tendency to social reform really join with imperialism or—to put it more broadly—does imperialism have its own social system? In trying to find an answer we must keep society as a whole in mind and not restrict ourselves to the "social question," in the narrower sense of relations between employers and workers. The problem of the workers is, however, the central social problem of the age and must be our starting-point.

No imperialist, of course, wanted a revolutionary change in social relationships, but, unlike the preceding generation and many of their contemporaries, the imperialists realized that some kind of change was necessary. What has already been said about imperialist entrepreneurs applies to imperialists as a whole: there was a marked tendency towards social reform on the part of their political and intellectual leaders. In many cases imperialism and socialism (reformist, not Marxist) seemed to be different sides of the same coin. Indeed, almost all the foremost theoreticians of imperialism held that a progressive view in social affairs was the correlate of successful world politics. Stimuli came from various directions: from the social caesarism of Napoleon III and German social legislation; from Carlyle and the English Christian socialists. Social imperialism underwent a consistent development in both theory and practice particularly in Britain and Germany. There was, however, no question of a doctrine comparable to Marxism. The Liberal Imperialists associated with Lord Rosebery, Dilke, Asquith, Grey and Haldane were determined advocates of social reform. As champions of protective tariffs, Joseph Chamberlain and his supporters, including Halford Mackinder, political economist and geographer who was converted from Free Trade to Protectionism, William Cunningham, theologian and economic historian, and W. J. Ashley, another political economist, emphasized the social progress to be expected from the abandonment of Free Trade. It was an active and distinguished minority that devoted itself to the triple aims of Protectionism, imperialism and social reform. An imperialist socialism was also advocated by individual leading members of the Fabian Society and fairly influential personalities without affiliations like the "military socialist," Robert Blatchford. They too have to be mentioned here, though there is certainly a discrimination to be made between imperialists who conducted progressive social policies and social reform, and socialists who were also receptive to imperialist ideas.

In Germany, the democratic imperialists Max Weber and Friedrich Naumann supported social imperialism, and this was true also of the academic group known as the "Kathedersozialisten" (professorial socialists), scholars and economic leaders who comprised the Verein für Sozialpolitik. It was not by chance that men like Gustav Schmoller, the economic historian who was Chairman of the Verein für Sozialpolitik for many years, the political economist Adolf Wagner, and many others, worked together with Max Weber and Friedrich Naumann to improve social conditions at the same time that they supported power politics; on the contrary, they established and energetically defended the mutual necessity of both.

The social element in the thinking of those Italian and German socialists who were won over (with appropriate reservations) to imperialist policies can be taken for granted. They too may be added to the broad and many-layered current of social imperialism. Marxist socialists and, for the most part, the British labour movement rejected social imperialism as a deception and a fraud; in many of their concepts they proved themselves a continuance of English radicalism, just as many of Hobson's radical views on imperialism flowed into the Marxist criticism of imperialism.

Imperialist Germany extended Bismarck's social legislation, and liberal-imperialist Britain likewise carried out a programme of social reform. In connection with individual social-political measures, such as the introduction of increasingly graded scales of social insurance, housing schemes, protective labour legislation, the beginning of shorter working hours, improved educational facilities and, particularly, the growing middle-class

appreciation of the trade unions, more comprehensive social reform projects must be attributed to imperialism.

The reasoning of Cecil Rhodes sounds rather primitive today,
although at the time it was defended even in scientific quarters
and can be regarded as almost a *communis opinio* of imperialism. That great colonial pioneer summarized it as follows during a conversation with his friend W. T. Stead:

"Yesterday I attended a meeting of the unemployed in London
and having listened to the wild speeches which were nothing
more or less than a scream for bread I returned home convinced
more than ever of the importance of imperialism . . . the great
idea in my mind is the solution of the social problem. By this
I mean that in order to save the forty million inhabitants of
the United Kingdom from a murderous civil war the colonial
politicians must open up new areas to absorb the excess population and create new markets for the products of the mines and
factories. I have always maintained that the British Empire is a
matter of bread and butter. If you wish to avoid civil war then
you must become an imperialist."

Joseph Chamberlain's organization, the Tariff Reform League,
put forward a programme according to which the Protectionist
course would not only brihg about economic prosperity and
secure national unity, but also, at the core of social-political
promises, would achieve full employment—a tempting prospect
indeed in view of prevalent unemployment. The workers, however, would have had to carry the main burden of the indirect
taxes proposed by the Protectionists, while Liberal Imperialists
continued their adherence to direct taxation in the most varied
forms. Labour maintained the tradition of Free Trade radicalism and opposed the plans of Chamberlain and his supporters.

The social concept of imperialism, however, went even further than Rhodes' remarks to Stead or than the Protectionists'
agitation would lead one to suppose. The national-minded
middle class in the age of imperialism saw themselves faced with
the basic fact of a class war that had become conscious and universally acknowledged. As for the workers, they went over to the
Marxist camp in great numbers on the Continent. This was not
the case in Britain where large groups of the working class continued to be represented by the Liberals even after the turn of

the century. But there too the emergence of an independent workers' party signified a break in the community of political interests between employers and workers which had lasted for decades under the banner of radical Liberalism. Confronted with this situation, it was Liberal Imperalism that sought an answer to the class war, a new possibility of national integration, since simple patriotism had obviously failed to fulfil this function for a considerable time. In this context many people proclaimed imperialism as the alternative to socialism. A good number believed, as E. Goulding put it, that "the greatest obstacle that could be erected against the policy of the Labour Socialist Party was the policy of tariff reform linked with imperialism." Imperialist answers to the class war differed in details according to their national and ideological origins; they could be liberal or anti-liberal, but the unifying and obligatory characteristics of all these efforts were the rejection of a revolutionary solution, maintenance of the existing form of society as far as ownership of the means of production was concerned, and devotion to one's own country. The imperialists as a whole countered the class-war formula with the idea of a national community with its national efficiency. It sometimes seemed as if foreign political activity and efforts towards imperial integration were being employed as a means to set national solidarity against class solidarity. In a related context, it was conjectured that the need to strengthen national consciousness was one of the reasons Bismarck turned to a colonial policy. Of course, imperialism frequently used power politics purely for the achievement of its own ends. But the subsidiary aim of establishing and consolidating the idea of a national community by such means was also pursued, and was openly acknowledged, by the most perceptive intellectuals of imperialism, such as the British-Canadian educationalist George Robert Parkin, one of the founders of the Imperial Federation League. Certain moral conquests in imperialism's favour were even gained in the party political camp of British, German, and Italian socialism. A national socialism linked with imperialism began to take shape in several European countries long before the First World War. A special case in the extensive repertoire of this national socialism was the portrayal of a nation in arms as the ideal community of life. In Germany, of course, there were many initiatives in this direction, but advocates of such thought patterns were by no means lacking elsewhere (for example Robert Blatchford in England). These protagonists not only drew their countrymen's attention to the model of the German military organization, but also perceived in militarism the most expedient principle of social order if the nation was to be kept healthy and efficient. A further variant on the interdependence of social and national concepts was put forward by German and Italian publicists: the concept of transforming the class struggle into a national struggle, the view that the "haves" and "have-nots" of the world, proletarian and propertied nations, confronted each other. Such thoughts, of course, were entirely lacking in Great Britain, where the idea of organizing and elevating society so as to breed a truly imperial race became increasingly widespread. All these outlines had one common denominator: imperialism was trying to counter the class struggle with what Viscount Milner called "a nobler socialism" and what international fascism was later to use with some success against international socialism—the idea of a national community.

Friedrich Naumann gave significant expression to the common denominator in the connection between imperialism and social reform. The manifesto of the Nationalsozialer Verein begins:

"We stand on nationalism in our belief that the unfolding of economic and political power by the German nation abroad is the prerequisite for all far-reaching social reforms at home. At the same time we are convinced that external power devoid of national consciousness cannot in the long run satisfy the politically interested masses. We therefore seek a power policy abroad and reform at home."

Many of Naumann's subsequent publications read like a simple paraphrase of this programme. In his *National Social Catechism* published in 1897, Naumann posed the question: "How much does the spread of German influence around the globe depend on the national consciousness of the masses?" The answer: "The tremendous sacrifices which must be made for the navy and the army if Germany is to mean anything in Asia, Africa, America and especially in Europe itself, cannot be imposed for long against the will of the working population." Naumann expected a period of great wars caused by imperialist rivalry, and represented the view that Germany would be erased from history unless she took part. The question: "Cannot the influence of all civilized peoples be spread in harmony?" was answered: "No, because the market for these nations' goods is not large enough. This market grows more slowly than the urge of the civilized nations to expand. The struggle for the world market is a struggle for existence."

Naumann could foresee success for Germany in world politics, but only if the German constitution were democratized and the working masses won over. He fought for the "nationalizing of social democracy" and the setting up of a bloc from Bassermann to Bebel, that is, from the liberal right to the social democrats, excluding the conservatives and the ultramontanes [Catholic zealots]. Conversely he felt that social progress could be guaranteed only if it was integrated into the nation's struggle for world power. "Is there a good prospect for social reform in Germany? Yes, as soon as it is pursued in connection with the expansion of German power." In 1900 Naumann summarized his views in a book called *Demokratie und Kaistertum* ("Democracy and Empire"). In it he again took up the view originated by Lorenz von Stein and Lassalle of a "social royalty" and the close inner connection between the monarchy and the fourth estate. He applied this to the Hohenzollern Empire, whose imperialist character he attempted to delineate more closely by reference to the caesaristic, anti-reactionary and generally modern features of the system and, in particular, of Wilhelm II's personality. "By raising the physical, mental and moral standards of the German worker," he wrote, "the democratic movement is making a direct contribution to the German policy of expansion."

PART THREE

Rich Lands, Poor Lands

11 FROM *Herbert Feis*
Loans to Poor Countries: An Imperialist
Entering Wedge

Herbert Feis is an historian who has acted as an adviser for several government agencies during a long and highly distinguished career. He has written many works on the economic and financial aspects of American foreign relations. The book from which the following selection is taken is our standard scholarly work on the export of capital from Europe during the era of "new imperialism."

As in Tunis, so in the larger Mohammedan state of Morocco, the borrowings of the government ended in bankruptcy, the advent of foreign capital brought conflict. The vision presented to the ruler when the purse strings were opened was too large for his incompetent and reckless character; when the purse strings closed, Morocco was within the purse.

The Sultan held only a loose and uncertain authority over the tribes of the interior. Commerce was scanty and hazardous, roads poor, currency mixed and fluctuating. The taxes were mostly

SOURCE. Herbert Feis, *Europe, the World's Banker, 1870–1914* (New Haven: Yale University Press, Publisher, for the Council on Foreign Relations, 1930), pp. 397–412. Reprinted by permission of the Council on Foreign Relations.

direct, collected by tribal authorities who used whatever means were necessary. The principal tax was the "achour" imposed upon landowners—one-tenth of the harvest or flocks in money or in kind. The public expenditures were small and highly variable, going mainly for the support of the Sultan's civil list and the army. The judicial system was complex, corrupt, and accustomed to administer a law far different from that of European countries. Under it foreign commerce and business felt insecure and soon discovered that economic advantage was to be obtained by personal favor or the support of their governments. Such was the country which put itself in debt. . . .

In 1902 the Sultan had miscellaneous debts to local and European bankers, and no adequate means of paying them. Tribes were in rebellion, and their rebellion interrupted commerce between Morocco and Algiers. The Sultan desired to increase taxes and change their administration. He wished, too, to end the tax exemption of the numerous subjects and *protégés* of the European powers who lived in Morocco. For the contemplated changes the permission of these Powers, especially of France, was not immediately forthcoming. The Sultan turned to European bankers. Three loans were contracted by a French bank, an English bank, and a Spanish syndicate. They paid 6 per cent, were secured by a special assignment of the customs duties, and were purchased by the bankers at 62 per cent of their nominal value; in other words, their effective interest cost was about 10 per cent, as high as the Sultan's credit was doubtful. This did not improve after the European governments gave consent to part of this plan of tax reform. The state expenditure still outran the state income. The tribes refused to pay the new taxes despite the pressure of the Kaids [tribal chiefs]. Nor did the deliberate debasement of the currency prove a more effective way of meeting too large a need. By the end of 1903 suspension of the debt service was again imminent. Assistance at such a time, under such circumstances, inevitably carried its price. Lenders would provide no more unless their loans were given protection. The French government had prepared by a series of understandings with other European governments to assume direction of affairs in the foreshadowed crises. . . .

English official policy was hesitant but traditionally opposed to French aggrandizement, though relatively indifferent to Moroccan trade. But the interested British groups feared that the establishment of a French protectorate would shut Morocco to English trade and investment, as the French Congo had been shut. . . .

The two countries adjusted their interests in a joint declaration of April 8, 1904. In return for freedom of action in Egypt, Great Britain stepped aside in Morocco. The British Government recognized "that it appertains to France as bordering power [i.e., in French Algeria] to keep order in Morocco, to lend its assistance in administrative, economic and financial reforms." France pledged itself not to discriminate as regards tariffs, taxes, and railroad rates, while reserving a right to see that concessions for roads and ports were made under conditions that would leave the authority of the state over these great enterprises of general interest intact. . . . But the treaty had secret clauses, published only seven years thereafter, which provided that when the Sultan ceased to exercise sovereignty over Morocco, the northern part should come within the sphere of influence of Spain, the rest under French influence. . . .

While the French Government was executing these agreements . . . a French banking group headed by the Banque de Paris et Pays Bas was discussing with the Sultan terms of the loan essential to the financial and military reorganization of Morocco. The group had already made short-time advances at the instance of the French Government. A representative of the French Government, under instructions from the Foreign Office, participated in the discussion of loan terms. The loan as arranged was of nominal total of 62.5 million francs, sold to the bankers at 80 and to the public at 96. The customs revenues were pledged as guaranty. These revenues were placed under the supervision of the bondholders, whose representative was given the right to appoint an assistant in each port to watch over the collection. . . .

This prospect of financial control (combined with that provision of the Anglo-French Declaration that seemed to imply control over concessions) was undoubtedly among the matters which moved the German Government to intervene, and thus to make the financing of Morocco an issue of grave international concern. German business and financial circles were stirred by the conviction that opportunity in Morocco was being foreclosed. As early as 1880 Germany had insisted upon the open door in that country. When a change in the status of the country seemed likely, the government apparently decided at first to put the best possible face on the event. The German Chancellor upon being informed of the Anglo-French Declaration asserted "that the interests of Germany in Morocco were mainly of an economic order. . . Germany had no reason to fear that her economic interests in Morocco will be injured by any other power." But behind this assertion there was some disappointed hope and displeasure. The government, apparently on the suggestion of its representative in Morocco, tried to induce the German banks to compete for the 1904 loan, but they refused. An attempt had also been made to have the concession for the State Bank [of Morocco] given to a German firm. German displeasure grew as the complaints of German enterprise were heard and the scope of French plans became clear. Besides, the German Government, despite its public statement, probably felt cheated on political grounds. Great Britain, Spain, and Italy had all been consulted and had received some political compensation for standing aside in Morocco; Germany had been passed over in these respects. The Foreign Office proposed a naval demonstration but this the Kaiser opposed. Instead, after grave hesitance, he landed in March, 1905, at Tangier and in two speeches affirmed the independence of the Sultan and warned him against the acceptance of the French plans of reforms. The move immediately checked their application.

The Sultan, after rejecting the French plans, then proposed that they be submitted to an international conference, and Germany made the same demand. . . . French consent was given in July, 1905, and the conference of Algeciras was arranged. The task of the conference was to determine what reforms were necessary for Morocco and the proper means and agents for executing them. Public finance and currency, public administration, especially the police and military branches all obviously required attention and new plans. Before the deliberations began, the German representative in Morocco, Count Tattenbach, secured concessions for German enterprise to build port works. This action the French Government asserted to be in contravention of an agreement that no concessions would be sought until the conference ended. French firms were charged by Germany with similar violations. The German banks made a short-time advance to the Sultan which, it was asserted, violated the priority privilege of the French banks. Only after protracted days of conciliatory efforts were these matters patched up in compromise, and the conference enabled to begin its anxious course.

In the outcome of the conference (January to April, 1906) German expectations were poorly met, and France was able to a substantial degree to work its will. The Powers with which she had alliances and those which had benefited by treaties dealing with Morocco brought the necessary support. Still Germany succeeded in submitting the process of economic and political penetration of Morocco to a certain measure of international control. The General Act of Algeciras, which issued from the conference (April 7, 1906), in laying down a political *régime* for Morocco, recognized its independence. The State Bank was made into an elaborate international institution in which the distribution of influence was decided only after intense diplomatic effort. Its ownership was lodged in the hands of banking syndicates of twelve countries, each nominated by the government of its own country. . . .

The notions of international control of Moroccan affairs . . . expressed in the Act of Algeciras, were soon to fail of effect, and the state of Morocco to grow more disturbed than before. During 1906–7 the disorder among the tribesmen grew chronic and widespread and the Sultan's government grew less able to subdue it. The revolt was, in part, induced by the opposition to the measures of European control which had been accepted. In 1907 the Sultan was forced to yield to his brother, Moulay-Hafid. This tumult of revolt had reduced the finances of the former Sultan to the last extremity and made him dependent once again upon French financial aid. Three times before his overthrow the French Government had persuaded the French banks to grant him advances. The State Bank of Morocco had loaned him almost all its capital. The new ruler had no funds to conduct his operations. Large claims for damages faced him. The French Government assessed the throne with the cost of a military expedition undertaken after the murder of five Frenchmen by tribes excited by a rumor that a railroad was to be run through a Moslem cemetery at Casablanca. The Spanish Government presented a similar demand. Due debts and claims of all sorts at the beginning of 1909 totaled about 150 million francs. The new Sultan had a total disposable revenue of about 9 million francs. Obviously the whole structure of government and reform had gone to pieces before the internal and external difficulties. . . .

The new Sultan, Moulay-Hafid, was made to face the debts and claims. The only means by which this could be done even temporarily was by contracting another large external loan which was certain to be conditioned upon an extension of the creditors' control over his revenues and actions. If this firmer control had been imposed earlier when the debt burden was smaller, it might have worked to the ultimate advantage of the country, but combined with too large a debt, it inevitably meant future difficulties. The Sultan endeavored to evade his responsibilities and for a time refused to accept the proffered loan terms. But a French ultimatum ended his resistance. . . . French evacuation was delayed until the loan was arranged. The French Government appears to have forced the issue partly out of fear that German firms, with the support of the German Government, might resort to direct seizure of Moroccan property. These fears centered upon the firm of Renschausen to whom the Sultan was indebted for port construction work at Tangier, for which debt seacoast property had been pledged under terms which gave the creditors power to sell it. The French Government feared too that the creditors might suggest another international conference thus taking the lead again out of French hands. The French ultimatum was effective. The loan contract was signed. The private claims were submitted to an arbitral commission upon which the Moroccan representative was in reality nominated by France. Thus, the new sovereign was forced to meet the expenses of his climb to power, and thereby prepared his fall from power.

The loan contract was signed with the same group of banks that had secured the 1904 loan. It was accompanied by accords between the two governments which provided for French evacuation, the appointment of a French engineer as adviser on public works to the Finance Minister, and the use of French instructors in the Moroccan army which was to be reorganized along with the police. These were constructive arrangements which at the same time increased French power. The German Government in disarming the criticism of their terms that arose in Germany indicated that it had asked the German banks to consider the loan business, but that they had not been disposed to do it. At the time the two governments were pledged to a measure of joint economic activity in Morocco, and the German Government was agreeable to the loan and convinced of its necessity. The loan was for 107 million francs and bore 5 per cent interest. It was sold to the bankers at 89, and to the public at 97. To its service and to the annuity due the French Government there was pledged most of the still disposable revenue of the Sultan. The creditors' control of customs was turned into a general debt control. Their powers of supervision of customs revenues had been incomplete and unsatisfactory. Now they were made effective by being extended to the actual work of collection. The new ceded revenues —the remainder of the customs, the net product of the tobacco taxes, of the tax on landed property in port areas, of the urban tax, and others—were put under their direct administration. An increase of 2.5 per cent in customs duties was permitted and this revenue was left outside the loan pledges. It was reserved for public works under a plan formulated in collaboration with the Powers and controlled by a special international committee.

The French Government of the day held the view that these obligations were within the capacity of the Sultan, and that these plans would pave the way to peace and foster economic development. The State Bank had stabilized currency; the control would increase revenues, the public works plan would stimulate economic activity, the new loan funds would permit the reorganization of the army and thereby assure order. But events immediately disproved these conclusions, if they were genuinely held. The Sultan's expenditures soon outran the disposable revenue. This was but little over 3 million francs in 1910. Out of a total revenue of 24 million francs, approximately 16.5 millions were required to meet the annuities of the debt service and war cost payments to the French and Spanish governments. It was on the evidence of these facts that M. Jaurès [a leader of France's socialists] remarked of the 1910 loan that it took away from the Sultan all financial autonomy, all military strength, and all moral authority. It was almost inevitable that some responsible power should step in to assume charge of events; anarchy could not indefinitely continue.

The Sultan within a few months was without resources. An attempt to borrow further in Paris did not succeed because of the lack of further security to offer. The French Government re-

mitted part of the annual payment due to it. The Sultan tried
to impose new taxes and increase existing ones. The Powers still
opposed the taxation of their subjects and the growing number
of their *protégés,* arguing that the administration could not be
trusted to be just. The new taxes were imposed upon the tribes
that remained loyal, and the tax rights were sold to chiefs who
sought to increase their yield by the use of force and cruelty.
When the Sultan tried to turn some of the taxes payable in kind
into a money tax and create a register of taxable people, both
the chiefs and the religious orders opposed, and aroused the
tribes. Tax receipts fell rather than rose. The tax gatherers resorted to pillage. The French commander of the expedition that
ushered in the French protectorate declared, "It is to the crying
abuses and shameful exactions that the revolt of the tribes must
be attributed."

Before the spreading revolt, the bankrupt Sultan was helpless.
On March 13, 1911, to keep himself in power he offered France
a complete and intimate understanding to inaugurate a *régime*
of general reform. The tribes around Fez joined in revolt and
threatened the Sultan, the city, and its European colony. The
French Government, asserting that Europeans were in danger
and promising to evacuate when the danger was ended, dis-
patched an expeditionary army of 10,000 men which occupied
Fez. The course of bankruptcy and borrowing, the anarchy, had
come to its inevitable end.

12   FROM   *H. W. Singer*
      Overseas Trade and Investment Patterns Can
          Reinforce Exploitation

Hans Wolfgang Singer was one of the first to realize that neo-classical and Keynesian theory have serious deficiencies for understanding what we need to know about the economic development of poor countries. In addition to teaching economics in England, he has served for many years as an economist for United Nations agencies concerned with underdeveloped nations.

International trade is of very considerable importance to underdeveloped countries, and the benefits which they derive from trade and any variations in their trade affect their national incomes very deeply. The opposite view, which is frequent among economists, namely, that trade is less important to the underdeveloped countries than it is to industrialized countries, may be said to derive from a logical confusion—very easy to slip into—between the absolute amount of foreign trade which is known to be an increasing function of national income and the ratio of foreign trade to national income. Foreign trade tends to be proportionately most important when incomes are lowest. Secondly, fluctuations in the volume and value of foreign trade tend to be proportionately more violent in that of underdeveloped countries and therefore *a fortiori* also more important in relation to national income. Thirdly, and *a fortissimo*, fluctuations in foreign trade tend to be immensely more important for underdeveloped countries in relation to that small margin of income over subsistence needs which forms the source of capital formation, for which they often depend on export surpluses over consumption goods required from abroad.

SOURCE. H. W. Singer, "The Distribution of Gains between Investing and Borrowing Countries," *The American Economic Review*, May 1950, pp. 473–485. Reprinted by permission of the American Economic Association and the author.

In addition to the logical confusion mentioned above, the great importance of foreign trade to underdeveloped countries may also have been obscured by a second factor; namely, by the great discrepancy in the productivity of labor in the underdeveloped countries as between the industries and occupations catering for export and those catering for domestic production. The export industries in underdeveloped countries, whether they be metal mines, plantations, etc., are often highly capital-intensive industries supported by a great deal of imported foreign technology. By contrast, production for domestic use, specially of food and clothing, is often of a very primitive subsistence nature. Thus the economy of the underdeveloped countries often presents the spectacle of a dualistic economic structure: a high productivity sector producing for export coexisting with a low productivity sector producing for the domestic market. . . .

The previously mentioned fact, namely, the higher productivity of the foreign-trade sector in underdeveloped countries might, at first sight, be considered as a cogent argument in favor of the view that foreign trade has been particularly beneficial to underdeveloped countries in raising their general standards of productivity, changing their economies in the direction of a monetary economy, and spreading knowledge of more capital-intensive methods of production and modern technology. That, however, is much less clearly established than might be thought. The question of ownership as well as of opportunity costs enters at this point. The productive facilities for producing export goods in underdeveloped countries are often foreign owned as a result of previous investment in these countries. Again we must beware of hasty conclusions. Our first reaction would be to argue that this fact further enhances the importance and benefits of trade to underdeveloped countries since trade has also led to foreign investment in those countries and has promoted capital formation with its cumulative and multiplier effects. This is also how the matter is looked at in the economic textbooks—certainly those written by nonsocialist economists of the industrialized countries. That view, however, has never been really accepted by the more articulate economists in the underdeveloped countries themselves, not to mention popular opinion in those countries; and it seems to the present writer that there is much more in their view than is allowed for by the economic textbooks.

Can it be possible that we economists have become slaves to the geographers? Could it not be that in many cases the productive facilities for export from underdeveloped countries, which were so largely a result of foreign investment, never became a part of the internal economic structure of those underdeveloped countries themselves, except in the purely geographical and physical sense? Economically speaking, they were really an outpost of the economies of the more developed investing countries. The main secondary multiplier effects, which the textbooks tell us to expect from investment, took place not where the investment was physically or geographically located but (to the extent that the results of these investments returned directly home) they took place where the investment came from. I would suggest that if the proper economic test of investment is the multiplier effect in the form of cumulative additions to income, employment, capital, technical knowledge, and growth of external economies, then a good deal of the investment in underdeveloped countries which we used to consider as "foreign" should in fact be considered as domestic investment on the part of the industrialized countries.

Where the purpose and effect of the investments was to open up new sources of food for the people and for the machines of industrialized countries, we have strictly domestic investment in the relevant economic sense, although for reasons of physical geography, climate, etc., it had to be made overseas. Thus the fact that the opening up of underdeveloped countries for trade has led to or been made possible by foreign investment in those countries does not seem a generally valid proof that this combination has been of particular benefit to those countries. The very differential in productivity between the export sectors and the domestic sectors of the underdeveloped countries, which was previously mentioned as an indication of the importance of foreign trade to underdeveloped countries, is also itself an indication that the more productive export sections—often foreign owned—have not become a real part of the economies of underdeveloped countries.

We may go even further. If we apply the principle of opportunity costs to the development of nations, the import of capital into underdeveloped countries for the purpose of making them into providers of food and raw materials for the industrialized countries may have been not only rather ineffective in giving them the normal benefits of investment and trade but may have been positively harmful. The tea plantations of Ceylon, the oil wells of Iran, the copper mines of Chile, and the cocoa industry of the Gold Coast may all be more productive than domestic agriculture in these countries; but they may well be less productive than domestic industries in those countries which might have developed if those countries had not become specialized to the degree in which they now are to the export of food and raw materials, thus providing the means of producing manufactured goods elsewhere with superior efficiency. Admittedly, it is a matter of speculation whether in the absence of such highly specialized "export" development, any other kind of development would have taken its place. But the possibility cannot be assumed away. Could it be that the export development has absorbed what little entrepreneurial initiative and domestic investment there was, and even tempted domestic savings abroad? We must compare, not what is with what was, but what is with what would have been otherwise—a tantalizingly inconclusive business. All we can say is that the process of traditional investment taken by itself seems to have been insufficient to initiate domestic development, unless it appeared in the form of migration of persons.

The principle of specialization along the lines of static comparative advantages has never been generally accepted in the underdeveloped countries, and not even generally intellectually accepted in the industrialized countries themselves. Again it is difficult not to feel that there is more to be said on the subject than most of the textbooks will admit. In the economic life of a country and in its economic history, a most important element is the mechanism by which "one thing leads to another," and the most important contribution of an industry is not its immediate product (as is perforce assumed by economists and statisticians) and not even its effects on other industries and immediate social benefits (thus far economists have been led by Marshall and Pigou to go) but perhaps even further its effect on the general level of education, skill, way of life, inventiveness, habits, store of technology, creation of new demand, etc. And this is perhaps precisely the reason why manufacturing industries are so universally desired by underdeveloped countries;

namely, that they provide the growing points for increased technical knowledge, urban education, the dynamism and resilience that goes with urban civilization, as well as the direct Marshallian external economies. No doubt under different circumstances commerce, farming, and plantation agriculture have proved capable of being such "growing points," but manufacturing industry is unmatched in our present age. . . .

It is a matter of historical fact that ever since the [eighteen-] seventies the trend of prices has been heavily against sellers of food and raw materials and in favor of the sellers of manufactured articles. The statistics are open to doubt and to objection in detail, but the general story which they tell is unmistakable. What is the meaning of these changing price relations?

The possibility that these changing price relations simply reflect relative changes in the real costs of the manufactured exports of the industrialized countries to those of the food and primary materials of the underdeveloped countries can be dismissed. All the evidence is that productivity has increased if anything less fast in the production of food and raw materials even in the industrialized countries but most certainly in the underdeveloped countries, than has productivity in the manufacturing industries of the industrialized countries. The possibility that changing price relations could merely reflect relative trends in productivity may be considered as disposed of by the very fact that standards of living in industrialized countries (largely governed by productivity in manufacturing industries) have risen demonstrably faster than standards of living in underdeveloped countries (generally governed by productivity in agriculture and primary production) over the last sixty or seventy years. However important foreign trade may be to underdeveloped countries, if deteriorated terms of trade (from the point of view of the underdeveloped countries) reflected relative trends of productivity, this could most assuredly not have failed to show in relative levels of internal real incomes as well.

Dismissing, then, changes in productivity as a governing factor in changing terms of trade, the following explanation presents itself: the fruits of technical progress may be distributed either to producers (in the form of rising incomes) or to consumers (in the form of lower prices). In the case of manufactured commodities produced in more developed countries, the former method, *i.e.*, distribution to producers through higher incomes, was much more important relatively to the second method, while the second method prevailed more in the case of food and raw material production in the underdeveloped countries. Generalizing, we may say that technical progress in manufacturing industries showed in a rise in incomes while technical progress in the production of food and raw materials in underdeveloped countries showed in a fall in prices. Now, in the general case, there is no reason why one or the other method should be generally preferable. There may, indeed, be different employment, monetary, or distributive effects of the two methods; but this is not a matter which concerns us in the present argument where we are not concerned with internal income distribution. In a closed economy the general body of producers and the general body of consumers can be considered as identical, and the two methods of distributing the fruits of technical progress appear merely as two formally different ways of increasing real incomes.

When we consider foreign trade, however, the position is fundamentally changed. The producers and the consumers can no longer be considered as the same body of people. The producers are at home; the consumers are abroad. Rising incomes of home producers to the extent that they are in excess of increased productivity are an absolute burden on the foreign consumer. Even if the rise in the income of home producers is offset by less than the gain in productivity so that prices remain constant or even fall by less than the gain in productivity, this is still a relative burden on foreign consumers, in the sense that they lose part or all of the potential fruits of technical progress in the form of lower prices. On the other hand, where the fruits of technical progress are passed on by reduced prices, the foreign consumer benefits alongside with the home consumer. Nor can it be said, in view of the notorious inelasticity of demand of primary commodities, that the fall in their relative prices has been compensated by its total revenue effects.

Other factors have also contributed to the falling long-term trend of prices of primary products in terms of manufactures, apart from the absence of pressure of producers for higher incomes. Technical progress, while it operates unequivocally in favor of manufactures—since the rise in real incomes generates

a more than proportionate increase in the demand for manufactures—has not the same effect on the demand for food and
raw materials. In the case of food, demand is not very sensitive
to rises in real income, and in the case of raw materials, technical
progress in manufacturing actually largely consists of a reduction
in the amount of raw materials used per unit of output, which
may compensate or even overcompensate the increase in the
volume of manufacturing output. This lack of an automatic
multiplication in demand, coupled with the low price elasticity
of demand for both raw materials and food, results in large price
falls, not only cyclical but also structural.

Thus it may be said that foreign investment of the traditional
type which sought its repayment in the direct stimulation of exports of primary commodities either to the investing country
directly or indirectly through multilateral relations, had not only
its beneficial cumulative effects in the investing country, but the
people of the latter, in their capacity as consumers, also enjoyed
the fruits of technical progress in the manufacture of primary
commodities thus stimulated, and at the same time in their
capacity as producers also enjoyed the fruits of technical progress
in the production of manufactured commodities. The industrialized countries have had the best of both worlds, both as
consumers of primary commodities and as producers of manufactured articles, whereas the underdeveloped countries had the
worst of both worlds, as consumers of manufactures and as producers of raw materials. This perhaps is the legitimate germ of
truth in the charge that foreign investment of the traditional type
formed part of a system of "economic imperialism" and of
"exploitation."

Even if we disregard the theory of deliberately sinister machina-
tions, there may be legitimate grounds in the arguments set out
above on which it could be maintained that the benefits of foreign trade and investment have not been equally shared between
the two groups of countries. The capital-exporting countries have
received their repayment many times over in the following five
forms: (a) possibility of building up exports of manufactures and
thus transferring their population from low-productivity occupations to high-productivity occupations; (b) enjoyment of the
internal economies of expanded manufacturing industries; (c)
enjoyment of the general dynamic impulse radiating from in-

dustries in a progressive society; (d) enjoyment of the fruits of technical progress in primary production as main consumers of primary commodities; (e) enjoyment of a contribution from foreign consumers of manufactured articles, representing as it were their contribution to the rising incomes of the producers of manufactured articles.

By contrast, what the underdeveloped countries have to show cannot compare with this formidable list of benefits derived by the industrialized countries from the traditional trading-*cum*-investment system. Perhaps the widespread though inarticulate feeling in the underdeveloped countries that the dice have been loaded against them was not so devoid of foundation after all as the pure theory of exchange might have led one to believe. . . .

If our view is accepted (namely, that the traditional type of foreign investment as it was known prior to 1929 was "foreign" only in the geographical sense and not in the relevant economic sense), does it then follow that foreign investment has failed to fulfill one of the functions traditionally ascribed to it (and hoped for from it in the future): *i.e.,* to spread industrialization more widely and more evenly throughout the world? It would be premature to jump to this conclusion. What has been maintained in the preceding part of this argument is that past foreign investment, and the type of foreign trade which went with it, failed to spread industrialization to the countries in which the investment took place. It may be, however, that for a full understanding of the process we have to consider not merely the investing and the invested countries but a third group of countries as well.

It is an interesting speculation that European investment overseas was the instrument by which industrialization was brought to North America. Roughly speaking, the supplies of food and raw materials pouring into Europe as the result of the investment-*cum*-trade system and the favorable terms of trade engendered by this system enabled Europe to feed, clothe, educate, train, and equip large numbers of emigrants sent overseas, principally to the United States and Canada. Thus the benefits to the investing countries of Europe arising out of the system described above were in turn passed on to the United States—the converse of the Marshall Plan—and were the main foundation of the enormous capital formation the result of which is now to be observed in North America. This "macroeconomic" analysis is, of course, in no way contradicted by the fact that the individual migrant was motivated by the prospect of raising his standards of living by the transfer.

Attention may be drawn to the interesting statistical computation of Corrado Gini that even the enormous capital-stock characteristic of the United States economy is not more than the equivalent of the burden in consumption goods and in such services as health, education, and other provision for the immigrants—a burden which the United States was enabled to save by shifting it to the European mother countries of the immigrants. Perhaps in the final result it may be said that the ultimate benefits of the traditional investment-*cum*-trade system were not with the investing countries of Europe but with the new industrial countries of North America.

If this analysis is correct, the industrialization of North America was made possible by the combination of migration and the opening up of underdeveloped overseas countries through European investment and trade. To that extent, Point Four and technical assistance on the part of the United States would be a gesture of historical justice and return of benefits received in the past.

It may be useful, rather than end on a wild historical speculation, to summarize the type of economic measures and economic policies which would result from the analysis presented in this paper. The first conclusion would be that in the interest of the underdeveloped countries, of world national income, and perhaps ultimately of the industrialized countries themselves, the purposes of foreign investment and foreign trade ought perhaps to be redefined as producing gradual changes in the structure of comparative advantages and of the comparative endowment of the different countries rather than to develop a world trading system based on existing comparative advantages and existing distribution of endowments. This perhaps is the real significance of the present movement toward giving technical assistance to underdeveloped countries not necessarily linked with actual trade or investment. The emphasis on technical assistance may be interpreted as a recognition that the present structure of comparative advantages and endowments is not such that it should be considered as a permanent basis for a future international division of labor.

In so far as the underdeveloped countries continue to be the source of food and primary materials and in so far as trade, investment, and technical assistance are working in that direction by expanding primary production, the main requirement of underdeveloped countries would seem to be to provide for some method of income absorption to ensure that the results of technical progress are retained in the underdeveloped countries in a manner analogous to what occurs in industrialized countries. Perhaps the most important measure required in this field is the reinvestment of profits in the underdeveloped countries themselves, or else the absorption of profits by fiscal measures and their utilization for the finance of economic development, and the absorption of rising productivity in primary production in rising real wages and other real incomes, provided that the increment is utilized for an increase in domestic savings and the growth of markets of a kind suitable for the development of domestic industries. Perhaps this last argument, namely, the necessity of some form of domestic absorption of the fruits of technical progress in primary production, provides the rationale for the concern which the underdeveloped countries show for the introduction of progressive social legislation. Higher standards of wages and social welfare, however, are not a highly commendable cure for bad terms of trade, except where the increment leads to domestic savings and investment. Where higher wages and social services are prematurely introduced and indiscriminately applied to export and domestic industries, they may in the end turn out a retarding factor in economic development and undermine the international bargaining strength of the primary producers. Absorption of the fruits of technical progress in primary production is not enough; what is wanted is absorption for reinvestment.

Finally, the argument put forward in this paper would point the lesson that a flow of international investment into the underdeveloped countries will contribute to their economic development only if it is absorbed into their economic system; *i.e.,* if a good deal of complementary domestic investment is generated and the requisite domestic resources are found.

13 FROM *Gunnar Myrdal*
Poverty—Imperialism—Poverty

Gunnar Myrdal is a Swedish social scientist famous for his studies of American race relations and of the outlook for the welfare state. In all his work he resolutely cuts across traditional lines separating economics, sociology, and political science in his search for explanations of and cures for the dilemmas of our day. His book from which this selection is taken has profoundly influenced our thinking about the dynamics of poverty and affluence. It is an examination of the role of inequality in economic change. In this selection Myrdal first treats regional inequalities and then applies his analysis to relations between countries. He shows us that the forces working for imperialism are not confined to "foreign affairs" but also operate between regions inside a nation, and—some persons would add—between races. One of the reasons for neocolonialism, therefore, is the inability of certain nations to break out of the vicious circle of poverty and dependency.

I have suggested that the principle of interlocking, circular inter-dependence within a process of cumulative causation has validity over the entire field of social relations. It should be the main hypothesis when studying economic under-development and development.

Suppose that in a community an accidental change occurs which is not immediately cancelled out in the stream of events: for example, that a factory, where a large part of the population gets its livelihood, burns down and that it becomes clear that it would not repay to rebuild it, at least not in that locality. The immediate effect of this primary change is that the firm owning

SOURCE. Gunnar Myrdal, *Economic Theory and Under-Developed Regions* (London: Gerald Duckworth & Co., 1957), pp. 23–32, 57–60. American title is *Rich Lands and Poor.* Copyright © 1957 by Gunnar Myrdal. Reprinted by permission of Harper & Row, Publishers, Inc.

it goes out of business and its workers become unemployed. This will decrease incomes and demand.

In its turn the decreased demand will lower incomes and cause unemployment in all sorts of other businesses in the community which sold to, or served, the firm and its employees. A process of circular causation has so been started with effects which cumulate in the fashion of the "vicious circle."

If there are no other exogenous changes, the community will be less tempting for outside businesses and workers who had contemplated moving in. As the process gathers momentum, businesses established in the community and workers living there will increasingly find reasons for moving out in order to seek better markets somewhere else. If they do, this will again decrease incomes and demand. It will usually also change the age structure of the local population in an unfavourable direction. . . .

A cumulative process of the same general character, going downwards or upwards as the case may be, will also be generated by a change in the terms of trade of a community or a region, if the change is large and persistent enough or, indeed, by any other change having as its effect a substantial decrease or increase in the inter-related economic quantities: demand, earning power and incomes, investment and production. The main idea I want to convey is that the play of the forces in the market normally tends to increase, rather than to decrease, the inequalities between regions.

If things were left to market forces unhampered by any policy interferences, industrial production, commerce, banking, insurance, shipping and, indeed, almost all those economic activities which in a developing economy tend to give a bigger than average return—and, in addition, science, art, literature, education and higher culture generally—would cluster in certain localities and regions, leaving the rest of the country more or less in a backwater.

Occasionally these favoured localities and regions offer particularly good natural conditions for the economic activities concentrated there; in rather more cases they did so at the time when they started to gain a competitive advantage. For naturally economic geography sets the stage. Commercial centres are, of course, usually located in places where there are reasonably good natural conditions for the construction of a port, and centres for heavy industry are most often located not too far away from coal and iron resources.

But within broad limits the power of attraction today of a centre has its origin mainly in the historical accident that something was once started there, and not in a number of other places where it could equally well or better have been started, and that the start met with success. Thereafter the ever-increasing internal and external economies—interpreted in the widest sense of the word to include, for instance, a working population trained in various crafts, easy communications, the feeling of growth and elbow room and the spirit of new enterprise—fortified and sustained their continuous growth at the expense of other localities and regions where instead relative stagnation or regression became the pattern.

It is easy to see how expansion in one locality has "backwash effects" in other localities. More specifically the movements of labour, capital, goods and services do not by themselves counteract the natural tendency to regional inequality. By themselves, migration, capital movements and trade are rather the media through which the cumulative process evolves—upwards in the lucky regions and downwards in the unlucky ones. In general, if they have positive results for the former, their effects on the latter are negative.

The localities and regions where economic activity is expanding will attract net immigration from other parts of the country. As migration is always selective, at least with respect to the migrant's age, this movement by itself tends to favour the rapidly growing communities and disfavour the others.

In the historical epoch—which is only just now coming to its end in the very richest and most advanced countries—when birth-control is still spreading to lower economic and social strata, the poorer regions will also have a relatively higher fertility. This adds its influence to that of the net emigration in making the age distribution in these regions unfavourable; in the longer run it may also cause a less favourable relation between total working population and resources. The poverty in rural regions of Europe during the long period of net emigration to the industrial centres—and to America—has a main explanation in the unfavourable age distribution there, caused by migration and in part also by higher fertility rates.

Capital movements tend to have a similar effect of increasing inequality. In the centres of expansion increased demand will spur investment, which in its turn will increase incomes and demand and cause a second round of investment, and so on. Saving will increase as a result of higher incomes but will tend to lag behind investment in the sense that the supply of capital will steadily meet a brisk demand for it. In the other regions the lack of new expansionary momentum has the implication that the demand for capital for investment remains relatively weak, even compared to the supply of savings which will be low as incomes are low and tending to fall. Studies in many countries have shown how the banking system, if not regulated to act differently, tends to become an instrument for siphoning off the savings from the poorer regions to the richer and more progressive ones where returns on capital are high and secure.

Trade operates with the same fundamental bias in favour of the richer and progressive regions against the other regions. The freeing and widening of the markets will often confer such competitive advantages on the industries in already established centres of expansion, which usually work under conditions of increasing returns, that even the handicrafts and industries existing earlier in the other regions are thwarted. The hampering of industrial growth in the poorer southern provinces of Italy, caused by the pulling down of internal tariff walls after Italy's political unification in the last century, is a case in point which has been thoroughly studied: industry in the northern provinces had such a lead, and was so much stronger that it dominated the new national market, which was the result of political unification, and suppressed industrial efforts in the southern provinces.

As industrialisation is the dynamic force in this development, it is almost tautological to state that the poorer regions remain mainly agricultural: the perfection of the national markets will even, as I have just mentioned, tend to frustrate earlier beginnings of industrial diversification in agricultural regions. In the backward regions of Southern Europe about three quarters of the population get their livelihood from agriculture. In these regions also, not only manufacturing industry and other non-agricultural pursuits but agriculture itself show a much lower level of productivity than in the richer regions. . . .

On the same assumption the poorer regions, unaided, could

hardly afford much medical care and their populations would be less healthy and have a lower productive efficiency. They would have fewer schools and their schools would be grossly inferior— in Southern Europe the population of the poorer regions is actually still largely illiterate.

The people living there would on the average be believers in the more primitive variants of religion, sanctioning traditional *mores* by taboos and functional magic, and they would be more superstitious and less rational generally. Their entire systems of valuations would take on such an imprint of poverty and backwardness that they would become even less susceptible to the experimental and ambitious aspirations of a developing society. . . .

For easy reference I shall refer to all relevant adverse changes, caused outside [a particular] locality, as the "backwash effects" of economic expansion in [another] locality. I include under this label the effects *via* migration, capital movements and trade as well as all the effects *via* the whole gamut of other social relations exemplified above; and the term refers to the total cumulative effects resulting from the process of circular causation between all the factors, "non-economic" as well as "economic." . . .

Against the backwash effects there are, however, also certain centrifugal "spread effects" of expansionary momentum from the centres of economic expansion to other regions. It is natural that the whole region around a nodal centre of expansion should gain from increasing outlets of agricultural products and be stimulated to technical advance all along the line.

There is also another line of centrifugal spread effects to localities farther away, where favourable conditions exist for producing raw materials for the growing industries in the centres; if a sufficient number of workers become employed in these other localities even consumer goods industries will be given a spur there. These, and also all other localities where new starts are being made and happen to succeed, become in their turn, if the expansionary momentum is strong enough to overcome the backwash effects from the older centres, new centres of self-sustained economic expansion.

The spread effects of momentum from a centre of industrial expansion to other localities and regions, operating through increased demands for their products and in many other ways, weave themselves into the cumulating social process by circular causation in the same fashion as the backwash effects in opposition to which they set up countervailing changes. They represent a complication of the main hypothesis that in the normal case the changes in other factors which are called forth as reactions by a change in one factor, always tend to move the system in the same direction as the first change.

In no circumstances, however, do the spread effects establish the assumptions for an equilibrium analysis. In the marginal case the two kinds of effects will balance each other and a region will be "stagnating." But this balance is not a stable equilibrium, for any change in the forces will start a cumulative movement upwards or downwards.

In reality, the expanding, stagnating and regressing localities are arranged in a fairly continuous series on different levels, with all possible graduation between the extremes. Insofar as in the aggregate all the dispersed industrial advances amount to something considerable, economic standards in the whole country are given a lift.

It is quite possible that all the regions in a country may be inside this margin of balancing forces—if the initial starts are many and strong and successful enough and if the centrifugal spread effects work relatively effectively. The problem of inequalities then becomes a problem of the different rates of progress between regions in a country. But ordinarily, even in a rapidly developing country, many regions will be lagging behind, stagnating or even becoming poorer; and there would be more regions in the last two categories if market forces alone were left to decide the outcome. . . .

On the international as on the national level trade does not by itself necessarily work for equality. It may, on the contrary have strong backwash effects on the under-developed countries. . . .

Many of the under-developed countries were until recently under the political domination of a metropolitan power, and some still are. In addition, almost all those under-developed countries which were not colonies were, and many still are, economically dominated from abroad with effects in the economic field which closely resemble those in the colonies themselves. . . .

A metropolitan country had, of course, an interest in using the dependent country as a market for the products of its own manufacturing industry. If it took special measures to hamper the growth of indigenous industry—which often happened— this was a natural commercial policy of a country which had political domination over another country. Usually such measures, however, were not necessary, as in the absence of protective duties—which the colony was not permitted to impose—the home industry could easily undersell any colonial competitors.

Likewise, the metropolitan country had a clear and obvious interest in procuring primary goods from its dependent territory, and even in investing so as to produce them in plenty and at low cost, thereby exploiting in its own interest local natural resources and indigenous cheap labour.

A metropolitan country had also a self-evident interest in monopolising the dependent country as far as possible for its own business interests, both as an export and an import market. Its control of trade and payments policy provided a ready means of securing preferential treatment for them. But in a natural and normal way it got the protection of its monopolistic interests fortified even more by the whole structure of legislation and administration, and the entrenched institutional system of business connections which was gradually built up. "Enforced bilateralism," as I have called this phenomenon in another connection, characterised all colonial empires, though in different degrees. It was a natural result of political and economic dependency, and it now tends to retain its hold even after political liberation.

In the metropolitan countries this bilateral tendency was often idealised as "close cultural and economic ties" to a mother country. And . . . there were very substantial advantages to the dependent country connected with it. But at the end of the process it must normally mean a considerable economic disadvantage to the dependent country, as it tends to worsen its terms of trade by restricting artificially the scope of the markets where it buys and sells.

It gives an interesting sidelight on the power situation in the world up till recently to note, in passing, that when occasionally this enforced bilateralism was challenged, it was not usually by the dependent countries themselves, but by other industrially developed countries which demanded open access to their markets as sources of raw materials, and as outlets for their exports of manufactured goods.

The capital, enterprise and skilled labour a metropolitan country sent to a dependent country tended for natural reasons to form enclaves, cut out and isolated from the surrounding economy but tied to the economy of the home country. Their economic relations with the indigenous populations were restricted to their employment as unskilled labour. Racial and cultural differences, and the very much lower level of wages and modes of living made strict segregation a natural consequence even within the enclaves themselves.

Segregation hampered the transfer of culture, including technical skills and the spirit of enterprise, to the indigenous population. It is one of the main reasons why these economic starts of colonialism remained enclaves, and why the spread of expansionary momentum was extremely weak or altogether absent.

When employment opportunities were expanded in the mines and on the plantations, the new demand for labour was rapidly filled by population increase, which was also spurred on by the unquestionably beneficial policies . . . of preserving internal order and peace and improving sanitation. As the colonisers had an interest in a plentiful labour supply and low wages for their enclaves, they were not likely to be disturbed by a rapid population increase and lack of real development in the much larger agricultural subsistence economy outside.

A main interest of a metropolitan country was order and social stability. By an almost automatic logic it therefore regularly came to ally itself with the privileged classes in the dependent country; sometimes such classes were created for this purpose. These favoured groups were, by and large, primarily interested in preserving the social and economic *status quo* under which they were privileged, and they would not normally press either for a national integration policy aimed at greater equality within the country, or for progressive economic development in the main subsistence sector of the economy.

From one point of view, the most important effect of colonialism was related to the negative fact that the colony was deprived of effective nationhood, and had no government of its own which could feel an urge to take constructive measures to promote the balanced growth of a national economy. True, in most cases it was only the fermenting influences of the changes brought into the colony by the activity of the colonisers which had gradually brought into existence a situation where such aspirations could be in any degree realistic and reasonable. At that stage, however, lack of political independence meant the absence of a unifying and integrating purpose for the community —except, at a still later stage, the negative aim of expelling the foreign rulers.

The country and the people were laid bare and defenceless to the play of the market forces as redirected only by the interests of the foreign metropolitan power. This by itself thwarted individual initiatives, at the same time as it prevented the formation of a public policy motivated by the common interests of the people.

For all these reasons, colonialism meant primarily only a strengthening of all the forces in the markets which anyhow were working towards internal and international inequalities. It built itself into, and gave an extra impetus and a peculiar character to, the circular causation of the cumulative process.

It had—and in some countries still has, not least in the dependent countries themselves—its close parallels in certain institutional power structures within individual countries: the caste system, racial and religious chasms, the dependence of the regions upon the richer city and, in the feudal or semi-feudal order, the dependence of the peasants upon the landlord, the merchant, the moneylender or the tax collector.

Such hardened institutions of inequality are inimical to economic progress in individual under-developed countries. If they hamper the spread effects within those countries, they inhibit, at the same time, the spread of expansionary momentum from the advanced countries abroad. As I have also mentioned, they have offered to the metropolitan governments a power basis for maintaining colonialism and, in fact, have been promoted by those governments. In these intimate ways internal and international inequalities are inextricably woven together by mutual causation in a circular fashion.

14   FROM   *Michael Barratt Brown*
       Imperialism Feeds on "Backwash Effects"

Michael Barratt Brown is an economist at the University of Sheffield. One of his purposes in the book from which this selection is taken is to show that, apart from a small minority, the people in rich countries also suffer from the continued poverty in poor countries. Therefore the British, he argues, can expect to benefit from the end of empire—provided that the "backwash effects" which took place under imperialism now can be reversed by encouraging planning in the former colonies and by extending them really efficacious aid.

In 1700 the East India Company had been reconstituted on a wider basis and thereafter its fortunes recovered. The famous three-cornered trade was begun—manufactures from England to Africa, slaves from Africa to the Americas, silver from Mexico to India and China, silks and spices from the East for Europe. . . . The fact is that trade, and particularly the slave-trade, was too profitable for capital to be attracted into manufacturing. The profit on each slave was between £20 and £30 and it is estimated that some three millions were transported in British ships in the eighteenth century. As a result, capital which might otherwise have been attracted to industry went back into financing more trade. The Dutch, who at the beginning of the eighteenth century were the greatest traders in the world, never developed their own manufactures, so profitable were their trading enterprises; and they never, therefore, changed from the old colonial system until their rivals had leapt far ahead of them. . . .

Yet, while the young [English] manufacturing interest was developing a new kind of trade with North America, albeit held back by old mercantilist ideas of monopoly restraint, the old system received a new and fabulous lease of life in the conquest of

SOURCE. Michael Barratt Brown, *After Imperialism* (London: Heinemann, 1963), pp. 40–48, 159–177. Reprinted by permission of the publisher. Copyright by Michael Barratt Brown, 1963.

India. After Clive's defeat of the Nawab of Bengal at Plassey in 1757, gold and jewels and other forms of tribute began to flow back to Britain on a scale that makes the plunder of the early adventurers look paltry indeed. Under the treaties that followed Plassey, treasure valued at £4 million sterling . . . was received by the Company and its servants. Clive took nearly a quarter of a million and an estate which brought him in £27,000 a year. For fifty years after Plassey, the tribute drained from Bengal may have amounted to £15 million a year and certainly exceeded £5 million, most of it going not to the Company but to establish the private fortunes of its servants. . . .

. . . It was in the West Indies and North America that the young manufacturers were developing in peaceful trade their new interests, and especially their interest in the growing of cotton, which was to be the catalyst of the industrial revolution. The East India Company, like so many imperial agencies that were to follow, was the happy hunting-ground for the rascals, the misfits, the spivs and speculators, who found the home country either too dull or too "hot" for them. . . .

. . . What had happened meanwhile in India? The great Mogul Empire had begun to disintegrate. An alien court drawing heavier and heavier tribute from the land had been opposed by peasant revolt, internal separatism and external attack.

Indian metallurgy anticipated European developments by several centuries, not only in copper and brass but in high-grade steels. Indian textiles had been selling in Europe at an immense profit to the traders ever since the eastern trade had begun. When the English manufacturers wished to protect their textiles from Indian competition, nothing less than 75 per cent duties were needed to do the job. There was, however, no strong and independent merchant or manufacturing class capable of replacing the decaying imperial rule in India. . . . Part of India's tragedy was that the merchants in Bengal and elsewhere had already become oriented towards the trade with Europe. . . .

. . . One thing still remained to be done before the English manufactures could establish their dominant position, before the industrial revolution could be completed: competition from eastern and particularly from Indian textiles and other handicrafts had to be ended. The East India Company had to be destroyed. At the same time, new overseas markets had to be added to the American market for the large scale of investment in manufacture to be realised. . . .

From 1720 the East India Company had been prohibited by British Government act from importing Indian silks and calicoes, and increasingly heavy duties were imposed upon Indian cotton manufactures as a result of the pressure of the Lancashire manufacturers. The Company's trade with India thereafter consisted mainly of reexports to the rest of Europe, always one of the most profitable sides of its business and the justification for its export of bullion. After Plassey no more bullion was exported; in fact practically nothing was taken *to* India, while exports *from* India were valued at well over £6 million a year. Dacca exported three million rupees' worth of muslin in 1787.

After Bengal had been devastated, the English manufacturers turned once more to attack the East India Company. The reasons advanced by their spokesmen, such as Fox in the House of Commons, were corruption, maladministration and peculation of the Company's servants. This led to the impeachment of Warren Hastings, but the real objective was the end of the Company's monopoly of the Indian trade, the elimination of Indian competition and the opening-up of this vast new market to English manufactures. . . .

Between 1814 and 1835, British manufacturers increased their exports of cotton goods to India from a million yards valued at £26,000 to 51 million yards at £400,000; that was a quarter of all their cotton exports. Exports of silk and woollen goods, iron, pottery, glass and paper increased likewise. India provided a captive market for British manufactures. Meanwhile, Indian spinners, weavers and metal-workers were steadily driven out of business. Dacca exported nothing in 1817. Total Indian exports of cotton goods, amounting to a million and a quarter pieces in 1814 and valued at £1.3 million, had fallen to 300,000 pieces valued at £100,000 by 1832, and to 63,000 pieces by 1844. The population of Dacca, Surat, Murshidabad and other centres for manufacture in India was decimated in a generation and India's balefully increasing dependence on agriculture had begun. . . .

The great Indian . . . markets were now wide open to the English manufacturers. The village handicraft industries were destroyed—the same which had supplied the eastern trade of more than a thousand years and had provided Greek and Ro-

man, Arab and Venetian, English and Portuguese traders with
their wealth. "The bones of the weavers,"—and an English Gov-
ernor-General said it—"were bleaching the plains of India."
Manchester and Birmingham ruled supreme, distorting even the
great centralised states of the irrigated plains of Asia to their
ends. Capitalism, which had grown from the tiny villages and
valleys of England, had achieved world dominion and divided
the nations into rich and poor—advancing industrial manufacturers and declining primary producers. It was the freeing of the
trade, not the building of the empire, that was the essence of
the process. . . .

In the earliest period of colonial rule the crucial element in
the relationship between Europe and the overseas dependencies
was the flow of tribute from the Americas and India to Europe.
This was followed by the no less important elimination of native
industries, above all in the opening-up of India and China to
British manufactures. It is this actual destruction of competitors
that is missed in Professor Rostow's theory of the incapacity of
traditional societies, as he calls them, to organise a surplus for
export without the help of Western European business, or to
develop anything but raw materials for export. The main exports entering world markets for two thousand years before 1800
were precisely the textiles and spices of China and India. The
same point is missed in the otherwise infinitely more valuable
theory of Professor [Ragnar] Nurkse and Dr Gunnar Myrdal
that the widening gulf between rich and poor nations results
from the vicious circle of free trade: that rich lands attract
wealth and poor lands repel it.

Dr Myrdal, in his *Economic Theory and the Underdeveloped
Regions,* quotes the biblical phrases, "For unto everyone that
hath shall be given, and he shall have abundance; but from him
that hath not shall be taken away even that which he hath," to
illustrate Nurkse's concept of a process of circular and cumulative causation that is involved in the unregulated free play of
economic forces. In the nineteenth century, free trade froze the
world division of labour between primary producers and manufacturers; but the division had first to be made by the opening-up of the world's markets to European manufacturers. This
artificial division of labour was the essence of the unequal relationship between advanced and underdeveloped lands. . . .

What has been the disadvantage, then, in being confined to primary production? Canada, Australia, New Zealand and South Africa all seem to have done well out of it. . . . But none of them has in fact been a colony, in this century at least. All have used the wealth from their primary production to establish many of their own industries. It is an extremely important fact that, by 1938, none had a majority of its population engaged in agriculture. Only countries for whose natural products there has been a steadily growing world demand have been in a position to begin industrialising. But more than this was needed. To industrialise requires economic independence, so that the wealth produced may be retained for internal development, and political independence, so that infant industries may be protected.

These courses have not been open to colonies, whose wealth was remitted to the investors of capital away in the metropolitan country, and who were often specifically prevented from introducing protective tariffs, and whose natural resources were developed by an artificially created proletariat at low wages from migrant, indentured and poll-tax labour. Colonial countries, along with other primary producers, have, in addition, suffered . . . in the terms of their trade with manufacturers for two reasons. Their exports were generally limited to one or two crops or minerals upon which their whole livelihood increasingly depended, and in which productivity was difficult to raise; at the same time, the markets for their products were generally restricted to the metropolitan investing country. This "enforced bilateralism" is, as Myrdal points out, what the imperialists call "close cultural and economic ties with the mother country." . . .

The free operation of market forces has been the cause of the violent instability of primary-commodity prices. High prices in the First World War encouraged . . . an excessive extension of crop areas, particularly of rubber, and also of some mining capacity. The subsequent slump in prices left a trail of ruin among primary producers which in the end reacted back on the manufacturing countries too. What must also not be forgotten is that the control of the production of many colonial exports came in this period increasingly into the hands of great imperial companies, such as Unilever, Imperial Tobacco, Dunlop, or Tate and Lyle, whose business has been to obtain cheap raw materials for processing.

Was there no advantage at all to colonies, then, from European investment in them? The answer . . . was that the position differed completely in the lands colonised by European settlers, and in the Asian and African lands brought under colonial rule. The greater part of overseas investment was in railways, ports and harbour installations, roads, telegraph and telephones, plantations and mining. To determine how far European investment actually advanced the condition of the peoples in the regions concerned, however, it is necessary to find what spread took place from the investment to the rest of the economy.

The object of the investment in such mining installations, plantations and transport was chiefly to facilitate the extraction of primary products for export. If the investment created enclaves of development within a largely-unchanged subsistence economy then it might well happen that the net result might be to leave the region as a whole poorer than it was before. . . .

The colonisers of [the U.S.A., Canada, Australia, New Zealand, and South Africa] were all lucky in the products they had to offer on the world market, but the crucial factor was their freedom to develop their own agricultural and mineral output and build up their own industries. Control over their own trade and industry enabled them to import capital equipment from Britain and develop their own economies without running into debt. For they had all won the political freedom to protect their own infant industries against British competition and to spend their earnings of foreign currency much as they wished. . . .

The settler lands of Africa provide a halfway house between the empty lands of white settlement, and the mining and plantation colonies. One can see the two elements side by side in Southern and Northern Rhodesia, or in the mining and settler communities in South Africa. The Dutch voortrekkers and the early British settlers in Southern Rhodesia employed native labour in a more or less servile state, but brought their own capital to develop the land for their own needs and to produce a surplus for export. Rhodes and his successors obtained capital in far larger amounts to mine the diamonds and gold of South Africa and the copper of Northern Rhodesia. But the capital came largely from investors in Britain and the return on this capital flowed back to Britain. Gold-mining dividends paid overseas between 1887 and 1932 were £190 million; investment including reinvestment £120 million. Thus, although the wealth produced by these British companies was immensely greater than that which the settlers contributed, it was largely the settlers and not the mining companies in both South Africa and Rhodesia who stimulated the industrialisation of the economies.

The settlers, however, were able to make use of the mines to develop the economy in South Africa, not only by direct and indirect taxation but by meeting many of the demands of the mines for stores of clothing, food, explosives, and similar necessities from local production instead of from imports. They had to fight for this, but, as Europeans themselves, it was not an impossibly unequal struggle. In South Africa and the Rhodesias there has for long been strong antagonism between the mine-owners and the white settlers, particularly the European trade unionists, who have fought for higher wages, for the exclusion of Africans from skilled jobs and for the retention of a larger share of the profits inside the colony. It was Sir Roy Welensky [later to become] Prime Minister of the Central African Federation, who, as a Northern Rhodesian railway-union leader, used to complain bitterly that more than 45 per cent of the colony's whole national income went to outside investors every year. . . .

The conclusion would seem to be that the wealth produced from mines, or from plantations, will not of itself generate economic development, no matter how great the wealth may be. It took two World Wars and a non-mining settler community to develop local industry in South Africa. This is not perhaps surprising when it is remembered that the average wage paid to African labour in the mines, in addition to his keep, remained at 2s. a day from 1890 to 1940. The spending of such pay as this was not likely to create demand for goods on a scale which would stimulate local industry. Here is the dilemma: industrial and economic development must be slow, indeed, where the market is so poor, but the basis of mining and planting overseas has always been cheap labour.

The wages paid in mines and plantations were based on the assumption that the worker's family stayed in the subsistence economy. Mining in Africa, and elsewhere too, largely depends on migrant labour, and the mine-owners want to keep it that way. Hence their support in the past for *apartheid* policies, which imply the restriction of native Africans to special reserves of land. . . .

. . . Where there were no European settlers, in West Africa for example, there was before the war virtually no development. We may take Nigeria as a case in point. The wealth of Unilever was based to a considerable extent on Nigerian vegetable oils, yet the Nigerians remained one of the poorest peoples of a poor continent. Half the children in Niger province did not survive their fifth year. After three-quarters of a century of British rule in West Africa, where 80 per cent of the population suffer from malaria, the British authorities had built only one fever hospital for a population of 30 million Nigerians. Compared with Britain's ration of a doctor to every thousand inhabitants, Nigeria had one to 60,000.

Nonetheless, for all that we have said, investment in primary production brought some advantage to a colony. The infrastructure of ports and railways involved some extra employment. Mining and plantation wages added something to subsistence. Urban centres did establish themselves, despite segregation policies, and the growth of towns, which received a great impetus during the Second World War, became the basis of African nationalism. . . .

Rates of profit for investors were high partly because wages were desperately low, and wages were low because there was no alternative employment. Mines and plantations were enclaves in a subsistence economy. Sometimes they were quite large enclaves: in Malaya, half the arable land was under rubber; two-thirds of the crop-area in Ceylon was taken up with the three export crops —tea, rubber and copra; a quarter of the cultivated land in Indonesia was covered by rubber, tea, sugar, copra, tobacco, all crops for export. The total value of Indonesian exports was equal to a quarter of the national income in 1938 and exceeded the value of imports by 50 per cent. Exports formed an even higher proportion of income in Burma (41 per cent), Ceylon (48 per cent) and Malaya (about 75 per cent); in the case of Burma, exports were more than double the value of imports. The result of the concentration on export crops was that food had to be imported. Before the war, Indonesia, Ceylon and Malaya all relied on imports for a third of their consumption of rice.

The earnings from the sale of these export crops accrued largely to Europeans. The wealth from the rubber and tobacco plantations, and from the tin and petroleum workings in Indonesia, which flowed back to the Netherlands, was estimated to be equal to a sixth of the Dutch national income before the war. Yet, so small was the spread from these enclaves of development to the rest of the Indonesian economy that every kind of iron goods, even to every nail used for building and packing, had to be imported. Britain . . . was far less dependent on her colonies than Holland. Less than 5 per cent was added each year to Britain's national income from overseas investment during the 1930s, and only a fifth of this was drawn from investment in colonial territories including India. . . . But this did not necessarily mean that no really large sums were taken from the colonies. Out of a value of £60 to £70 million of exports from Malaya in the middle 1930s, the return on tin and rubber investments valued at about £100 million probably amounted to £10 million a year, which would be somewhat over a tenth of Malaya's national income. . . .

Between 1891 and 1931, the population of India dependent upon agriculture rose from 61 per cent to 75 per cent, and this was after the main blows at the handicraft industry had already been absorbed. At the same time, yields per acre were falling, in rice, for instance, from nearly 1,000 pounds in the First World War to just over 700 pounds in the second, and similar steady falls were recorded for other crops. Moreover, more and more land was being taken for export crops and, while before the First World War the area under food crops was also being increased by irrigation works and reclamation, after 1920 the food-crop acreage actually declined—by two million acres in the succeeding twenty years. The area under export crops rose to almost a fifth of the total cultivated land. Exports, mainly of cotton, jute and tea, rose steadily until, in the five years after 1931, they were on average, including bullion, £60 million a year in excess of imports.

This difference between the value of exports and imports went each year to pay the "Home Charges," loan interest and dividends. The so-called "Home Charges," drawn from Indian revenues for British services, rose from £2.5 million in 1851 to £33 million in 1937, and with them the remittances of individual

Britons rose steadily. This was the estimate of a semi-official American report in 1945, which added the loans made to the Indian Government for building the railways and telegraph system carrying annual payments of interest of nearly £50 million, and also incomes of another £50 million earned by British companies in trade and shipping, from which Indians were excluded. Thus, by the Second World War, the annual flow of wealth from India to Britain amounted to over £130 million. The average flow of tribute for the first seventy-five years of British rule in India had been between £2 million and £3 million a year, and the difference between that and the 1945 figure can only in some small part be accounted for by the depreciation in the value of the Pound.

The Indian tribute may have been a small addition to Britain's national wealth in the 1930s, perhaps of the order of 3 per cent. . . . It was a larger loss to India—about a tenth of her national income. In the 1930s, India was forced to cover her losses with gold, which was paid into Britain's reserves to the astonishing amount of £240 million during the six years from 1931 to 1937. The traditional savings of the Indian peasantry, the heirlooms of an ancient people, were melted down and shipped to London and then to America to cover Britain's own deficit on her foreign trade.

There was, however, one important difference between what happened in India and in the smaller plantation and mining colonies. Some part of the crops for export were produced by Indian peasants rather than on British or other European-owned plantations. A rather larger proportion of the earning from the sale of these crops, therefore, stayed in India. Some of the processing of the crops and the secondary industries associated with them were also established in India. Many of these were British-owned and thus their British owners tended to take the profits made in them out of the country. Some, however, were Indian-owned, and this development led to the emergence of a small Indian capitalist, manufacturing class.

The Indian textile industry had first been established in the 1850s, but made little progress until the late 1880s. Expansion up to 1913 was rapid, when . . . exports of cotton yarn and jute manufactures became of major importance. During the First World War, Indian cotton- and jute-mills enjoyed high profits and attracted a new flow of investment immediately after 1918, partly owing to the government's over-valuation of the rupee, but mainly to war-time demand and high prices. Capital equipment was exported to India, and Indian owned as well as British companies flourished. The boom crashed in 1921, the smaller Indian firms being the worst hit, and the proportion of the population engaged in industry actually declined during the next decade. It had been over 11 per cent in 1911; by 1931 it was under 10 per cent. Exports of yarns collapsed but exports of piece-goods grew.

The development of Indian industrialisation had been recommended in 1918 in the light of war-time experience by the Montagu-Chelmsford report; and for strategic, economic and political reasons it was decided to give protection first to cotton manufacture and then to the infant iron and steel industry. When, after 1921, other industries applied for protection, only the British-owned match industry received it. In 1927, the whole policy was reversed: the iron and steel tariff was lowered and a system of imperial preference for imports of British manufactures was introduced. In 1930, this was extended to cotton textiles and, after the Ottawa Conference of 1932, a measure of protection for Indian textiles was combined with protection for British exporters in the Indian market, albeit over strong Congress protests. Thus, not only was Indian economic development held back, until a second World War created conditions which encouraged it once more, but the share of imports from Britain in a much smaller total of trade after 1931 was steadily increased.

Despite the obstacles we have considered, Indian industry did develop between the wars, but very slowly. By 1937, the Tata mills were producing nearly a million tons of steel, enough at least for India's own restricted needs; and Indian mills were meeting three-quarters of the country's textile requirements. Cement and paper output had doubled in a decade but there had been practically no development in heavy engineering, chemicals and machinery manufacture. Thus, the initial impetus given to industrialisation by increased export earnings before and during the war was checked first by the collapse of export markets and then by imperial policies that worked against industrialisation.

PART FOUR

Neocolonialism and International Corporations

15 FROM *Harry Magdoff*
Modern Capitalism and the American Drive
for Empire

Harry Magdoff is the author of several works on American imperialism; he also is the coeditor of the Monthly Review, *a journal which publishes articles reflecting various strands of socialist opinion. In this selection he explains American involvement in Vietnam (and other militaristic aspects of American relations with weaker powers) as "the price being paid to maintain the imperialist network of trade and investment in the absence of colonialism"; and he argues that the deadly "twins," militarism and imperialism, are neither new nor peripheral features of American foreign policy.*

[In the United States] war-related expenditures have constituted the dominant sector of the federal budget throughout our history. Omitting the years of the Second World War and the postwar period, where the record is so well known, a tabulation of federal expenditures by decade, from 1800 to 1939, for army, navy, veterans' compensation and pensions, and interest on the debt—prior to the New Deal federal debt incurred was primarily

SOURCE. Harry Magdoff, "Militarism and Imperialism," *Monthly Review,* XXI, no. 9 (February 1970), pp. 3–11. Reprinted by permission of Monthly Review, Inc. Copyright © 1970 by Monthly Review, Inc.

a result of war spending—shows that except for one decade, at least 54 percent of federal expenditures were for military activities or preparations during the decade or to meet obligations arising from previous military activity. The one exception was the decade of the great depression (1930–1939) when the percentage dropped to somewhat below 40 percent. In seven of the fourteen decades the war-related share of the federal budget was 70 percent or more.

This almost continuous preoccupation with military affairs was clearly not inspired by fears of invading barbarians. Of course, the competing colonial and commercial interests of France, England, Spain and Russia were part of the reality in which the infant and adolescent United States had to operate. At times, self-defense had to be considered. Moreover, resolution of internal tensions, as in the Civil War, exercised a major influence on military aspects of U. S. life. All of this, however, occurred within a context of empire-building. For there has been a continuous thread in U. S. history, beginning with colonial and revolutionary days, of economic, political, and military expansionism directed towards the creation and growth of an American empire. The original expansionism, for which military investment was needed, concentrated on three main thrusts: (1) consolidation of a transcontinental nation, (2) obtaining control of the Caribbean area, and (3) achieving a major position in the Pacific Ocean. It should be noted that this expansionism was not confined to what is now considered the continental territory of the United States: striving for control of the seas, as a shield and promoter of international commerce, has been an ingredient of U. S. policy from its earliest days. In fact, the struggle to incorporate the West Coast into the United States was, among other things, prompted by the desire to control Pacific Ocean ports for the Asian trade.

The experience thus gained in the early stages of empire-building turned out to be most useful when the leading nations of the world entered the stage of imperialism. Several decisive and coinciding developments in the late nineteenth and early twentieth centuries mark off this new stage:

1. The onset of significant concentration of economic power in the hands of a relatively small number of industrial and finan-

cial giants in advanced nations. Competing interest-groups continued to exist, but now the success or failure of the advanced economies became closely identified with the prosperity of the new giant corporations whose *modus operandi* required control over international sources of supply and markets.

2. The decline of Great Britain's monopoly position as world trader and world banker. The burgeoning competitive industrial powers—notably, Germany, France, the United States, and Japan—pressed for a reshuffle of established trade relations and a redistribution of world markets.

3. Industrialization and new naval technology enabled competitive nations to build up their own naval strength to the point where Great Britain could no longer maintain unilateral control over the major sea lanes. . . . Control over sea routes also involved establishing military bases where naval units could be refueled and repaired. The availability of decisive mobile military power on the one hand required acquisition of strategic foreign territory to support bases, and on the other hand provided the means for aggressive pursuit of colonial possessions.

4. The earliest stage of the new imperialism engendered a race by the major powers for control of available foreign real estate. According to Theodore Ropp, after 1880 "every great power except Austria-Hungary . . . became involved in . . . active, conscious colonial expansionism. . . . [*War in the Modern World*, New York, 1962.]" Of the traditional colonial powers— the Netherlands, Portugal, Spain, Britain, France, and Russia— the last four continued to add to their holdings. (Spain, after losing Cuba and the Philippines, proceeded to conquer Spanish Morocco.) And at the same time five new powers entered the race for colonial territory: Germany, Italy, Belgium, Japan, and the United States. As for the United States, it was the Spanish-American War, of course, that placed it with both feet in the imperialist camp. And it was success in this war, plus the subsequent pacification of the Cuban and Philippine "natives," which satisfied two long-term U. S. expansionist ambitions: a leading position in the Caribbean, broadening the highway to the rest of Latin America, and a solid base in the Pacific for a greater stake in Asian business.

As far as the United States is concerned, there have been three distinct stages in the drive to empire: (1) the period when the United States was the supplier of food and raw materials to the rest of the world, when it was an importer of capital, and when maritime commercial interests were relatively very strong; (2) the period when the United States began to compete with other industrialized nations as an exporter of manufactured goods and an exporter of capital—a time when a small number of industrial and financial giants began to dominate the economic scene; and (3) the period when the United States becomes the major, dominant capitalist economy, the largest manufacturer, foreign investor, trader, the world's banker, and the dollar becomes the key international currency.

The energy and determination with which the expansionist strategy is pursued change from time to time. In the transition from one period to another, and because of internal as well as external conditions, it appears at times as if the United States is "isolationist" and uninterested in further extension of its influence and control. Yet it is especially noteworthy that the drive for business opportunities on a world scale is ever present. Even when, as in New Deal days, domestic solutions were sought for crises, the development of foreign business was high on the agenda of government and private enterprise. Given the structure of the economy, the major operating levers work in such a way as to repeatedly reassert expansionism as the dominant strategy. In this perspective, the history of the years since the end of the Second World War are far from a new departure; instead, they are a culmination of long-term tendencies which profited by and matured most readily in the environment created by the course of the last major war.

The postwar leap forward in empire-building and the transition of U. S. society to rampant militarism are associated with two phenomena: (1) the desire to resist and repress socialist nations and to defeat national liberation movements designed to release underdeveloped countries from dependence on the imperialist network, and (2) the extension of U. S. power to fill "vacuums" created by the decline of Western European and Japanese influence in Asia, Africa, and Latin America.

Combating the rise of socialism is of course not a new objective. The destruction of the Russian Revolution was a top priority of the imperialist powers beginning in 1917. In this connection, Thorstein Veblen's observations on the Versailles Treaty in his 1920 review of Keynes' *The Economic Consequences of the Peace* are most pertinent:

"The events of the past months go to show that the central and most binding provision of the Treaty (and of the League) is an unrecorded clause by which the governments of the Great Powers are banded together for the suppression of Soviet Russia—unrecorded unless record of it is to be found somewhere among the secret archives of the League or of the Great Powers. Apart from this unacknowledged compact there appears to be nothing in the Treaty that has any character of stability or binding force. Of course, this compact for the reduction of Soviet Russia was not written into the text of the Treaty; it may rather be said to have been the parchment upon which the text was written."

The failure of the United States to join the League of Nations reflected no slackness in its efforts to contain anti-imperialist revolutions: in Russia, these efforts took the form of armed intervention and support of anti-Bolshevik forces with food and other economic supplies; in Hungary, the manipulation of food supplies to help defeat the Bela Kun government. Surely the issue at that time was not fear of aggressive Russian or Hungarian militarism. Nor can much credit be given to political or religious idealism. The relevant motive, clearly, was recovery of territory lost to free enterprise and prevention of the spread of the contagious revolutionary disease to Western Europe and the colonies. Any such spread, it was recognized, would severely affect the stability and prosperity of the remaining capitalist nations.

Capitalism as an economic system was never confined to one nation. It was born, developed, and prospered as part of a world system. Karl Marx went so far as to claim, "The specific task of bourgeois society is the establishment of a world market, at least in outline, and of production based upon this world market." One might add that it has been the specific task of imperialism to fill out this outline and establish a complex international network of trade, finance, and investment. Given this network, it follows that limitation of opportunity to trade and invest in one part of the world restricts to a greater or lesser extent the freedom of action of private enterprise in other parts of the world. The dimensions of the defense of free enterprise therefore become world-wide.

The United States had long ago accepted its destiny to open and keep open the door for trade and investment in other parts of the world. The obstacles were not only the heathens who wanted to be left alone, but the preference systems established in the colonies of the older nations. The decline of political colonialism and the weakness of the other great powers thus placed upon the United States a primary responsibility for the defense of the capitalist system and at the same time afforded golden opportunities to obtain special beachheads and open doors for U. S. enterprise.

With a task of this magnitude, it is little wonder that the United States now has a larger "peacetime" war machine, covering a greater part of the globe, than has any other nation in all of past history. Imperialism necessarily involves militarism. Indeed, they are twins that have fed on each other in the past, as they do now. Yet not even at the peak of the struggle for colonies did any of the imperialist powers, or combination of powers, maintain a war machine of such size and such dispersion as does the United States today. In 1937, when the arms race in preparation for the Second World War was already under way, the per capita military expenditures of all the great powers combined— the United States, the British Empire, France, Japan, Germany, Italy, and the Soviet Union—was $25. (Germany's per capita of $58.82 was then the largest.) In 1968, the per capita military expenditures of the United States alone, in 1937 prices, was $132. This was only in part due to the Vietnam War: in 1964, our most recent "peace" year, the per capita military expenditures in 1937 prices was $103.

One of the reasons for this huge increase in military outlays is no doubt the greater sophistication of weaponry. (By the same token, it is the advanced airplane and missile technology which makes feasible the U. S. globe-straddling military posture.) An additional reason, of course, is the military strength of the socialist camp. I would like to suggest a third reason: that a substantial portion of the huge military machine, including that of the Western European nations, is the price being paid to maintain the imperialist network of trade and investment *in the absence of colonialism.* The achievement of political independence by former colonies has stimulated internal class struggles in the new states for economic as well as political independence. Continuing the economic dependence of these nations on the metropolitan centers within the framework of political independence calls for, among other things, the world-wide dispersion of U. S. military forces and the direct military support of the local ruling classes.

Precise information on the dispersion of U. S. forces is kept an official secret. However, retired General David M. Shoup, former head of the Marine Corps, who should be in a position to make a realistic estimate, stated in a recent article in *The Atlantic:* "We maintain more than 1,517,000 Americans in uniform overseas in 119 countries. We have 8 treaties to help defend 48 nations if they ask us to or if we choose to intervene in their affairs." The main substance of U. S. overseas power, aside from its present application in Vietnam, is spread out over 429 major and 2,972 minor military bases. These bases cover 4,000 square miles in 30 foreign countries, as well as Hawaii and Alaska. Backing this up, and acting as a coordinator of the lesser imperialist powers and the Third World incorporated in the imperialist network, is a massive program of military assistance. According to a recent study:

"U. S. military aid . . . since 1945 has averaged more than $2 billion per year. It rose to as much as $5 billion in fiscal year (FY) 1952 and fell to as low as $831 million in FY 1956. The number of recipient countries rose from 14 in 1950 to a peak so far of 69 in 1963. In all, some 80 countries have received a total of $50 billion in American military aid since World War II. Except for 11 hard-core communist countries and certain nations tied closely to either Britain or France, very few nations have never received military aid of one kind or another from the United States."

The above factual recital by no means exhausts the international functions of U. S. militarism. Space considerations permit no more than passing reference to (a) the active promotion of commercial armament sales abroad (contributing a sizable portion of the merchandise export surplus in recent years), (b) the extensive training of foreign military personnel, and (c) the use of economic-aid funds to train local police forces for "handling mob demonstrations and counterintelligence work." These are, in the main, additional instruments for maintaining adherence and loyalty of the non-socialist world to the free-enterprise system in general, and to the United States in particular.

The military forces of the politically independent under-developed countries frequently perform a very special function. This arises from the relative weaknesses of the competitive elite power groups: large landowners, merchants, industrialists and financiers—each with varying degrees of alliance to interest groups in the metropolitan center. When none of these ruling-class groups has the strength and resources to take the political reins in its own hands and assert its hegemony over the others, the social order is operated by means of temporary and unstable alliances. Under such circumstances, and especially when the existing order is threatened by social revolution, the military organizations become increasingly important as a focal point for the power struggle within the ruling classes and/or as the organizer of political arrangements. Space limitations do not permit a review of this special role of militarism in the under-developed world as, one might say, the skeletal framework of the imperialist system in the absence of colonies. It is this framework that is supported and nurtured by the practices mentioned above: military training and advisory services, the widespread military assistance programs, and the stimulus given to commercial sales of U. S. armaments.

16 FROM *Fred M. Gottheil*
Frantz Fanon on the Not-So-Dead Hand
of Imperialism

Frantz Fanon (1925–1961) was a Negro doctor from Martinique who studied psychiatry in France, was sent to Algeria during the war for independence there, and was won over to the side of the rebels. In spite of his short life and the demands of his career he found time to write three famous books, each a passionate indictment of imperialism. These works analyze the agonized psyche of colonized peoples and urge these peoples to take up continuing revolution against European overlordship and, indeed, against the entire European way of life. But Fanon's writings also contain a theory of class relations among colonial and excolonial peoples that has become important to the New Left. This theory holds that one of the main causes of neocolonialism is the economic interests of the bourgeoisie of the excolony and that these interests arose out of the institutions and attitudes developed during colonial times. In this selection Fred M. Gottheil, an economist who teaches at the University of Illinois, examines this view and concludes that it fits the facts.

During the past twenty years, old and seemingly permanent colonial empires have undergone some form of imposed or self-liquidation. In some areas of Africa, Asia, and Latin America, social, political, and economic revolutions of fundamental character have occurred; in others, change has been minimal. Whatever the extent of the particular revolutionary process, the structural relationships between the metropolitan centers of Europe-North America and the colonial regions of the third world have been irrevocably altered.

SOURCE. Fred M. Gottheil, "Fanon and the Economics of Colonialism: A Review Article," *Quarterly Review of Economics and Business,* vol. 7 (Autumn 1967), pp. 73–80. Reprinted by permission of the Bureau of Economic and Business Research, University of Illinois and the author. Copyright © 1967 by the Board of Trustees of the University of Illinois.

In spite of such dynamic societal transformations, the study of colonialism among academics has been virtually nonexistent, the term colonialism itself virtually taboo. True, the literature concerning the third world is rich on matters of economic development; but the focus of this research has generally been on strictly mechanical problems. However important these problems are, as a rule they have been examined in such a sterile framework that the entire colonial apparatus has been ignored.

The Wretched of the Earth [New York, 1965], however, places the issues of economic development into the context of colonialism. Fanon examines the economic processes as an integral part of the social and political ones. Alignments of classes, formations of indigenous political parties, and the development of national independence movements are seen as vital components of modern-day colonialism. Although *The Wretched of the Earth* is essentially an analysis of revolutionary Algeria, Fanon borrows liberally from the experiences of other African as well as Asian and Latin American countries to demonstrate the generality of his propositions.

This paper focuses upon the socioeconomic content of Fanon's evaluation of colonialism. Fanon, however, offers much more. A psychiatrist by profession, he finds colonialism as deeply rooted in the psyche of the colonized populations as it is in their socioeconomic structures. To this he attributes particular forms of tribal rituals and the sense of racial inferiority—and even self-hatred—that often become manifest in internal violence. . . .

During the two hundred years of colonial occupation, the native populations and geography were specifically tailored to meet the needs of the metropolitan centers. Capitalism extended itself into the heart of Africa, Asia, and Latin America, selected for itself those resources that could be marketed profitably, and left untouched the rest. As a result, economic growth in these regions was characteristically unbalanced; large urban centers—electrified, motorized, and commercialized—stood in sharp contrast to the still primitive hinterland. . . .

The populations of Africa also bear colonial markings. White officers, white administrators, white employers, and white clergymen imposed white values on the nonwhite populations until dominance and color fused into one. Further, the emergence of class structure reflected the inroads of implanted capitalism. Like its counterpart in the metropolitan centers, capitalism in the colonial world produced a bourgeoisie and a proletariat. But this type of bourgeois-proletarian class relation differed from the European variety in one important respect—color. White colonists alone controlled the principal economic resources and organizations in the colonial regions. They alone, by force of arms, became the major financiers, the industrial magnates, and the primary employers of native labor. For the most part, the native bourgeoisie was restricted to the intermediate types of

TABLE 1
LABOR FORCE IN ALGERIA, BY OCCUPATION AND BY ETHNIC GROUP, 1954

Occupations	Distribution by Occupation (Percent)		
	Europeans	Moslems	Total
Agricultural	9.2	73.2	64.3
Self-employed (including family workers)	6.8	47.3	41.7
Wage earners	2.4	25.9	22.6
Nonagricultural	90.8	26.8	35.7
Self-employed and artisans	5.6	1.4	2.0
Tradesmen	8.5	3.6	4.3
Industrialists	1.5	0.1	0.3
Liberal professions	3.1	0.1	0.5
Religious functionaries	0.6	0.3	0.4
Foremen and technicians	15.9	0.4	2.6
White-collar workers	15.8	0.7	2.8
Skilled workers	21.9	4.6	7.0
Fishermen and miners	0.7	0.5	0.5
Unskilled laborers	3.6	6.7	6.3
Domestics, personal service	4.9	1.9	2.3
Armed forces, police	4.7	0.3	0.9
No profession (unemployed and casual workers)	4.0	6.1	5.8
Total	100.0	100.0	100.0

Source. Harold Lubell, "Independent Algeria's Chances for Development," *Quarterly Review of Economics and Business,* Vol. 3, no. 4 (Winter 1963), p. 9.

economic activity, for example, shopkeeping, light manufacturing, and a scattering of the liberal professions. Even at the levels of managerial and working-class positions, the color differentiation was strikingly obvious.

Color polarization of the labor force in Algeria (see Table 1) is clearly marked. Compare particularly the color disparity among foremen and technicians, white-collar workers, and skilled workers. Such segregation characterizes most colonial regions. Fanon, of course, was by no means the first to note the racial factor. Economists generally emphasize the scarcity of indigenous managerial and industrial skills in colonial areas. Fanon's analysis differs from the rest in his attempt to explain *why* the scarcity exists. To him, the colonists gave the native population no choice in the matter.

Still, the aspiration of the native bourgeoisie is not to change the colonial system but to inherit it—to obtain from the European his production processes and consumption patterns. To Fanon, the emulation effect generated by consumption dichotomies, such as those revealed in Table 2, conditions both the attitudes and expectations of the bourgeoisie. This is a critical factor in Fanon's description of neocolonialism. Native populations have come to identify consumption patterns with economic control. Decolonization means to the native bourgeois the freedom to step into vacated shoes of white privilege.

TABLE 2
CONGO (LEOPOLDVILLE) PATTERNS OF CONSUMPTION IN PERCENTAGES

Item	African	Non-African
Subsistence	27	—
Domestic goods	40	8
Imports	22	24
Services	5	38
Taxes, savings, others	6	30

Source. United Nations, *Economic Bulletin for Africa* (Addis Ababa, Ethiopia), June 1962, p. 26.

The native proletariat, embryonic in size and servile in function, displays much the same bourgeois mentality. These workers, Fanon points out, are the least exploited faction of the non-propertied, nonprofessional colonial population. And yet, whatever comparative advantages they enjoy, their living conditions still reflect their subservient status in the colonial world: "The native town is a hungry town, starved of bread, of meat, of shoes, of coal, of light. The native town is a crouching village, a town on its knees, a town wallowing in its mire." Even trade unions, where they exist, have had little effect on working-class conditions. For they pursue much restricted goals and, in order to preserve their meager gains, serve consciously or otherwise the prevailing colonial structure. As a result, writes Fanon, there has developed "a traditional gap between the rank and file who demand the total and immediate bettering of their lot, and the leaders, who since they are aware of the difficulties which may be made by the employers, seek to limit and restrain the workers' demands." In this sense, the trade union movement in the colonial regions may represent a reactionary potential. The colonial towns are further populated by vast numbers of the chronically unemployed, many of them landless migrants from the countryside who form the unstable lumpenproletariat. And in spite of their conditions, even these people have come to live by, if not to accept the fundamental institution of capitalism: the wage system.

The barriers dividing the urban from the rural colonial populations are more than geographic. The peasant sees in the colonial proletariat the acceptance of the alien and hostile European values which indicates to him a betrayal of his native heritage. To the proletariat, on the other hand, and particularly to the small but politically active middle class, peasant attitudes seem out of step with socioeconomic progress.

Feudal chieftains, operating very much in an environment of medieval village life, still exercise considerable social, economic, and political control. Such feudal patterns, Fanon observes, are supported by colonial administrators, who see in them a source of internal stability. The abundant marketable agricultural and mineral resources of the interior, however, are integrated into colonial capitalism and fall in the domain of the colonialist and native land proprietor. Here, as in the towns, color domination of property ownership prevails. The primary aspiration of the native land proprietor is to acquire the resources held by the whites.

The first and foremost concern of the landless peasant, who represents the overwhelming proportion of the colonial population, is land. How to obtain it and end his history of hunger is uppermost in his mind. Writes Fanon: "They never cease to think of the problem of liberation except in terms of taking back land from the foreigner, in terms of national struggle and armed insurrection." The peasant learns early in life that in his pursuit he has nothing to lose. "The land belongs to those who till it. This is the principle which has become the fundamental law of the Algerian revolution." Accepting this law, peasants have developed into the foremost revolutionary class and are the first among the exploited classes to discover that in the struggle for land, only violence pays.

Such is Fanon's description of the colonial population. Basically, it is a society riven with class conflicts. Fundamentally, the antagonisms concern the ownership and control of property. *But here class alignments cross color lines*. The white settler and the black feudal chieftain, he notes, share common economic interests in maintaining the colonial apparatus: "[The chieftains'] enemy is not at all the occupying power, with which they get along very well, but these people with modern ideas who mean to dislocate the aboriginal society and who in doing so will take the bread out of their mouths." On the other hand, the black bourgeoisie and the black landowners find the existing colonial structure an impediment to the development of their specific class interests, and in the pursuit of these interests, they have successfully associated them with national interests. The national independence movements that emerge throughout the colonial world stem from this association. The native proletariat and peasant are ultimately drawn into this struggle on the side of the native bourgeoisie and in the name of national independence. Here is perhaps Fanon's major contribution to the understanding of colonialism and the decolonization process. He is able to penetrate below the color surface of colonialism to its class structure in order to relate the national independence movements to these class antagonisms.

Political parties in the colonial world have developed as almost exclusively middle-class, urban-centered, and urban-oriented institutions. These parties, composing the core of the national independence movement and controlling the decolonization process, have little interest in eliminating the exploitation of the great majority of the population—the peasants and the working class—but merely seek the control of the exploiting apparatus. An effective technique for acquiring the apparatus is nationalization: the transfer of property from private to public hands—in other words, from white to black. As Fanon sees it: "To them, nationalization quite simply means the transfer into native hands of those unfair advantages that are the legacy of the colonial period." And, "As far as doctrine is concerned, they proclaim the pressing necessity of nationalizing the robbery of the nation."

The use of the nationalization for class interests appears also in the agricultural interiors. Here, native land proprietors, claiming rights by color, "manage to make a clean sweep of the farms formerly owned by settlers, thus reinforcing their hold on the district."

For the peasant and the urban worker, however, political independence and the nationalization of property in most instances have proved to be impotent tools in solving their most pressing needs. Fanon writes:

"The peasant who goes on scratching out a living from the soil, and the unemployed man who never finds employment do not manage, in spite of public holidays and flags, new and bright though they may be, to convince themselves that anything has really changed in their lives."

In Fanon's view, nothing really has. The exodus of foreign troops and administrators, the unveiling of the new flag; the setting up of embassies, consulates, and UN delegations; and the participation in international conferences are the more visible symbols of decolonization. In Fanon's judgment such acts add up to very little. With independence achieved, the primary objectives of the native bourgeoisie alone have been attained. The structure remains intact.

Sectoral imbalance, one-crop specialization, and dependence on the metropolitan centers for capital and commodity markets continue. In fact, the urban-rural unity that was so vital in establishing the national independence movement and in winning the struggle against the white colonialists disappears. Now the divergence of class interests between the black bourgeoisie and the black peasant and proletariat stands out sharply. Whereas the workers and peasants once had come to understand that colonial wealth was the result of organized, protected robbery, they now learn that no color has a monopoly on such robbery.

A rapprochement with the metropolitan centers inevitably follows independence. Writes Fanon:

"The national bourgeoisie turns its back more and more on the interior and on the real facts of the underdeveloped countries and tends to look forward toward the former mother country and the former capitalists who count on its obliging compliance."

The compliance becomes all too clear.

"The economic channels of the young state sink back inevitably into neo-colonialist lines. The national economy, formerly protected, is today literally controlled. The budget is balanced through loans and gifts, while every three or four months, the chief ministers themselves or else their governmental delegations come to the erstwhile mother countries or elsewhere, fishing for capital."

This picture that Fanon paints of the newly independent nations, though not a flattering one, is perhaps accurate. The ineffectiveness of the bourgeoisie should not be viewed simply as an act of conspiracy but as an inability to cope with the problems of unemployment, land starvation, and low per capita incomes within the confines of the market system. To tamper with this system would be to negate its own fundamental interest: the accumulation of wealth.

However ineffective this initial stage of decolonization is in solving the basic problems of economic production and distribution, nonetheless it does represent, Fanon argues, a necessary step toward fundamental social emancipation, namely, the expulsion of foreign control and privilege. New conflicts, he argues, will sharpen the new class relations and, once again, the union of the dispossessed, the unemployed, and the destitute in the cities and countryside will come to understand the necessity for carrying the revolution further. The renewed conflict will reveal itself, not as racial, but more correctly as a struggle over the rights to property and the wealth that comes from property. "This is why," Fanon instructs, "we must understand that African unity can only be achieved through the upward thrust of the people and under the leadership of the people, that is to say, in defiance of the interests of the bourgeoisie."

Perhaps Fanon places too much reliance on the ability of "a people" to organize and execute successful revolution—that is, revolution that reshapes the production and market structure and property relations. Fanon certainly is not unaware of the complex processes and enormous tasks involved in the preparation of a people for this role. He notes:

"The awakening of the whole people will not come about all at once; the people's work in the building of the nation will not immediately take on its full dimensions: first because the means of communication and transmission are only beginning to be developed; secondly because the yardstick of time must no longer be that of the moment or up till the next harvest, but must become that of the rest of the world, and lastly because the spirit of discouragement which has been deeply rooted in people's minds by colonial domination is still very near the surface."

But Fanon has no doubt that the task can be done. The first hurdle is psychological:

". . . we must above all rid ourselves of the very Western, very bourgeois and therefore contemptuous attitude that the masses are incapable of governing themselves. In fact, experience proves that the masses understand perfectly the most complicated problems."

Fanon's analysis of the impending second stage of the decolonization process may be a reflection of self-delusion rather than an objective observation. Fanon was writing during the Algerian revolution and was, until his untimely death, its most articulate spokesman. Like Adam Smith in *The Wealth of Nations*, David Ricardo in *The Principles of Political Economy and Taxation,* and Karl Marx in *Capital,* Fanon functioned in the dual capacity of scholar and political activist. But if his anticipation of the people's control of the revolutionary process is more for political consumption than it is a reflection of reality, his sharp, critical analysis of the first stage of decolonization is not. His descriptions, though sweeping, have been borne out by events.

In the former colony of British Guiana, now independent Guyana, the Fanon analysis of decolonization holds up remarkably well. The struggles for political independence in the late 1940's combined the sectional interests of the Negro workers with those of the Indian sugar workers and rice farmers. This political unity, successful in the 1953 elections to the legislature, posed a serious threat to the native propertied class and colonialists. The unity, however, was to be short-lived. By 1955, internal friction, aided by colonial obstructionist policies (for example, dissolving the legislature and imprisoning its leaders) split the population along essentially racial lines. In the 1955–64 period, the splintered independence parties, jockeying for internal power, began to incorporate into their fold the once-excluded but strong bourgeois interests. Following the electoral success in 1964 of the more property-oriented of the parties (aided by CIA-AFL-CIO funds and by the English reorganization of the voting procedures), political independence was finally arranged.

The coalition government today represents the postindependence government that Fanon had described. In its first year, the government, although professing socialist goals, severed its lucrative rice trade with Cuba, drastically reduced its trade relations with the Soviet Union and Eastern European countries, reorganized its monetary and fiscal policies to accommodate its business community, and vigorously courted United States economic aid.

The effect of these measures was to produce as great a dependence on the metropolitan centers as that which had existed prior to political independence. The 8 percent increase in gross national product in the first year of the coalition government was largely due to the major infusion ($18 million) of US economic aid. Guyana's balance-of-payments difficulties have steadily worsened. The Bank of Guyana reported a sharp drain in foreign reserves from $50 million to $34 million in 1956. The reliance on foreign credit has already increased the Guyanese external indebtedness flow from $6 million annually in 1960 to $14.5 million in 1966. The increasing deficit must be financed through external aid or loans. The government tax reform reduced the tax base of personal and corporate income sources so that the available options were either foreign credit or greater tax burdens on the working and peasant classes.

In the area of long-range planning, the 1966–72 development plan was written by a team of Western economists headed by Sir Arthur Lewis. The plan calls for an expenditure of $294 million, and here too the purse strings are held by the US, the UK, and Canada. *The 1966–1972 Development Programme for Guyana: Economic Review,* a Ministry of Finance document, states clearly:

"This $294 million Development Plan will be financed mainly by loans and grants from friendly governments who are willing to help put the country back on its feet after the troubles of recent years."

Not unexpectedly, the plan provides a proper climate for foreign investment and de-emphasizes direct government participation in economic development.

The apparent reluctance to modify the production or distribution structures of Guyana and the continued reliance upon private and foreign economic development will provide little relief to the immediate pressures weighing on the nonpropertied classes. This was precisely Fanon's point. The characteristic problem in the urban area is unemployment. In 1965, the unemployment rate in Guyana was estimated to be 20.9 percent. Although the Lewis plan projects a reduction in unemployment to 10 percent by 1972, there is little likelihood of *any* reduction. Even granting the 5 percent annual increase in GNP that Lewis assumes, independent projections of unemployment in Guyana indicate a 25 percent rate by 1975.

Whatever the percentage may be, it is difficult to see that postindependence Guyana differs in any meaningful way from the preindependence British Guiana.

17   FROM   *James O'Connor*
     A New Form of Imperialism?

*James R. O'Connor is an economist at San Jose State College
who has written several works on Cuba. In this article he gives
us his analysis of the various types of practices of international
corporations. His essay is an example of how the New Left, in
addition to adding certain elements to Lenin's concepts concerning imperialism, has shifted our concern from European to American imperialism.*

. . . The general reasons for the expansion of foreign capital
during the 1950s and 1960s, especially capital organized by the
giant United States international corporations, are well known:
In the first place, the United Staes economy tends to generate
more economic surplus than large-scale business can profitably
absorb at home. Foreign investments absorb some of the surplus
in the short run, but generate even greater amounts of surplus
in the long run. The large corporations are thus compelled to
become even more expansion-minded and seek fresh investment
opportunities. As shown below, branch plant investments of U. S.
corporations absorb surplus generated in the United States by
providing major export markets for parent corporations.

In the second place, modern technology requires special raw
materials, mainly metals, many of which are found only in underdeveloped countries. In addition, short supplies of raw materials
in the North American continent have compelled U. S. corporations to exploit new sources in the underdeveloped world.
More, U. S. corporations are under constant pressure to develop
fresh raw material sources, as a hedge against competitors and
as a way to reduce business risk by diversifying supplies.

It is also well known that U. S. corporations have been operating in an especially favorable economic and political environ-

SOURCE. James O'Connor, "International Corporations and Economic Underdevelopment," *Science & Society*, pp. 43–59. Reprinted by permission of
Science and Society, Inc.

ment since the end of World War II. There have been few important political barriers preventing American capital from insinuating itself into the defeated empires of Germany and overseas Japan, and the decayed empires of Britain, France, and Holland in Asia and Africa. In Latin America, the failure of national-oriented import-substitution industrialization policies to promote ongoing economic development has accelerated the conquest of Latin American capital by U. S. corporations.

Another familiar story concerns the general political-economic effects of U. S. control of an increasing part of the capitalist world's economic resources. Canada's independent economic foreign policies are confined to the agricultural sphere, still under the control of Canadian capital. India's domestic economic policies are influenced at every turn by the United States, due to her dependence on U. S. "aid," U. S. government control of a large share of India's money supply, and the growing penetration of U. S. private capital. Fiscal and monetary policies in Brazil, Argentina, and many smaller countries are often dictated by the U. S.-dominated International Monetary Fund. Everywhere in the underdeveloped world the World Bank influences or controls development plans, due to the Bank's monopoly position in the international market for long-term capital funds. Only Cuba has escaped the bondage of U. S. imperialism, although in Guatemala, Colombia, Bolivia, Angola, and elsewhere revolutionary forces are fighting to free these countries as well.

Less familiar is the story of how U. S. corporations actually cause economic underdevelopment, or prevent on-going development in the underdeveloped countries. Thanks to the work of Andre Gundar Frank, Clifford Geertz, Gunnar Myrdal, and others, but above all due to Paul Baran's pathbreaking book, *The Political Economy of Growth*, the general historic mechanisms of the process of development-underdevelopment are understood. Almost invariably, when pre-capitalist societies were integrated or re-integrated into the world capitalist system the result was underdevelopment in the economically more backward poles and development in the advanced poles. Economic development and underdevelopment did not merely go hand in hand historically; the one *caused* the other. Only in a handful of regions, such as West Africa, where the existence of unused land and under-employed labor opened the possibility of expanding subsistence and export production simultaneously, did specialization in raw material production for export fail to undermine subsistence agriculture, small-scale local manufacturing, and, in general, any local base for autonomous development. Although not the typical case, Britain's relations with her economic and political colonies highlight the development-underdevelopment process. Britain developed a balanced industrial economy which was able to "capture" economies of large-scale production and external economies of scale *because* most of her colonies (including her Latin American economic colonies in the last half of the nineteenth century) were *underdeveloped*—that is, because they became unbalanced, nonindustrial economies specializing in the production of raw materials for export. . . .

As a beginning, it is well to list the main types of U. S. foreign investments, in rough order of their historic priority. First, of course, are investments in raw materials production, including the necessary infrastructure investments (e.g., Anaconda's copper mines in Chile and Reynolds' bauxite mines in Jamaica and Guyana). Second are investments in raw material processing, such as the nickel-processing facilities in pre-Revolutionary Cuba. Third are investments in manufacturing facilities, chiefly final assembly operations taking the form of branch plants of parent U. S. corporations. These are the so-called "tariff hopping" investments, which import many raw materials, intermediate goods, parts, and sometimes, even fuel from the parent corporation or elsewhere in the developed countries, and sell final products in the local market. Branch-plant investments have become increasingly popular since World War II, and, in fact, constitute the only way that many underdeveloped countries are able to acquire foreign private capital. A good example are the many automobile assembly plants in Latin America. Fourth, there are the true "multi-national" investments, plants that purchase inputs from one branch of a corporation located in the same or a different country and sell outputs to another branch of the same corporation located elsewhere—that is, investments characterized by "product-by-plant" specialization. Multi-national invesments are mainly confined to petrochemicals and computers, although electronic and other assembly plants in cheap labor havens such as northern Mexico, Puerto Rico, Formosa, and South Korea often produce for re-export to the parent company.

Many international corporations confine their foreign investments to only one or two of the above types, although a handful —International Telephone and Telegraph and Standard Oil of New Jersey are two examples—are represented in all four categories. For expository purposes, and because each type of investment works somewhat different effects in the underdeveloped regions, our analysis will focus on the specific effects of the various forms foreign investment takes.

Next, what is required is a general description of the world capitalist system from the standpoint of the international corporations. These companies provide the institutional framework— or the accounting framework for resource utilization—for many underdeveloped countries, especially the smaller, more vulnerable economies. Integrating more and more resources into their own structures, the international corporations are able to mobilize, transform, and dispose of capital on a regional, or even worldwide scale—in effect, constituting themselves as extra-territorial bodies.

Production goals and techniques, investment policies, labor relations, prices, profit allocation, purchasing, distribution, and marketing policies are all decided from the standpoint of the profit goals of the international corporation *whether or not these goals are consistent with local economic development*. The corporations are the channels for the diffusion of technology and consumption patterns; again, profits come first, local needs second. . . .

The effects of foreign investments in raw material production and processing are too well known to require more than brief mention. In a nutshell, raw material investments tend to make underdeveloped countries mere appendages of developed countries, depriving them of any opportunity for autonomous, ongoing economic development, and thwarting the development of industry and an industrial bourgeoisie.

Foreign investments in manufacturing in the form of branch plants and wholly or partially owned subsidiaries have less familiar effects. The basic purpose of these investments is to control markets by affording the large corporation the opportunity to retain and expand export markets in the face of high tariffs, that is, to control the market for parts, components, and raw materials. In India, for example, Pavlov [V. I. Pavlov, *Economic Freedom*

Versus Imperialism, 1963] has shown that Indian tariff policy largely determines the industrial and sectoral composition of joint ventures and wholly-owned subsidiaries of foreign corporations. Surveying the key international corporations, the National Industrial Conference Board concluded that "marketing strategy was clearly the dominant element in investment decisions." A study made by the U. S. Department of Commerce in 1963 disclosed that over one-third of the corporations sampled invested abroad mainly to expand exports. More evidence is provided by data on U. S. exports to Latin America: in 1964, of total U. S. exports to manufacturing affiliates of U. S. firms in Latin America, 57 per cent consisted of parent exports of capital equipment and materials for processing and assembly to affiliates. Profit figures provide more evidence of the importance of export markets for foreign investments; some parent corporations make most of their money abroad by exporting materials and equipment to their branch plants; next in importance are revenues from royalties and fees; dividend revenue for these corporations is marginal.

Put briefly, the significance of this for the underdeveloped countries is that investment decisions are not made on the basis of local priorities, or the ranking of alternative yields, but rather on the basis of promoting exports. Thus in an economy receiving private foreign capital in the form of branch plants there is a tendency toward overinvestment, high costs, and excess capacity—that is to say, there are too many production units, all of them too small for efficient operations. . . .

In addition, in the branch plant economies there is a tendency for existing local industry to be eroded away as a result of the effects of over-crowding on the rate of profit, particularly since local industry, unlike the affiliates, cannot charge losses back to a parent corporation. Foreign capital, in the words of David Felix, out-competes local capital partly due to its ability "to self-insure against risk and to inflate the capital base of subsidiaries by transferring to them already depreciated equipment and designs from their more advanced home plants." Local capital thus tends to be either co-opted by foreign capital, or confined to especially risky undertaking. Further, branch-plant savings are not ordinarily available to other sectors of the local economy, being reinvested, used to purchase facilities from local capital, or repatriated. All in all, branch-plant investments promote the misutilization of capital, and generate severe immobilities in the local capital market.

The third type of foreign undertakings are the pure "multinational" investments. Again, investments are not made on the basis of local priorities, or with an eye to the local resource base and local needs. Rather the motive is to minimize costs of production to the corporation. Thus, once a sizable market for a standardized commodity has been established in the advanced countries, the corporations are free to make long-term commitments to build production facilities in the underdeveloped countries where labor costs are low. The facility imports the bulk of its inputs, exports nearly all of its output, and hence remains totally unintegrated into the local economy.

Next we will consider the impact of corporate production policy on . . . underdeveloped countries. So far as raw materials are concerned, Baran has shown that production is optimum only from the standpoint of the needs of the developed countries. In Chile, for example, the two international corporations which monopolize copper production have acquired more profits by expanding output in competing areas, which also enables the monopolies to pressure the Chilean government for more favorable treatment locally. Examples could be mutiplied no end; two more are drawn from the Caribbean: in recent years, rivalries between metropolitan-based international corporations which dominate Caribbean banana production have helped to ruin small-scale peasant producers by promoting an unlimited expansion of production. Again in recent years, Bookers Sugar Estates Ltd. and the Demerara Co., which control nearly all of Guyana's sugar production, have established sugar plantations in Nigeria from profits made in, and in competition with Guyana.

The effects of corporate production policy in the industrial sphere presents somewhat different problems. Three key features stand out. First, it is clear that the international corporations have every motive to defend their export markets, and hence order their branch plants to discriminate against local supplies in favor of imports from the parent company. There is no evidence that the governments of the smaller underdeveloped countries have been able to compel the corporations to produce with local supplies, although some of the larger countries, such as Brazil, have partially succeeded in doing this.

Second, it is also clear that the international corporations— excepting the true multi-national companies—have little or no interest in producing for *export*, especially when export production competes with other branches of the same corporation in the international market. The significance of this is that an economy which is undergoing "branch-plant industrialization" is developing little or no export capacity, a process which was crucial to the growth of the developed countries of Europe, as well as Japan and the United States.

Third, in the underdeveloped countries the demand for commodities is increasingly based on the diffusion of "tastes" from the developed countries, together with the prevailing social structure and distribution of income. As Levitt has pointed out, the international companies seek to homogenize world demand in order to spread fixed costs and capture economies of scale in research, product design, and technology. ". . . The profitability of the parent corporation," she writes, "is assisted by every influence which eliminates cultural resistance to the consumption patterns of the metropolis. The corporation thus has a vested interest in the destruction of cultural differences and homogenization of the [U. S.] way of life, the world over." In addition, as Stavenhagen points out, "the diffusion of manufactured articles is directly related to the overall level of technology as well as to effective demand [in the underdeveloped country]." We must return to the basic Marxist theory of consumption to assess the significance of this for economic development. Marx demonstrated not only that production creates the objects that satisfy economic needs, but also the economic needs satisfied by the objects; in short, production determines consumption. Today consumption in the underdeveloped countries tends to be determined by production in the developed countries, and hence economic needs in the former are satisfied poorly or imperfectly. . . .

A general understanding of the impact of purchasing and sales policies on underdeveloped countries requires a brief review of corporate price policies. In general, the international corporation is an effective instrument for maximizing the appropriation of surplus from satellite economies by metropolitan economies.

On the one hand, the parent corporation charges its branch plants (both in the raw materials and manufacturing sectors) the highest price possible, in order to maximize profits on exports, as well as a hedge against local government restrictions on profit remittances. (The exceptions are corporations that intend to reinvest abroad and thus desire to maximize foreign profits and minimize profits reported at home, in order to escape U. S. taxes.) Meanwhile, the parent corporation's interests are best served by keeping final product prices in the underdeveloped country as high as possible, consistent with the role of the branch plant as the parent's export market.

On the other hand, the parent buys raw materials from its branches and subsidiaries at the lowest possible price. Bauxite, iron ore, and copper—among other minerals—all tend to be undervalued. The reasons are plain: first, the large corporations seek to purchase the outputs of small independent producers at depressed prices; second, low prices discourage the development of new independent producers, and hence potential competition; third, depressed prices reduce foreign exchange risks when local governments attempt to reduce profit remittances; and, last, low buying prices mean that the corporations pay fewer taxes and lower royalties and wages.

We have finally to discuss the impact of the international corporation on technological change in underdeveloped countries, as well as on the satellite economies' balance of payments. As we have seen, the international corporations seek to keep control over technology themselves. In Alavi's words, "typically, strict control is sought over the use to which the techniques imported are put. . . . The supplier of the new technique is often fully protected from imparting a complete technology by clauses which specifically exclude 'fundamental investigation and development' . . . the Indian concern is often effectively prevented from adapting products or processes to local conditions and materials, or from encouraging local ancillary industries and so becomes even more dependent on imported supplies." In effect, control of technology (foreign capital tends to be more technologically integrated than local capital, and foreign production more specialized) means control of markets.

Besides licensing agreements restricting local control of technology, the international corporations often discourage their

branches from applying technological resources to *local* technological bottlenecks. Thus U. S.-owned sugar firms in pre-Revolutionary Cuba conducted little research into the problems of
raising cane yields, increasing the sucrose content of cane, or
mechanizing the harvest. Again, U. S. aluminum companies in
Jamaica spend nothing on iron separation techniques, even
though Jamaican bauxite has a high iron content; on the other
side, the same companies finance intensive research into the
problem of recovering aluminum from high-alumina clays in the
United States. . . .

The international diffusion of technology is thus under the
control of the international corporations. Perhaps the most significant consequence for the underdeveloped countries is that
the large corporations make technological decisions with an eye
to the resource base (or "relative factor supplies") of the United
States or world capitalism as a whole, and not to the resource supplies of the underdeveloped country or region. In
Felix's words, "Despite their involvement in activities in which
sustained profits are supposed to depend on a continual replenish-
ment of technological advantages, neither domestic nor foreign-
owned firms [in Latin America] have tried to modify imported
technology or products through local research and development."
This has led to the use of techniques which generate little additional employment of labor in the underdeveloped world. Branch-
plant industrialization thus not only assures technological
backwardness and prevents the development of production processes and products more suitable to local conditions, but also
inhibits the growth of manufacturing employment. In Latin
America as a whole, for example, industrial production compared
with total production rose by 16.5 per cent from 1950 to 1960;
meanwhile industrial employment in relation to total employment *fell* by 10 per cent. . . .

Although the critical study of the role of international corporations in underdeveloped countries (especially in manufacturing industries) remains in its infancy, it may not be premature to
offer some general observations about the relationship between
economic development and underdevelopment in the present era.
The evidence at our disposal strongly suggests that the development of the large international corporation at home and abroad,
and hence the development of the advanced capitalist countries

causes the underdevelopment of the economically backward countries and regions. The relationship between the developed and underdeveloped poles in the world capitalist system thus has not been fundamentally changed, even though many of the forms of exploitation have been altered. . . .

Certainly in Brazil, Mexico, and India, governments have had a certain degree of success in "legislating" *national* economic integration by compelling the international corporations to purchase more and more of their supplies locally. Meanwhile, however, foreign capital, especially in Brazil, has taken over a larger share of the local economy. Further, even though from a strictly economic standpoint there is considerable scope in these countries for the development of a great number of capital goods industries, every country in the underdeveloped world remains largely dependent on imported machinery and other capital equipment. The truth is that nowhere has there been, nor can there be save by socialist revolution, the structural changes in agriculture, state policy (especially tax policy), wealth and income distribution, and so on necessary for on-going, self-generated development. Only Mexico has had a significant "agrarian reform"—that is, the displacement of the *ejido* sector by the capitalist sector dominated by large corporate farming. But income distribution in Mexico is far too unequal to sustain a domestic market for any length of time, and, as a consequence, Mexico is looking hungrily at Central America, long dominated by the United States. Tax reform in most of the underdeveloped world is a joke; the Chilean government, for example, has not used taxes and royalties to integrate the copper mining industry into the local economy (nor did Chile use nitrate royalties to this end in the nineteenth century), but rather to increase imports of consumer goods and to finance the government payroll. And of all the underdeveloped countries, only Cuba has promoted a deepgoing redistribution of wealth and income. . . .

SUGGESTIONS FOR FURTHER READING

I like to tell students that investigating the economic history of imperialism can be an exercise in self-discovery. The issues involved touch on so many vital features of human affairs, and the interpretations of these issues have been so abundantly thrashed out in easily accessible narratives and analyses, that assessing one's reactions to these readings makes it relatively easy to locate oneself on the various spectrums such as radical-conservative, optimist-pessimist, racist-color blind, elitist-egalitarian, materialist-idealist, and so on. Furthermore, a student puzzled as to the nature of his own philosophy of history will find that when he has formed up his opinions regarding the economic causes of imperialism in particular, he will be well on his way to knowing where he stands in general.

The following list is only a small selection of items of high value from the enormous number of excellent works touching on this issue. The items are ranked in descending order of usefulness for students needing both facts and arguments.

1. RECENT SURVEYS THAT TREAT THE ISSUE OF ECONOMIC CAUSES

D. K. Fieldhouse, *The Colonial Empires: A Comparative Survey From the Eighteenth Century,* London, 1966.

Hans Daalder, "Imperialism," *International Encyclopedia of the Social Sciences.*

Raymond F. Betts, *Europe Overseas: Phases of Imperialism,* New York, 1968.

George Lichtheim, *Imperialism,* New York, 1970.

Robert O. Collins, ed., *The Partition of Africa* ("Major Issues in History"), New York, 1969.

M. E. Chamberlain, *The New Imperialism*, Pamphlet no. G73 of the [British] Historical Association, London, 1970.

William Woodruff, *Impact of Western Man*, New York, 1967.

2. ON THE HOBSON-LENIN MODEL

Richard Koebner, "The Concept of Economic Imperialism," *Economic History Review*, 2nd ser., II, no. 1 (1949).

E. M. Winslow, *The Pattern of Imperialism*, New York, 1948.

John Strachey, *The End of Empire*, London, 1959.

Nikolai Bukharin, *Imperialism and World Economy*, New York, 1929.

Bernard Porter, *Critics of Empire: British Radical Attitudes to Colonialism in Africa, 1895–1914*, London, 1968.

Eric Stokes, "Late Nineteenth-Century Colonial Expansion and the Attack on the Theory of Economic Imperialism: A Case of Mistaken Identity?" *The Historical Journal*, vol. 12 (1969).

Paul M. Sweezy, *The Theory of Capitalist Development: Principles of Marxian Political Economy*, New York, 1942.

3. WORKS THAT CHALLENGE THE PRIMACY OF ECONOMIC CAUSES

William L. Langer, *The Diplomacy of Imperialism, 1890–1902*, 2nd ed., New York, 1956.

————, *European Alliances and Alignments, 1871–1890*, New York, 1931.

Richard J. Hammond, "Economic Imperialism: Sidelights on a Stereotype," *Journal of Economic History*, XXI, no. 4 (Dec. 1961).

W. K. Hancock, *The Wealth of Colonies*, Cambridge, 1950.

L. H. Gann and Peter Duignan, *Burden of Empire: An Appraisal of Western Colonialism in Africa South of the Sahara*, New York, 1967.

Grover Clark, *The Balance Sheet of Imperialism: Facts and Figures on Colonies*, New York, 1936.

W. David McIntyre, *The Imperial Frontier in the Tropics, 1865–75: A Study of British Colonial Policy in West Africa, Malaya and the South Pacific in the Age of Gladstone and Disraeli*, London, 1967.

Bernard Semmel, *Imperialism and Social Reform: English*

Social-Imperial Thought, 1895–1914, Cambridge, Mass., 1960.

Henri Brunschwig, *French Colonialism, 1871–1914: Myths and Realities,* London, 1966.

A. P. Thornton, *The Imperial Idea and Its Enemies: A Study in British Power,* London, 1959.

4. STUDIES THAT TREAT THE RELATIONSHIP BETWEEN UNDER-DEVELOPMENT AND IMPERIALISM

George Dalton, ed., *Economic Development and Social Change: The Modernization of Village Communities,* New York, 1971.

S. H. Frankel, *The Economic Impact on Under-Developed Societies: Essays on International Investment and Social Change,* Oxford, 1953.

Everett E. Hagen, *On the Theory of Social Change: How Economic Growth Begins,* Homewood, Ill., 1962.

J. H. Boeke, *Economics and Economic Policy of Dual Societies, as Exemplified by Indonesia,* New York, 1953.

Clifford Geertz, *Agricultural Involution: The Process of Ecological Change in Indonesia,* Berkeley, 1963.

Frederick Clairmonte, *Economic Liberalism and Underdevelopment: Studies in the Disintegration of an Idea,* New York, 1960.

5. IMPERIALISM AS SEEN BY THE NEW LEFT

Robert I. Rhodes, ed., *Imperialism and Underdevelopment,* New York, 1970.

Kwame Nkrumah, *Neo-Colonialism: The Last Stage of Imperialism,* New York, 1965.

Paul A. Baran, *The Political Economy of Growth,* rev. ed., New York, 1962.

Pierre Jalée, *The Pillage of the Third World,* New York, 1968.

Peter Worsley, *The Third World,* 2nd ed., London, 1967.

Richard D. Wolff, "Modern Imperialism: The View from the Metropolis," *American Economic Review,* May 1970.

K. T. Fann and Donald C. Hodges, eds., *Readings in American Imperialism,* Boston, 1971.

Jack Woddis, *Introduction to Neo-Colonialism,* London, 1967.

6. MATERIALIST INTERPRETATIONS OF IMPERIALISM

David S. Landes, "Some Thoughts on the Nature of Economic Imperialism," *Journal of Economic History*, XXI, no. 4 (Dec. 1961).

D. C. M. Platt, *Finance, Trade, and Politics in British Foreign Policy*, Oxford, 1968.

————, "Economic Factors in British Policy during the 'New Imperialism'," *Past and Present*, no. 39 (April 1968).

William Appleman Williams, *The Roots of the Modern American Empire: A Study of the Growth and Shaping of Social Consciousness in a Marketplace Society*, New York, 1969.

G. C. Allen and A. G. Donnithorne, *Western Enterprise in Indonesia and Malaya*, London, 1957.

David S. Landes, *Bankers and Pashas: International Finance and Economic Imperialism in Egypt*, Cambridge, Mass., 1958.

Donald C. Blaisdell, *European Financial Control in the Ottoman Empire*, New York, 1929.

EAKINS
Watercolors

EAKINS
Watercolors

by Donelson F. Hoopes

Watson-Guptill Publications/New York

Front cover: *Drifting* (detail)
            Collection of Mr. Thomas S. Pratt

Paperback Edition, 1985

First published 1971 in New York by Watson-Guptill Publications,
a division of Billboard Publications, Inc.,
1515 Broadway, New York, N.Y. 10036

Distributed in the United Kingdom by Phaidon Press Ltd.,
Littlegate House, St. Ebbe's St., Oxford

Library of Congress Catalog Card Number: 78-152785
ISBN 0-8230-1591-2 (pbk.)

Manufactured in Japan

1 2 3 4 5 6 7 8 9/90 89 88 87 86 85

Although his chief means of expression was painting, Eakins essayed many other techniques, including sculpture, photography (as an investigative tool for his studies of animal locomotion), and watercolor. The present volume is a record of the small, but intensely interesting facet of his work in watercolor, and contains illustrations of all of the known examples save one —a miniature portrait of his father made about 1870, which is not reproduced here for technical reasons. As many as half a dozen more watercolors may yet exist, but their whereabouts are unknown. In recent years, two examples have been located which were known, but presumed lost. A third, *The Pathetic Song*, related to the painting of the same title in The Corcoran Gallery of Art, was not even recorded until the Eakins retrospective exhibition at The Whitney Museum of American Art in 1970.

All of these discoveries, as well as the original pioneering study of Thomas Eakins which appeared in 1933, are the work of Lloyd Goodrich, Advisory Director of The Whitney Museum of American Art. Mr. Goodrich will shortly publish a revised edition of his biography of Eakins, the result of many years' diligent effort. While I have relied securely on Mr. Goodrich's chronicle of the life of Thomas Eakins—which anyone may, who has access to a copy of that now-scarce 1933 edition— I am personally and profoundly grateful to him for permitting me to consult his notes on the artist's works. Without his generous cooperation, the present effort—which is offered as a footnote to Eakins' prolific career—might have been incomplete.

To Donald Holden, Editorial Director of Watson-Guptill, who has responded to my appeals for additional time with a magnificent tolerance and compassion, I am grateful beyond measure. And to his Associate Editor, Margit Malmstrom, on whom the responsibility lies for coaxing this text out of the author's reluctant hands, no words are adequate to express the extent of my appreciation for her understanding and forbearance. But most of all, I wish to thank them for availing me of their time and skills—Mr. Holden in the inception and planning of this book, and Miss Malmstrom in the care and diligence with which she assembled the vital illustrative material and marshalled the many details connected with the project.

Once again, I am indebted to Geoffrey Clements for his superlative photography on the majority of the watercolors reproduced in this book. And my thanks, too, for the excellent work of the staff photographers who provided the color transparencies of works in the museum collections.

My thanks also go to the staffs of these museums, who made available photographic materials for the book: The Art Institute of Chicago; Art Museum of Princeton University; The Baltimore Museum of Art; The Corcoran Gallery of Art; The Brooklyn Museum; The Hyde Collection; Museum of Fine Arts of Boston; Museum of Art of The Rhode Island School of Design; The Metropolitan Museum of Art; The Philadelphia Museum of Art; Randolph-Macon Woman's College; Wichita Art Museum; and Yale University Art Gallery. I am especially obliged to the individual collectors who so graciously consented to have their works photographed and included in this volume: Mr. and Mrs. Paul Mellon; Mr. and Mrs. Elmer E. Pratt; Mr. and Mrs. C. Humbert Tinsman. Additional valuable assistance was given me by Mrs. Thomas B. Malarkey; Miss Beverly Carter, Secretary, Paul Mellon Collection; and Mr. Stuart P. Feld, Director, American Division of Hirschl and Adler Galleries, New York.

D. F. H.

American art in 1870 was dominated by the grandiose romanticism of the Hudson River School and the nostalgic sentiment of the native genre school. Into this art world, Thomas Eakins and his older contemporary, Winslow Homer, brought a new note—naturalism. Like the young generation in Europe, they looked at the life around them and painted what they saw, disregarding traditional styles. Eakins, spending almost his entire life in his native Philadelphia, built his art out of its everyday realities: men and women, their work and recreations, their existence as individual human beings. Few artists have been such complete realists; every figure was a portrait, every scene an actual one.

Eakins was an unusual combination of the artist and the scientist: an anatomist, a mathematician, a photographer, a student of perspective and visual phenomena, and the foremost teacher of his time. His work combined thorough knowledge of nature's forms and movement, an intense emotional attachment to the world in which he lived, and the deep sensuousness that is the basis of all vital art. Within naturalistic limits, his painting possessed the strongest architectonic and plastic qualities of any American of his period.

Among the less familiar aspects of Eakins' art are his watercolors. We usually associate his name with the solidity and weight of his oil paintings. His watercolors, while equally characteristic, show a different side of his artistic personality. Though far fewer in numbers than his oils, they are completely realized works of art in every respect.

Soon after his return in 1870 from his three and a half years of study in Europe, Eakins began to use watercolor. Most of his twenty-six works in the medium were painted in the ten years from 1873 to 1882. In subject matter, they paralleled his oils of these years. There were scenes of the outdoor sports and activities that he himself enjoyed: rowing on the Schuylkill River, sailing on the Delaware, hunting in the Cohansey marshes in southern New Jersey. There were the shad fisheries at Gloucester, across the Delaware. There were indoor genre subjects picturing his family, friends, and pupils. In the late 1870's appeared a series of watercolors of women in old-fashioned dresses, sewing, knitting, and working at spinning wheels. This unexpected development on the part of the most drastic of American realists was doubtless a result of the historic Centennial Exhibition of 1876 in Philadelphia, which had aroused general interest in everything Colonial and early American. These reminiscences of the past reveal a grave, intimate poetry, without any loss of the utter authenticity of his contemporary subjects.

Eakins' watercolors were far from the spontaneous, direct-from-nature works usual in the medium. They were as thoughtfully planned as his oils. As with the latter, the three-dimensional structure of the picture was often worked out in preliminary perspective drawings, such as the one for *John Biglin in a Single Scull*—drawings that have a precise beauty of their own. But though Eakins was a strong draftsman, strangely enough he made few drawings aside from his perspective studies. Instead, oil sketches in full color were painted directly from the subject, then squared off, and their forms transferred to the final surface. Even for his watercolors, his studies were in oil—a curious reversal of the usual procedure. (Winslow Homer, for example, often used his watercolors as source material for his oils.)

By these unorthodox methods, Eakins produced watercolors that were as finely designed and fully realized as any of his oils, and as complete works of art, allowing for differences in scale and complexity. The physical nature of the medium, of course, did not make possible the full substance and weightiness of oil; but in compensation, there were greater refinement and subtlety, and a higher, clearer range of color, thanks to the translucency of the water medium, with the white paper showing through.

Eakins himself evidently considered his watercolors equal to his oils; in the 1870's and early 1880's, he exhibited them extensively, not only in the annual shows of the American Society of Painters in Water Colors, but in other national exhibitions; and he priced them not much lower than his oils. It is significant that when in 1873 he wanted to show his revered master, Jean Léon Gérôme, what he had accomplished in America, he chose to send him a watercolor of a man rowing; and after receiving Gérôme's letter criticizing his attempt to represent full motion, he evidently painted a new version, also in watercolor, and sent it to Gérôme.

One tantalizing feature of Eakins' watercolors is that five of the twenty-six have not so far been found. Aside from the two given to Gérôme, three of those exhibited at the watercolor society are still unlocated, including one that may well have been among his most important, judging by its price and its title: *The Pair-oared Race—John and Barney Biglin Turning the Stake* —probably a watercolor version of the big oil in the Cleveland Museum.

Almost all of Eakins' watercolors were products of his early manhood—his late twenties and his thirties—and they have the varied subject matter and the healthy extroversion of those years. In his forties, he was to abandon such subjects, except occasionally, and to concentrate on portraiture, attaining an increased breadth and mastery in this more limited field.

In selecting for the present volume this unfamiliar, but essential side of Eakins' life work, and in writing his perceptive and illuminating comments on it, Donelson Hoopes has made an important contribution to our understanding of one of America's greatest artists.

Lloyd Goodrich

COLOR PLATES

PERIODICALS

Ackerman, Gerald M. "Thomas Eakins and His Parisian Masters Gérôme and Bonnat," *Gazette des Beaux-Arts,* LXXII (April 1969), p. 235 ff.

Burroughs, Alan. "Thomas Eakins, the Man," *Arts,* IV (December 1923), p. 303 ff.

Bregler, Charles. "Thomas Eakins as a Teacher," *Arts,* XVII (March 1931), p. 376 ff.; and (October 1931), p. 27 ff.

PAMPHLET

McHenry, Margaret. *Thomas Eakins Who Painted.* Overland, Pa., Privately Printed, 1945.

BOOKS

Barker, Virgil. *American Painting: History and Interpretation.* New York, 1950.

Goodrich, Lloyd. *Thomas Eakins, His Life and Work.* New York, 1933.

Novak, Barbara. *American Painting of the 19th Century.* New York, 1969.

Richardson, E. P. *Painting in America.* New York, 1956.

Schendler, Sylvan. *Eakins.* Boston, 1967.

EXHIBITION CATALOGS

Metropolitan Museum of Art, 1917. *Loan Exhibition of the Works of Thomas Eakins.* Introduction by Bryson Burroughs.

Pennsylvania Academy of the Fine Arts, 1917. *Memorial Exhibition of the Works of the Late Thomas Eakins.* Introduction by Gilbert S. Parker.

Museum of Modern Art, 1930. *Sixth Loan Exhibition of The Museum of Modern Art: Winslow Homer, Albert P. Ryder and Thomas Eakins.* Article on Eakins by Lloyd Goodrich.

Philadelphia Museum of Art, 1944. *Thomas Eakins.*

National Gallery of Art, Art Institute of Chicago, and Philadelphia Museum of Art, 1961. *Thomas Eakins, a Retrospective Exhibition.*

Whitney Museum of American Art, 1970. *Thomas Eakins.* Introduction by Lloyd Goodrich.

1844. Born July 25 in Philadelphia, Pennsylvania.

1846. Family moved to 1729 Mt. Vernon Street, Philadelphia.

1861. Graduated from Central High School in the upper quarter of his class. In the fall, began studying at The Pennsylvania Academy of the Fine Arts, principally under Christian Schussele in drawing. Took independent study of anatomy at Jefferson Medical College.

1866. To Paris in the autumn. Enrolled at the Ecole des Beaux-Arts. Studied under Jean Léon Gérôme and Léon Bonnat; studied sculpture under Augustin Alexandre Dumont. Classmates included Frederick A. Bridgman, Abbott H. Thayer, J. Alden Weir, and Wyatt Eaton.

1867. First use of oil color.

1868. Spent the summer traveling in France, Germany, Switzerland, and Italy.

1869. To Madrid and Seville in late November. His contact with the works of Velasquez and Ribera at this time became a formative influence in his work.

1870. Returned to Philadelphia in the late spring. Except for brief excursions to teach in New York and Washington, Eakins remained in Philadelphia for the rest of his life.

1871. Painted his first major canvas, *Max Schmitt in a Single Scull* (Metropolitan Museum of Art).

1872. His mother died. Became engaged to Katherine Crowell.

1875. Painted *The Gross Clinic* (Jefferson Medical College, Philadelphia).

1876. Five works accepted for exhibition at Memorial Hall, the Centennial Exhibition, Philadelphia. *The Gross Clinic* hung apart from his other works; considered too offensive for inclusion in the art section, and hung in the medical display. In April; The Pennsylvania Academy of the Fine Arts opened; Eakins became instructor in drawing in the Academy school.

1877. Painted first version of *William Rush Carving His Allegorical Figure of the Schuylkill River* (Philadelphia Museum of Art).

1879. Death of his fiancée, Katherine Crowell. Appointed Professor of Drawing and Painting in the Academy school. Painted *The Fairman Rogers Four-in-Hand* (Philadelphia Museum of Art).

1882. Appointed Director of the Academy school. Death of his sister Margaret.

1883. Painted *The Swimming Hole* (Fort Worth Art Association).

1884. Collaborated with Eadweard Muybridge at the University of Pennsylvania in the study of human and animal locomotion through sequential still photography. Married Susan Hannah Macdowell. Took up residence at 1330 Chestnut Street, Philadelphia, former studio of Arthur B. Frost.

1885. Returned to 1729 Mt. Vernon Street.

1886. Resigned Directorship of the Academy school under pressure from the Academy's board of directors, who objected to the use of nude models in the drawing classes. Art Students League (of Philadelphia) founded by some of Eakins' pupils from the Academy. Met Samuel Murray, with whom he formed a lifelong friendship.

1887. Trip to North Dakota in July; painted views of cowboy life. Returned to Philadelphia in October. Met Walt Whitman and began painting his portrait.

1889. Painted *The Agnew Clinic* for The School of Medicine, University of Pennsylvania. Death of his sister, Caroline Eakins Stephens.

1891. *The Agnew Clinic* rejected from exhibition at the Pennsylvania Academy.

1892. Art Students League disbanded. *The Agnew Clinic* rejected from exhibition of the Society of American Artists;

Eakins resigns his membership in protest. Painted *The Concert Singer* (Philadelphia Museum of Art).

1893. Exhibited at the Columbian Exposition, Chicago; awarded a gold medal.

1894. Published a paper on human musculature in the journal of The Academy of Natural Sciences, Philadelphia.

1896. Given a one-man exhibition (his first) at the Earle Galleries, Philadelphia. First invitation to exhibition of the Carnegie International, Pittsburgh.

1898. Painted important boxing picture, *Salutat* (Addison Gallery of American Art).

1899. Death of his father, Benjamin Eakins. Invited to serve on jury of the Carnegie International Exhibition.

1902. Elected Associate, then full Academician, National Academy of Design, New York. Began a series of portraits for St. Charles Seminary, Overbrook, Pennsylvania.

1903. Painted *Archbishop William H. Elder*, which won him a gold medal from The Pennsylvania Academy of the Fine Arts. Met John S. Sargent through a mutual friend, Dr. William White. Last year as a juror for the Carnegie International Exhibitions.

1905. Portrait of Professor Leslie Miller, painted in 1901, awarded prize by National Academy of Design.

1908. Returned to paintings on the theme *William Rush Carving His Allegorical Figure of the Schuylkill River*.

1910. Gradual deterioration of his health; few works completed from this year until his death.

1914. Philadelphia collector, Dr. Albert Barnes, purchased an oil study for *The Agnew Clinic*, paying a record price and helping to confirm Eakins' importance.

1916. Death of Thomas Eakins, June 25.

Thomas Eakins has achieved a paramount place among American artists, not because of the novelty of his particular vision of the world or his formidable technique as a painter but because of the penetrating truth of his statements. In the very pronounced academic way that Eakins approached his art, he is revealed as an exponent of a kind of science of recording visual phenomena, in contrast with the free, romantic spirit of his contemporary, James A. M. Whistler. Eakins always thought of himself as a "scientific realist," a term which summarizes aptly the clear assessment he made of his career. He was what we would call today an inner-directed person, and one of the very few American artists who did not allow his European training and experience to dominate his work.

Eakins successfully integrated European influences (Velasquez and Murillo from the past, Gérôme and Bonnat from his own time) with a strong, native American luminism to achieve a unique pictorial expression. Luminism sought to intensify the experience of reality by a heightened rendering of light and color, combined with linear precision and extreme clarity of detail. The luminist tendency is revealed particularly in his landscape and sporting pictures, and is most consistently maintained in his watercolors. In the watercolors, one is impressed with Eakins' almost compulsive concern with minute detail. There is the suggestion of a miniaturist at work; yet, largely because of his sensitivity to delicate nuances of tone, the watercolors take on an importance quite beyond their physical size.

Rather than simply employing watercolor as a sketching tool (as it had been regarded generally in the 19th century), Eakins frequently used the medium to achieve a final result. Winslow Homer seized on watercolor in the early '70s at exactly the same moment as did Eakins. But in spite of Homer's surer handling of the medium, Eakins' papers—barely a score of them in existence today—are much more intense creations.

The color scheme for *John Biglin in a Single Scull* (Plate 1), for example, was worked out in an oil study (Figure 2) before Eakins attempted the subject in watercolor. Yet the watercolor does not betray even the slightest suggestion of the laborious framework on which it was constructed, such as the mathematically precise perspective study (Figure 1). Moreover, Eakins achieved a sense of light and atmosphere in the sporting watercolors that many of his oils lack. Perhaps only the oil painting of *Max Schmitt in a Single Scull* (Metropolitan Museum of Art) completed in 1871, attains equal luminosity.

Eakins made very few watercolors, perhaps no more than thirty examples in all. They all date from the decade of the '70s and the early '80s, with two examples made as late as 1890. The production of watercolors corresponds roughly with the period in which Eakins was engaged mainly in painting outdoor subjects, before he turned to portraiture as his main activity. But why so few watercolors? The limitation on size imposed by the medium may be a partial explanation, since Eakins tended to paint portraits life size or nearly life size. And during the '90s, Eakins turned to portraiture almost exclusively. Few artists have been so insightful about human character, and for Eakins, portraiture seems to have been the logical culmination of his art.

Thomas Eakins was born in Philadelphia in 1844. His family derived from a working class background of farmers and craftsmen. His father, Benjamin Eakins, earned a modest living by teaching handwriting—"penmanship," as it was termed—in the fashionable private schools of the city. In a time when the manual arts were still flourishing, "Master" Benjamin supplemented his income by engrossing documents and presentation testimonials with his elegant steel-pen script. Son and father had a close personal relationship, and the elder Eakins imparted a love of drawing and his craftsman's diligence. The son became highly proficient as a draughtsman in school. Looking at his early drawings of simple machinery, such as lathes, one recognizes in them the same precisionist bent in American art which became formalized later in the work of Charles Sheeler (1883-1965). Other genial influences of the father are reflected in Eakins' early love of sports; rowing his single scull on the Schuylkill River or sailing on the Delaware and hunting for rail birds in the Cohansey marshes of New Jersey also said much about Eakins' individualism.

The pervading atmosphere of the Eakins house on unfashionable Mt. Vernon Street was one of companionship and a liberal parent-child exchange. Thomas was the firstborn and only son; his three sisters, Frances, Margaret, and Caroline, ranged in age from five to fifteen years younger. Parents and children were extraordinarily close in their affection for one another. Probably no other single influence sustained Eakins so well against the hostility his critics directed toward him in later years. The family house was the warm heart of his entire creative life; the integrated quality of his personality as an artist was due in no small measure to the benign and sustaining influence of his early home life.

Eakins graduated from Central High School in Philadelphia in July 1861, as the Confederacy dealt the Union forces its first defeat at Bull Run. He enrolled in the school of The Pennsylvania Academy of the Fine Arts and there he remained throughout the war; perhaps his excellence as a student earned him exemption from duty, or when military conscription loomed in 1863 his family may have been able to pay for a substitute.

The Academy was America's oldest continuing art museum, having been established in 1804 by Charles Willson Peale. It contained works of art of widely disparate merit—paintings of Biblical and allegorical subjects by Benjamin West were exhibited on an equal footing with plaster casts of classical sculpture. Instruction of students centered on drawing "from the antique," as the casts were called. Exactitude in rendering a charcoal drawing of the chipped and dusty plasters was stressed by the Academy's small faculty, headed by the ailing Christian Schussele (1824-1879), whose specialty was painting pictures laden with historical anecdote. There was drawing from the live model also, but this was mostly an extracurricular activity, paid for separately by the students, with the Academy lending the studio space.

Eakins hated the routine of the Academy, but deadly as the drawing classes were, he persisted in a methodical study of the human figure. Even at this early date, Eakins' concern for accurate scientific inquiry into human anatomy characterized the seriousness of his studies. On his own initiative, he applied to Jefferson Medical College in order to acquire a more thorough knowledge of human musculature and bone structure. Dissection of cadavers became a regular experience for him at Jefferson, and he probably acquired as complete a working knowledge as any medical student. In his respect for the human body, Eakins manifested a kind of Renaissance attitude: man was the center of all things, and the measure of creation. His art became consecrated to the human condition; without reference to people, even the landscape which he loved as a sportsman held no interest for him as an artist.

The Academy gave Eakins much practice in drawing the figure, and his studies at the medical college equipped him with a superb technical background—but he had no experience with handling color or with painting. He had exhausted the resources of the Academy and appealed to his father to send him to Paris. Although this must have placed a considerable strain on the family's finances, he was allowed to go.

During his time as a student at the Academy, Eakins had seen exhibitions dominated by grandiose history paintings, largely the works of popular European academicians. The native American landscape and genre painters—descendants of the Hudson River School tradition—merely looked old fashioned to Eakins' generation. The Barbizon School of Millet, Corot, and Daubigny, with its gentle, poetic view of the world, was just beginning to appear in the United States, especially in the more advanced private collections. Neither the pompous history paintings of older Europeans, nor the quaint and often sentimental pictures of the older native painters had anything to do with the world of these younger men.

Eakins saw the work of Jean Léon Gérôme (1824-1904) for the first time in the Academy's annual exhibitions. Although Gérôme was an exact contemporary of the fusty Schussele, his paintings seemed modern and exciting in Eakins' eyes. Gérôme practiced a precise style of drawing and painted in clear colors—a kind of commitment to realistic definition that touched a sympathetic response in Eakins. Gérôme's *Egyptian Recruits Crossing the Desert* was shown at the Academy in 1861 and 1862, and the harshly realistic subject must have seemed particularly strong when compared to the more usual exhibition fare, such as the *Birth of Venus* by Alexandre Cabanel (1823-1889), which the Academy bought for its own collection in 1863. The Cabanel was a replica of the original in the Musée du Luxembourg and represented the kind of official academic French painting that was attuned to the saccharine taste of Louis Napoleon's court; the Gérôme, on the other hand, was a painting created by a master of dramatic action and aimed for an emotional response, rather than a sentimental one. Gérôme was also unusual in that he did not require vast areas of canvas to present his themes; his highly charged and compact composition was perhaps the key that Eakins was looking for. Clearly, Gérôme was in Eakins' mind when he embarked for Europe from New York in September, 1866.

Until the decade of the '70s, very few Americans had ventured to Paris to study art. James Whistler had gone there to study under Charles Gabriel Gleyre in 1855, but virtually no other American followed him until Eakins. Eakins arrived in Paris with a knowledge of the French language gained from books and a determination to be accepted into the schools of the Académie des Beaux-Arts. The method of instruction at the school was rigid, and even to be accepted as a student required an entrance examination, followed by an interrogation by a faculty member. Classes were given in studios presided over by a roster of notable teachers which, besides Gérôme, included Léon Bonnat (1833-1922), William Adolphe Bouguereau (1825-1905), Benjamin Constant (1845-1902), and Jules Bastien-Lepage (1848-1884).

After a month of waiting, Eakins was finally accepted into Gérôme's class. Gérôme had been a pupil of Paul Delaroche (1797-1856), who was a contemporary and rival of Delacroix and was even preferred to the latter by critics in his time. Delaroche, a member of the new romantic school, tended to return to academic modes of expression; thus his historical paintings for which he was famous really lacked the movement and force of true romanticism and have a decided penchant for merely descriptive and literary values. Gérôme owed as much to Delaroche as he did to Ingres whose dictum, "the integrity of art lies in drawing," he pursued relentlessly. Into this mixture of historical academicism and neo-classicism, Gérôme incorporated a third element, Orientalism. This was one of the most pervasive influences of mid-19th century academic painting; unfortunately for Gérôme, the exotic appearances of Oriental life appealed primarily to his sense of the picturesque and rarely evoked a more profound expression.

Gérôme had other American students—Frederick A. Bridgman (1847-1927) and Edwin Lord Weeks (1849-1903)—on whom he exerted an overwhelming influence, but Eakins resisted the seduction of the picturesque-romantic mode. Gérôme was a dedicated craftsman, whose disciplined working methods Eakins found useful for improvement in drawing. Not until the following spring, in March 1867, was Eakins permitted to use color in his studies of the life class models. The problems he found in handling color relationships, complicated by learning how to use a new medium of oil paint, discouraged him. In the fall, he rented a private studio and threw himself into the task of mastering problems of light and form with oil color. He wrote home, "Gérôme told me . . . to paint some bright-colored objects, lent me some of his Eastern stuffs, which are very brilliant, and I am learning something from them faster than I could from the life studies."

These letters to his family reveal an ambivalence toward his dogmatic teacher, but the overall impression is that Eakins benefited from the experience. Eakins regarded color as a perplexing mystery. If he could only solve that mystery, he would cease making studies and begin to paint pictures in earnest. When he erred, as in a portrait class, the master applied a perfunctory correction, "Gérôme just painted [the] head right over again, and this I take as an insult to my work." Years later, as a teacher himself, Eakins often instructed by the same kind of direct demonstration, painting into his students' work. Gérôme showed him that painting instruction is largely a matter of practical example, not theory. As for problems of composition and style, Gérôme gave scant advice, preferring that the student work out his own solutions.

The manner in which Eakins made analogies between life and art in his letters reveals the practical, homespun way in which he approached problems of aesthetics in art. He compared adjusting his palette of colors to tuning a fiddle; learning painting technique by trial and error to learning how to ice-skate; and improvising on nature's realism to sailing a boat. Eakins was no aesthetician, but he was able to translate the abstract principles of aesthetics into practical terms which became a part of his daily life.

The phrase, "solid work," appears frequently in his letters and reveals the overriding passion of his artistic life, which was to create a palpable realism in his paintings. During these student days, this preoccupation led him into an admiration for technical proficiency irrespective of the ends it might serve. He once commented that a painting by Mariano Fortuny (1839-1874) was "the most beautiful thing I have ever seen." Today, Fortuny's pictures seem parodies of candy box style and puerile subject matter, but Fortuny was a master at creating the semblance of an incredible variety of textures, and he could incorporate and control a prodigious range of color. Clearly, Eakins was blind to Fortuny's subject matter and saw only his virtuoso technique. And compared with the vaguely salacious, pseudo-classical female nudes that abounded in the Salon exhibitions, the highly finished realism of Gérôme and Fortuny must indeed have seemed like "solid work."

At the moment when Eakins was discovering his own way as an artist, there was another kind of realism in the air of the Paris art world. Gustave Courbet and Edouard Manet led the advance against official art by rejecting history painting and other forms of sentimental fiction in favor of the world as they saw it around them. Eakins took no evident notice of them, nor did he report to his family the sensation they created at the Exposition Universelle of 1867. The jury of the Exposition had rejected their works, and in an act of defiance, both artists constructed temporary wooden sheds in which they displayed their paintings outside the Exposition grounds. As a curious comment on the times, a portrait of Manet by Fantin-Latour could be seen at the Salon of 1867; the artist portrayed Manet as a respectable gentleman, fastidiously tailored and in a top hat, which was acceptable to the genteel jurors of the Salon, while the artist's real self, as reflected in his rejected paintings, was officially discredited.

As if to underscore the pervading mood of official repression in Paris that year, Manet could not exhibit his *Execution of Emperor Maximilien* for political reasons. Napoleon III was not prepared for such graphic reminders of the transitory history of imperial dynasties. Manet survived the war that toppled Napoleon III in 1870, and went on to draw scenes of the aftermath of civil disorder. During this same period, all of those artists who were struggling toward that other revolution which would come to be called "Impressionism"—Pissarro, Cézanne, Monet, Renoir, and Sisley—constituted the vital center of artistic activity in Paris.

There is no evidence that Eakins had taken any notice of these movements or the personalities associated with them. His point of view was precisely opposed to Impressionism—the object of his studies was to isolate and define the particular; while the element of light was important to these studies, it was the quality of light in sharp focus that created individual character. Thus, Eakins' search was not for general truths about nature as the Impressionists would have it, but for a humanist approach to the specific. Landscape painting and still life, whether that of the Academicians or of the Independents, could hold little interest for him. Moreover, in his abhorrence of the work of the great majority of traditional Salon painters, Eakins belonged to no identifiable group.

His admiration for Gérôme led him to look at those masters of the past who were admired by his teacher. Gérôme was part Spanish and so was Sargent's teacher, Carolus-Duran. It is interesting to note how Gérôme inculcated Eakins' admiration for Murillo and how Carolus-Duran imparted to Sargent an enthusiasm for Velasquez. Manet had begun the craze for Spanish subject matter in the '60s, with his exhibition of a number of paintings of Spanish dancers, notably his portrait of *Lola of Valencia*. But Eakins was the first important American painter to "discover" 17th century Spanish art. In the fall of 1869, he wrote to his father, "I feel now that my school days are at last

over and sooner than I dared hope . . . I am as strong as any of Gérôme's pupils, and I have nothing now to gain by remaining." With the onset of the late autumn rains in Paris, Eakins decided that this was the moment to seek a more agreeable climate. He set out for Spain, arriving in Madrid on the first of December, 1869.

In the Prado, he saw for the first time the full scope of 17th century Spanish painting, and the impact of these pictures moved him deeply. He wrote, ". . . what a satisfaction it gave me to see the good Spanish work, so good, so strong, so reasonable, so free of every affectation." Lloyd Goodrich, in his biography of Eakins, identified the magnetic attraction between Eakins and the Spanish masters: ". . . the closest to his own temperament was [that of] the Spaniard, with his naturalism, his concern with the facts of everyday life, his love of character more than ideal beauty, his scientific objectivity." Rembrandt and Titian also became more important to Eakins as he began to explore the techniques of painting in transparent glazes. He saw immediately the limitations of Gérôme's opaque technique, and was mature enough to understand that Gérôme, with all of his obvious faults as an artist, had been a good and necessary step in his own development. He remained in Spain—mostly in Seville—for six months. Then, in the spring of 1870, he returned to Paris for a brief visit before taking ship to New York.

His three and one half years in Europe were marked by an intense application to art that permitted him little time for making many friends or engaging in the Bohemian life of the typical art student. His best friends during these years were, curiously, Philadelphians also. William Sartain (1843-1924) had been a fellow student at the Pennsylvania Academy and had followed Eakins to Paris, where he became a student of Bonnat. Sartain's father, John Sartain (1808-1897), was an English mezzotint engraver who had emigrated to Philadelphia and established himself as editor of *Sartain's Union Magazine of Literature and Art*. Eakins' other companion in Europe was Henry H. Moore (1844-1926), who was already a pupil of Gérôme when Eakins arrived in Paris. Moore's family had come with him to care for him, since he was totally deaf since birth and could converse fluently only in hand signs. Eakins learned sign language in order to communicate with Moore, perhaps enjoying the challenge of learning a new language as much as he had enjoyed teaching himself French. These Philadelphians provided Eakins with the necessary spiritual ties to his home;

the importance of this tie is demonstrated by his effort to overcome the difficulties involved in communicating with Moore.

Eakins returned to Philadelphia in July 1870 and immediately resumed residence in his father's house on Mt. Vernon Street. A studio was fitted out for him on the top floor and he began painting immediately, choosing his sisters in the family parlor for his subject matter. In 1871, he began work on a picture of a boyhood friend rowing on the Schuylkill River: *Max Schmitt in a Single Scull* (Metropolitan Museum of Art). Such a subject had never appeared before in American painting. At twenty-seven, Eakins already showed a prodigious mastery; he had successfully established a bridge between his own heritage of luminism and the clarity of color and precision of drawing of his European teachers. He surpassed Gérôme in this picture precisely because he understood that light is transparent and must be rendered transparently. Moreover, his sense of spatial relationships is refined in the Schmitt picture to a point which vindicates his scientific realism in both a pictorial and a mathematical way.

In the early '70s, Eakins was painting pictures from two distinct points of departure. The intimate world of his family, with its enclosed space, was being handled in a controlled studio manner, employing a single source of light, while his landscape subjects—mostly Schuylkill River scenes with rowers—were statements concerning the quality of diffused, enveloping light. The emphasis of his work was upon the study of the broad light of nature, whether he was painting his many versions of the professional oarsman or his scenes of hunting in the New Jersey marshes.

Eakins resumed his studies of anatomy at Jefferson Medical College and formed friendships with members of the teaching staff. In particular, the strong, independent character of Doctor Samuel Gross appealed to Eakins, who saw in the surgeon something of his own self-reliance. It has been suggested that Eakins determined to paint Gross in emulation of Rembrandt's *The Anatomy Lesson of Dr. Tulp*. Rembrandt had created an immediate reputation on the basis of this picture, and Eakins, returning from Paris full of confidence in his own powers, needed to call attention to himself in some dramatic way.

In *The Gross Clinic* of 1875, Eakins turned from his accustomed bright palette to somber colors and dramatic chiaroscuro that strongly suggested not only Rembrandt, but also the Spanish masters of the 17th century. The painting is not a portrait in the conventional sense, but was conceived as a pictorial environment with lifesize figures, expressing the artist's heightened ideal of realism. Though clearly based on well-established precedent, the Gross portrait was highly innovative. Eakins knew this painting to be a most important work and submitted it to the art jury of the Centennial Exhibition of 1876. The painting was rejected, presumably because of its uncompromising realism in treating the subject of a surgical operation in progress. *The Gross Clinic* was finally exhibited in the medical section of the Centennial Exhibition, along with displays of equipment. The painting received abusive criticism in the press, reflecting moral outrage at a subject that offended the public's genteel sensibility. Eakins found it impossible to sell the painting until three years later, when Jefferson Medical College bought it for two hundred dollars.

Eakins must have been profoundly disturbed by the treatment accorded *The Gross Clinic* and by the invective heaped upon him personally as one who had created "a degradation of Art." While he understood the basis of such criticism, he knew it to be utterly irrelevant to art. Realism, if it were to be a viable form of expression, could not shrink into comfortable pictorial pleasantries. Above all, his art was an expression of his own personality; and he spoke, behaved, and painted with equal candor and disregard for meaningless conventions.

It would be wrong to assume, from *The Gross Clinic* fiasco, that Eakins had been banished, like some American Courbet, from the great official exhibition. Quite the opposite, for inside the art section of the exhibition were five works by him, duly passed and accepted by the jury of selection. These pictures—including two watercolors, *Baseball Players Practicing* (Plate 6) and *Whistling for Plover* (Plate 3)—offered no disturbing scenes. One of them, a small oil painting showing three distinguished elderly men in an ornate parlor—*The Chess Players* (Metropolitan Museum of Art)—was a very model of dignity and good taste.

Despite his unwillingness to paint a merely conventional portrait of Doctor Gross, Eakins' aim was not to offend public sensibility. He was making his way in the Philadelphia art world through the very doors of its conservative establishment, The Pennsylvania Academy of the Fine Arts. The new Academy building at Broad and Cherry Streets, which had been erected uptown from its old location on Chestnut Street (not far from the Eakins house on Mt. Vernon Street), was designed by a young Philadelphia architect, Frank Furness. The Academy opened its doors in April, 1876, with exhibition space over the ground floor where the school was located. The new Academy building was a kind of masterpiece of inspired compromise in design; and Eakins might well have read the portents for the future in it. Furness had created an imposing eclectic facade out of Gothic and Renaissance motifs, with an interior inspired by the fashionable formulas of Eastlake's principals of decorative design. The psychological effect of having the school space dominated by the museum was ever to be subtly demonstrated in the years ahead.

Eakins became an assistant to his old instructor, Christian Schussele, in 1878, and succeeded him as professor of drawing and painting in the fall of 1879, following Schussele's death. Eakins was regarded as a radical by the conservative Philadelphia gentlemen who underwrote the Academy's operations and who sat on its autocratic board of directors, guiding its future. Eakins' appointment probably reflected the inertia of the board, which kept them from looking for a less controversial figure; however, when he was appointed to assume control of the school's teaching, Eakins accepted and immediately advanced his own beliefs over the established teaching process. Fixing an experienced and disillusioned eye on many of the "antique" casts he had been obliged to draw as a student, Eakins said: "I don't like a long study of casts . . . the beginner can at the very outset see more from the living model in a given time than from the study of the antique in twice that period." He also determined to shorten the period of drawing from plaster casts which typified Schussele's approach; "I think [the student] should learn to draw with color; the brush is a more powerful and rapid tool than [the pencil] . . . There are no lines in nature . . . only form and color."

Thus began Eakins' revolution in teaching at the Academy. Dedicated as he was to arriving at a scientifically truthful, yet artistic solution to the problem of figure painting, Eakins encouraged his students in ways that the administration was certain to resent and fear. Whereas Eakins regarded the human body as a thing of beauty, the society in which he lived equated nudity with sin. Eakins himself was not inclined to paint a nude for its own sake: "I can conceive of few circumstances wherein I would have to paint a woman naked," he wrote to his father in 1867. When he finally came to the right "circumstance" ten years later, Eakins produced one of the most beautiful paintings of his career. *William Rush Carving his Allegorical Figure of the Schuylkill River* (Philadelphia Museum of Art) is a title invented to dispel any possible suspicion in the mind of the public that the painting might not be a representation of a purely historical scene, rather than the ravishing nude study that is really the subject of the composition. Eakins admired the colonial sculptor William Rush (1756-1833) as a kindred spirit who looked to the human figure for his inspiration also. Rush's model did not pose nude: that was pure invention by Eakins.

Eakins was sustained in his position at the Academy by its board chairman, Fairman Rogers. Besides his attainments in engineering, which gave him a solid basis of respectability in the community, Rogers held a keen interest in art and scientific studies. He upheld Eakins' teaching methods as appropriate for a school which sought to develop professional artists, rather than amateurs. Rogers engaged in the elegant sport of coaching and maintained a large stable of horses at his farm west of Philadelphia. Out of their friendship and mutual interests—Eakins studied equine anatomy and offered additional lessons on this subject at the Academy—the painting *The Fairman Rogers Four-in-Hand* (Philadelphia Museum of Art) was conceived.

Up to this time, horses in motion were generally represented in art by a convention which showed leg movement in a stylized way that the trained observer knew to be false. Few artists before Eakins had bothered to investigate the actual conformation of a horse in motion. This he did in many preparatory studies, made while the coach-in-four passed before him as he studied each of the horses one by one. In order to better his understanding of this complicated subject, Eakins made wax models of the horses. But it was not until 1884 and his association with Eadweard Muybridge at the University of Pennsylvania that Eakins was fully able to realize scientific exactitude in the study of motion.

Muybridge's method was to set a series of still cameras in line, a few feet apart, and to actuate each camera in sequence as the moving subject passed before them. Eakins' modifications produced the first true motion picture—proved many theories about animal and human motion and gave Eakins an important tool in his search for a realistic representation of life. However, Eakins did not use photographs directly to paint pictures; the photograph was only a tool in his hands. When he was ready to paint a picture, he did so directly with the brush and with no elaborate preparatory drawing.

With the resignation of his good friend Rogers from the

Academy's board came a turning in Eakins' fortunes. Rogers had prevailed in getting Eakins appointed director of the school in 1882, but an unfortunate matter occurred that spring. One of the young ladies in the life classes wrote a lengthy diatribe to the president of the Academy, protesting the exposure of the "horrid nakedness" of male and female models. The following year, Eakins was commissioned to paint *The Swimming Hole* (Fort Worth Art Association) for one of the Academy's board members, who then rejected the painting in favor of one with more conventional subject matter. Perhaps the enthusiasm and liberalism that Rogers had brought to the Academy's board had been momentarily infectious, but with his departure, stodgy industrialists resumed their normal attitudes about art.

In *The Swimming Hole*, Eakins portrayed a group of six men, nude and enjoying nature in a kind of Whitmanesque abandonment to sunshine and water. Eakins knew that the nude figure was best observed and sketched outdoors in the context of sunlight and landscape, rather than in the artificial light of the studio. Other scenes of nude figures set against landscapes—mostly on the theme of Arcadia—suggest Eakins' yearning to be free of the restraints that his society had placed upon the human spirit. (Henry Adams, reflecting on this problem, had observed that the repression of sensuality had been one of the principal triumphs of society.)

By 1882, death had come to three persons who had been very close to Eakins: his mother, in 1872; his fiancée of seven years, Katherine Crowell, in 1879; and his sister Margaret, in 1882. Margaret had posed for many of his pictures, including the two watercolors which bear the title, *Spinning* (Plates 19 and 21). With the outside world setting itself against him, Eakins must have cherished the warmth of family ties more than ever. In 1884, he married one of his students, Susan Macdowell, and for the first and only time, took up residence away from the family house on Mt. Vernon Street. The new studio-apartment on Chestnut Street had belonged to the illustrator, Arthur B. Frost (1851-1928), whose portrait Eakins painted at about this time. Frost had studied under Eakins at the Academy night school and considered this instruction the most important influence in his career. But the Eakinses gave up the studio after only one year and moved into the family house. The old attachments were strong. His career was not going well—there were intimations of trouble with the Academy administration and he had not been able to realize the kind of income from his painting that would

have granted him independence. Eakins kept a notebook of his transactions between 1870 and 1880, which recorded the sale of only eight paintings in this period, for a total income of something more than $2000. He had shown his work at every possible opportunity, from the prestigious exhibitions of the National Academy of Design, the Society of American Artists, and the American Watercolor Society to regional fairs and industrial exhibitions.

1886 was a lean year for Eakins. He painted only three portraits and one of these was not a commission—the sitter was his brother-in-law, Frank Macdowell. All of the minor incidents relating to the study of the nude at the Academy, under Eakins' leadership, came to a crisis point that year. A full-blown scandal finally erupted when Eakins, demonstrating the muscle function of the pelvis of a male model, removed the loincloth before the eyes of some women students. Eakins had determined that the business of studying the human figure was ". . . not going to benefit any grown person who is not willing to see or be seen seeing the naked figure . . ." and he had at last thrown aside all caution as an impediment to his teaching. The ensuing uproar lead to his censure and an admonition from the board to refrain from using a totally nude model ever again. Rather than compromise his standards, Eakins rejected the conditions under which he could remain at the Academy and resigned under pressure in February 1886.

A loyal group of students immediately formed an independent school with Eakins at its head. They found quarters in a commercial building a few blocks south of the Academy on Market Street. It was called The Art Students League, probably emulating the independent school of this name founded in New York in 1875 as a reaction against the National Academy of Design. There was a feeling of revolution in the air among art students in the two cities. In Eakins' new school were men who had seen action in the Civil War; the school's first curator had been a captain of cavalry. These were mature men who resented the patronizing attitude of the art establishment toward students. The release from his struggle with the Academy administration was good for Eakins and for the students who came over to him. The League was operated in an egalitarian fashion; Eakins accepted no pay for his teaching, and the tuition was kept to a minimum, although operating funds were often short.

Out of the League experience, Eakins acquired a lifelong friend in Samuel Murray, a young sculptor who stayed on with him to share his studio for ten years. Eakins assisted Murray in creating architectural sculpture for new buildings in Philadelphia. This was a field which Eakins entered in the '90s, making bas-relief sculpture for Memorial Arch at the entrance to Brooklyn's Prospect Park and for the Battle Monument at Trenton, New Jersey.

His involvement in the creation of the Art Students League must have helped to heal the psychological wounds caused by his dismissal from the Academy. But nearly a decade after the event, he still recalled the incident with mild, but unmistakable bitterness: "I taught in the Academy from the opening of the school until I was turned out, a period much longer than I should have permitted myself to remain there. My honors are misunderstanding, persecution and neglect, enhanced because unsought."

After the conclusion of the first year of the League's operation in 1887, Eakins decided to spend the summer at the Dakota ranch of his friend Dr. Horatio Wood, a distinguished faculty member of the University of Pennsylvania School of Medicine. He went alone—Susan Eakins remained in Philadelphia and their parting for the first time in three years of marriage suggests the depth of his discouragement. Eakins evidently needed a solitude that would not admit even of his wife. In 1885, Eakins had painted a portrait of his bride, *A Lady with a Setter Dog* (Metropolitan Museum of Art), full of rich, glowing color that distracts attention from the melancholy expression of the face and the listless posture of the figure. Eakins' portraits, to a remarkable extent, are reflections of his own somewhat dour personality. His perception of the tragic element in the human experience was profound. In Dakota, Eakins engaged fully in the outdoor life, taking daily horseback rides and sketching scenes of cowboy life and the landscape of the Badlands. Several of these sketches became fully realized the following year in his studio in Philadelphia, notably one of his rare landscape pictures, *Cowboys in the Badlands* (private collection), and the subject of the cowboy singing received a number of treatments.

Eakins returned to Philadelphia refreshed and apparently ready to make another serious commitment to his art. In view of the dismal fate of *The Gross Clinic*—it had been exhibited once at the Academy in 1879 under the most unpleasant circumstances for Eakins—it seems particularly optimistic of him to embark upon a second composition whose character is so similar to the Gross subject. In 1889, Eakins accepted a commission to paint *The Agnew Clinic*, paid for by students of Dr. D. Hayes Agnew,

who was retiring from his teaching position at the Medical School of the University of Pennsylvania. Once again, Eakins chose to show the doctor at work in an operating amphitheater, rather than giving him a conventional portrait treatment. And again Eakins described in vivid detail an operation in progress—this time exposing a breast to view. The painting was finished in three months and came under attack from the conservative art establishment almost at once, when it was shown for the first time in a commercial gallery. In 1891, the Academy quite predictably refused to hang the painting in its annual exhibition, explaining that the rejection was based upon its having been shown previously. The real reason came forward eventually: the painting was "not cheerful for ladies to look at." Twelve years had elapsed between the Academy's rejection of *The Gross Clinic* and its triumph in excluding *The Agnew Clinic;* the Academy still regarded Eakins as an outlaw of art.

His friend Harrison Morris, who became managing director of the Academy, was much the same kind of influential friend as Fairman Rogers had been. Morris believed that "A city with Eakins living in it detached from its Fine Arts Academy was a . . . farce. You might as well try to run a wagon on three wheels . . ." Morris lured Eakins out of his isolation and from 1894 until the end of his painting career, Eakins exhibited in the Academy's annual exhibitions on a more or less regular basis. The Academy officially ended its vendetta against him in 1897 with the purchase of *The Cello Player*.

Eakins lived to see his values as an artist vindicated, but he continued to suffer discouragements. 1892 had been a particularly disappointing year; his Art Students' League was forced to disband after six years because of lack of financial support. The Society of American Artists—that once-liberal group turned conservative with whom Eakins had exhibited regularly since its inception—rejected *The Agnew Clinic* in 1892. Eakins resigned his membership in the Society in protest.

He was not dismayed by others' lack of confidence. Eakins had worked laboriously for two years on *The Concert Singer* (Philadelphia Museum of Art) and perhaps the aria, *O rest in the Lord*, from Mendelssohn's *Elijah*, sung to him by the model every day during the sittings, gave him more than just the observation of throat muscles in action. The painting proved to be one of his most poetic and colorfully resonant. Eakins began to concentrate on portraiture in the '90s; even though fashionable members of Philadelphia society shunned his services, he found plenty of patronage from doctors, professional men, and musicians in the community. Toward the end of the decade, Eakins returned to sporting scenes—boxing and wrestling interested him now. He gave to boxing, as in *Salutat* (Addison Gallery of American Art), the same immediacy in paint that he had bestowed on the drama of the surgical amphitheatre. The boxing scenes are faithful mirrors of the atmosphere of the ring at the turn of the century, straightforward and free of clichés.

The decade of the '90s also produced for him the first stirrings of national recognition: a gold medal at the Columbian Exposition in Chicago in 1893 and, three years later, an invitation to exhibit at the Carnegie International Exhibition in Pittsburgh. At home, too, he had a measure of public acclaim: the Academy of Natural Sciences published his paper, *The Differential Action of Certain Muscles Passing More than One Joint*. His first one-man show occurred in 1896 at the Earle Galleries in Philadelphia, and it could not be said that he was ignored by his city. Just after the turn of the century, Eakins became a full member of the National Academy of Design in New York—a place where he had given much of his time in teaching—and respect-

ability seemed to be conferred on him at last. John S. Sargent sought him out and was introduced to Eakins by a mutual friend, William White, with whom Sargent was staying while completing a portrait of Mrs. Joseph Widener of Philadelphia.

Honored in New York, Eakins was still a prophet without much honor in his own land, however. It was not the monied classes of Philadelphia's Main Line who sought his services, but a group of Catholic prelates of St. Charles Seminary. The collection of Eakins portraits accumulated at the seminary during the latter part of Eakins' career represent some of his finest achievements in the art of portrait painting.

At the last, Eakins reached back over thirty years to recall the theme of William Rush and the allegory of the Schuylkill River. His ideal of representing the human body in art with monumentality and dignity—an ideal which had caused him a lifetime of ostracism—was reaffirmed in the 1908 version of the Rush theme with an undiminished force and beauty. Until his health began to fail in 1910, Eakins remained a powerful artist, a clear eye, and a perceptive mind in an uncompromising search for a vision of the truth.

PLATES

JOHN BIGLIN IN A SINGLE SCULL
1873-74
17⅛″ x 23″ (43.4 cm. x 58.4 cm.)
The Metropolitan Museum of Art, Fletcher Fund, 1924

John Biglin in a Single Scull. Shortly after Eakins returned from Paris in 1870, he began working on a series of pictures whose subjects were the Biglin brothers. The Biglins were professional oarsmen whom Eakins got to know because he himself enjoyed rowing in the single scull. Eakins' meticulous care and attention to detail in constructing a picture is perhaps nowhere better demonstrated than in the step-by-step preparation for this watercolor.

In its creation, Eakins seems to have continued to rely upon the guidance of his former teacher in Paris, Gérôme, maintaining a frequent correspondence with him. In the spring of 1873, Eakins sent Gérôme a trial watercolor whose subject was also the rower, Biglin. Although this first version is now lost, a letter from Gérôme to Eakins, in which the master gives a critique of the picture, reveals its probable appearance.

Gérôme commented: "The individual who is well drawn in his parts lacks a total sense of movement; he is immobile, as if he were fixed on the water; his position I believe is not pushed far enough forward—that is, to the extreme limit of movement in that direction. There is in every prolonged movement, such as rowing, an infinity of rapid phases, and an infinity of points from the moment when the rower, after having leaned forward, pulls his upper body back as far as it will go. There are two moments to choose from for painters of our sort, the two extreme phases of action, either when the rower is leaning forward, the oars back, or when he has pushed back, with the oars ahead; you have taken an intermediate point, that is the reason for the immobility in the work."

The first watercolor was presumably returned to Eakins, who may have destroyed it. He immediately began work on a second version, incorporating into it the suggestions made by Gérôme. In the perspective drawing (Figure 1) for this watercolor, it may be seen how Eakins approached the subject with mathematical precision. It is drawn almost exactly twice the size of the finished watercolor. With such an enlargement, Eakins could more precisely study the problem of perspective involved in this very complicated subject. While superficially appearing to be a profile view of the rower and his boat, it is actually not a profile, but a very subtle three quarter view. As the perspective

drawing shows, the imaginary lines which create depth in the picture all vanish at a point directly behind the head.

In order to work out the problems of form involved in the figure of the central subject, Eakins resorted to oil paint. The oil study is larger than the watercolor and notably richer in color, due to the greater strength of the oil medium. Yet the transparency of the watercolor permits a much more subtle range of tones, giving a much more convincing atmospheric perspective. The figure of Biglin is rendered with solidity and with such attention to detail that it runs the risk of being a static thing. By injecting such elements into the composition as the water dripping from the blade of the oar and the prow of a scull entering the picture from the left, Eakins has suggested the transistory moment.

Eakins also sent this second version to Gérôme in Paris and it was returned to him with a letter from his master, which said: "Your watercolor is wholly well-made." In 1874, Eakins entered the work in the annual exhibition of the American Society of Painters in Water Colors, an organization which had been established in New York in 1867, in recognition of the growing interest in watercolor among American artists.

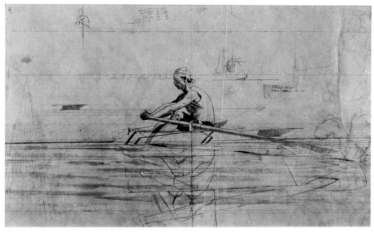

Figure 1. *Perspective Study for John Biglin in a Single Scull*, ca. 1873-74, pencil, ink, and wash on paper, 27⅜″ x 45³⁄₁₆″ (69.5 cm. x 114.8 cm.). Museum of Fine Arts, Boston, Gift of Cornelius Vanderbilt Whitney.

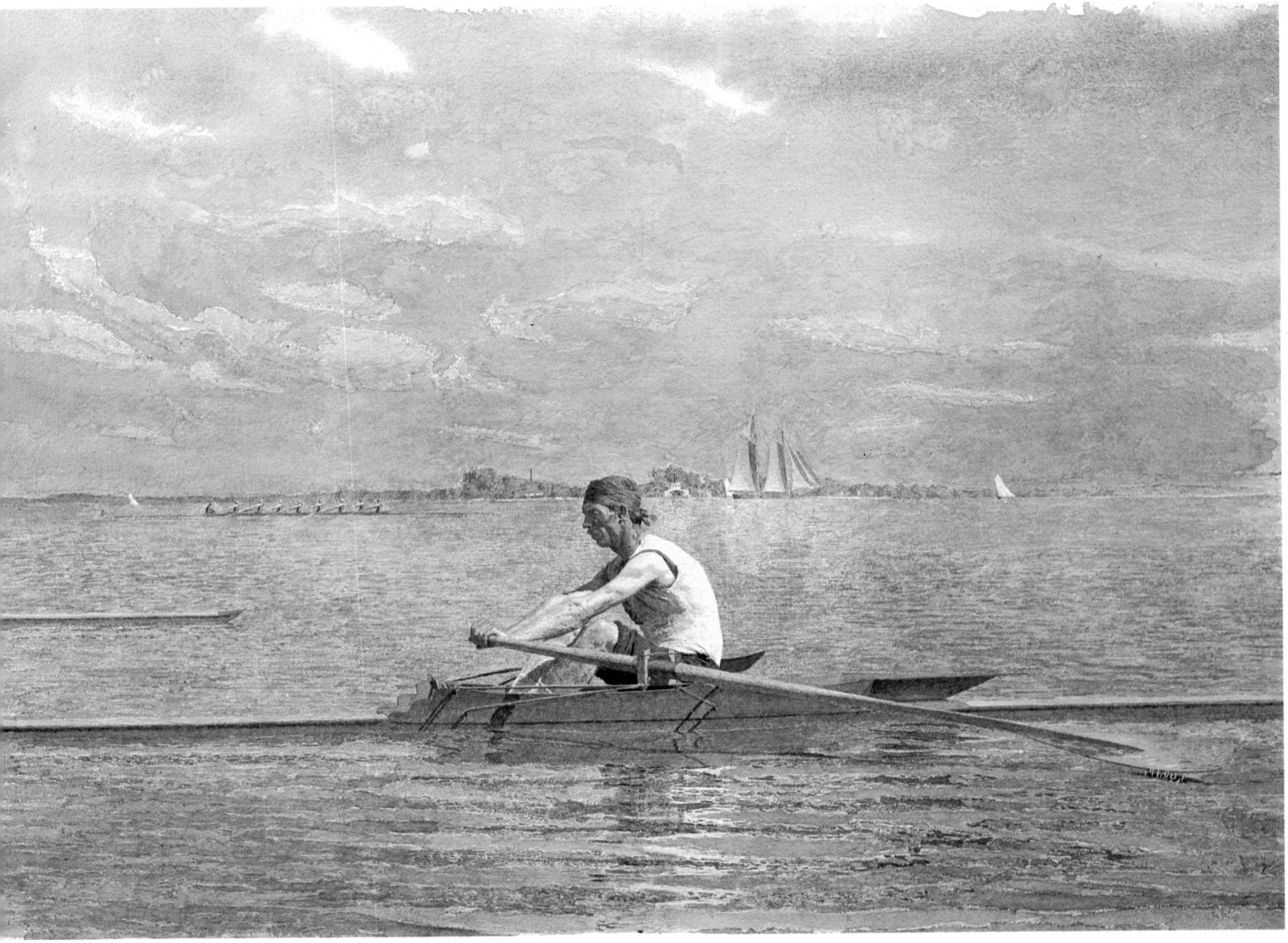

Plate 2
JOHN BIGLIN IN A SINGLE SCULL
Detail of Plate 1, Actual Size

Figure 2. *John Biglin in a Single Scull*, 1874, oil on canvas, 24⅝″ x 16″ (61.8 cm. x 40.6 cm.). Yale University Art Gallery, Whitney Collection of Sporting Art.

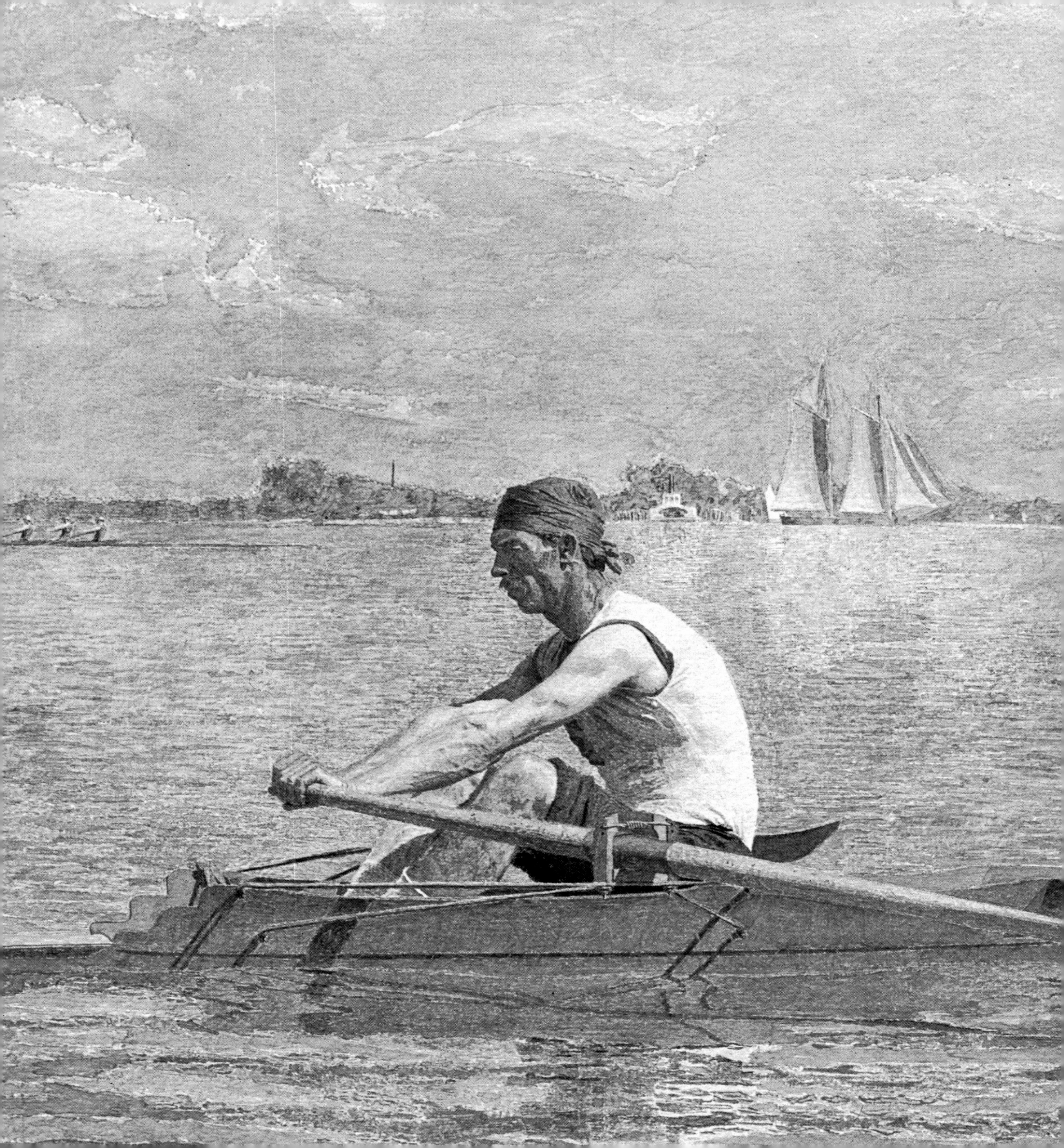

Plate 3
WHISTLING FOR PLOVER
1874
11" x 16½" (27.9 cm. x 41.9 cm.)
The Brooklyn Museum

While Gérôme was assisting Eakins in Paris—not only through constructive criticism, but also with his help in placing Eakins' work in collections and in the Salon exhibitions—another friend, Earl Shinn (1838-1886), was helping him in New York. Shinn was a native Philadelphian and he had also been a student of Gérôme in Paris. But most important, he was the art critic for *The Nation* between 1868 and 1886.

In January, 1875, Eakins wrote to Shinn from Philadelphia: "You will see in the watercolor exhibition [American Society of Painters in Water Colors] three little things of mine . . . a negro whistling for plover. This is the same subject as my oil and the selfsame Negro William Robinson of Backneck but in a different position. It is not near as far finished as the little oil one but is painted in a much higher key with all the light possible." The "little oil one" is a reference to an oil painting which Eakins sent to the Salon in Paris that year. The oil version was sold through Goupil, and its whereabouts are unknown today.

It is interesting to note that Eakins' letter refers to the watercolor as being painted "in a much higher key with all the light possible." The watercolor has an overall pearly light, achieved by a very high keyed color scheme. To judge from the letter, Eakins must have been looking for a means of painting light in a way that he found impossible in oils. But because of his manner of working—with close attention to minute detail—the creation of a finished watercolor must have been extremely tedious. Even more than in the Biglin watercolor (Plate 1), Eakins seems to have depended on drawing, rather than on broad washes of color. The areas of local color are rendered with staccato touches of the brush. Eakins has taken Gérôme's idea about the phases of action in rowing, translating it into the terms of this picture. We are given a split second in time—the moment when the hunter utters a whistle to call the birds and is preparing to close his shotgun and aim at them. In a moment, he will rise from his crouching position and fire. The sense of expectation that this small image creates is extraordinarily powerful.

Whistling for Plover was one of the five works Eakins exhibited in the Centennial Exhibition in Philadelphia in 1876. Shortly thereafter, he presented the watercolor to a man he admired greatly, Dr. Silas Weir Mitchell (1829-1914) the Philadelphia physician, novelist, and poet.

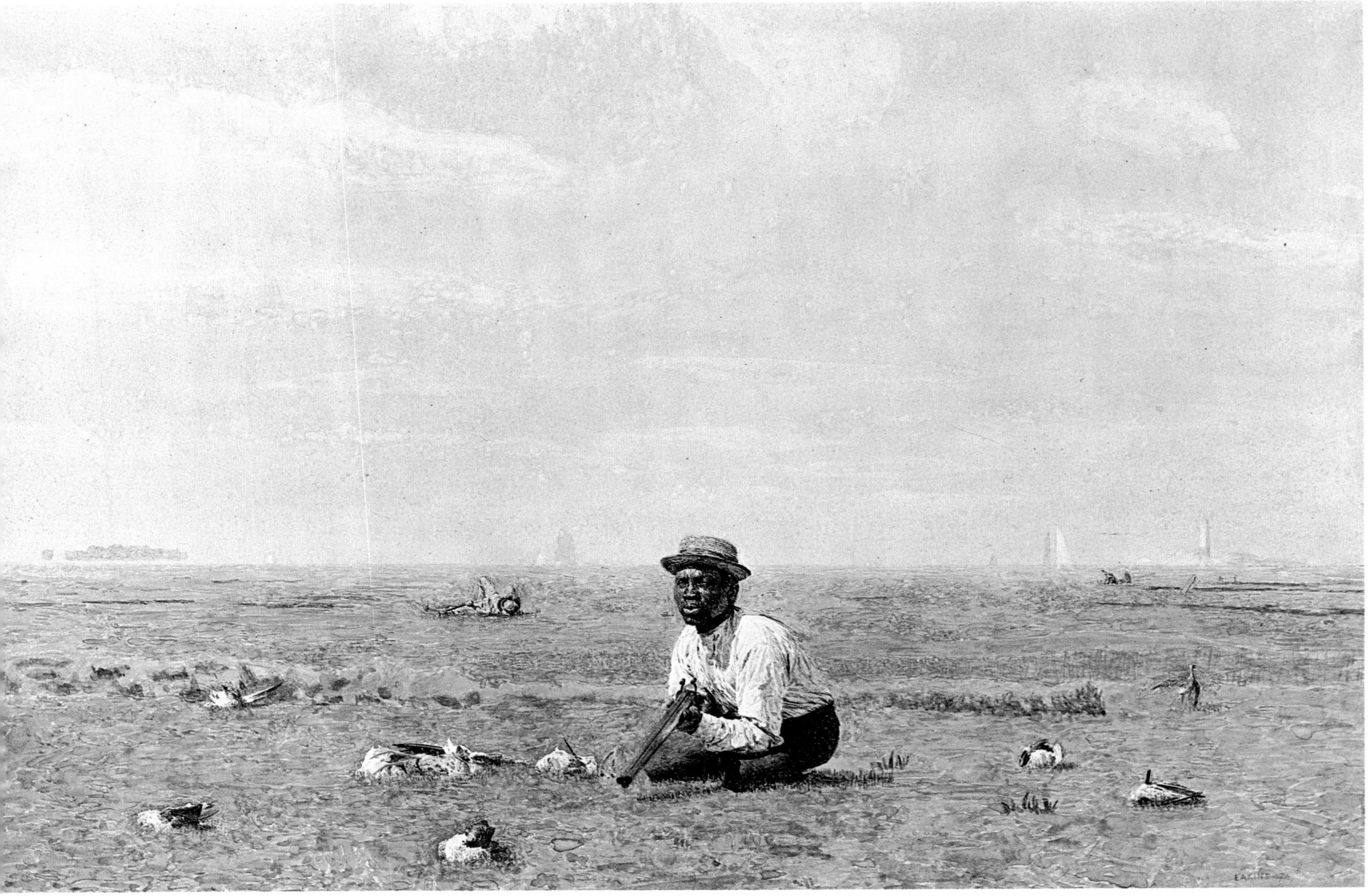
EAKINS

Plate 4
STARTING OUT AFTER RAIL
1874
25″ x 20″ (63.5 cm. x 50.8 cm.)
Wichita Art Museum, Murdoch Collection

Two versions in oil preceded the watercolor that Eakins finally painted in 1874. The first version was a horizontal composition, rather sketchily painted. This he gave to his close friend, William Merritt Chase (1849-1916), in 1900. The second composition is identical with the watercolor, both in composition and in size. It was the second and more finished oil painting that Eakins sent to Goupil, his dealer in Paris, in 1874. The watercolor version, however, was exhibited at the Seventh Annual Exhibition of the American Society of Painters in Water Colors in New York, during the spring of 1874. In the exhibition catalog, Eakins identified the picture as *Harry Young, of Moyamensing, and Sam Helhower, "The Pusher," Going Rail Shooting.* (A pusher is a poleman in a punt.) The watercolor was later shown at the 52nd annual exhibition of The Pennsylvania Academy of the Fine Arts in 1881.

The picture shows two of Eakins' friends setting out in a small catboat across the Delaware River to the hunting marshes in New Jersey. Eakins once remarked in a lecture: "I know of no prettier problem in perspective than to draw a yacht sailing. A vessel sailing will almost certainly have three different tilts. She will not likely be sailing in the direct plane of the picture. Then she will be tilted over sideways by the force of this wind, and she will most likely be riding up on a wave or pitching down into the next one." Nowhere is Eakins' interest in the subject better demonstrated than in this picture.

Figure 3. *Starting Out After Rail*, 1874, oil on canvas, 24″ x 20″ (60.9 cm. x 50.8 cm.). Museum of Fine Arts, Boston, Charles Henry Hayden Fund.

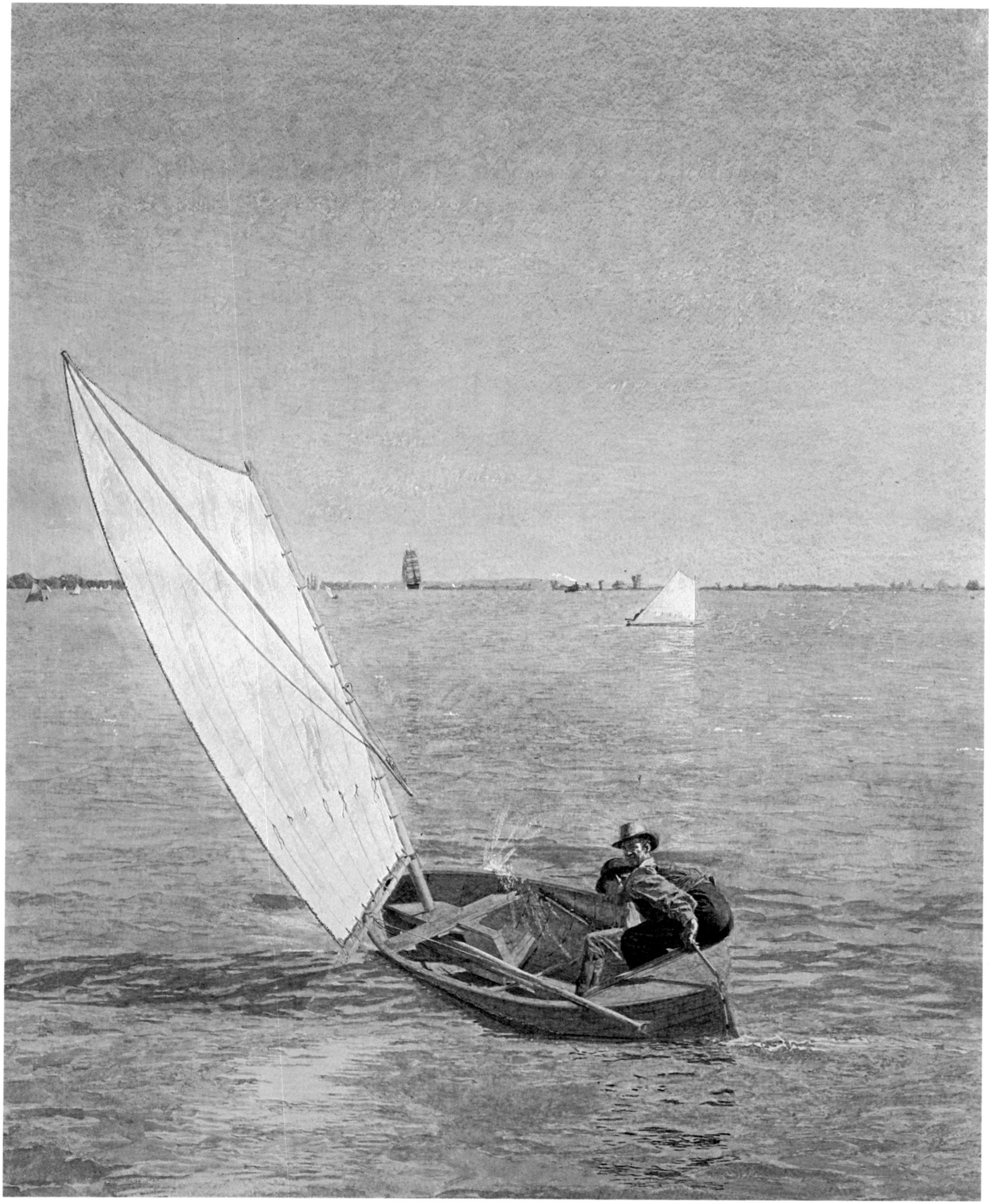

Plate 5
STARTING OUT AFTER RAIL
Detail of Plate 4, Actual Size

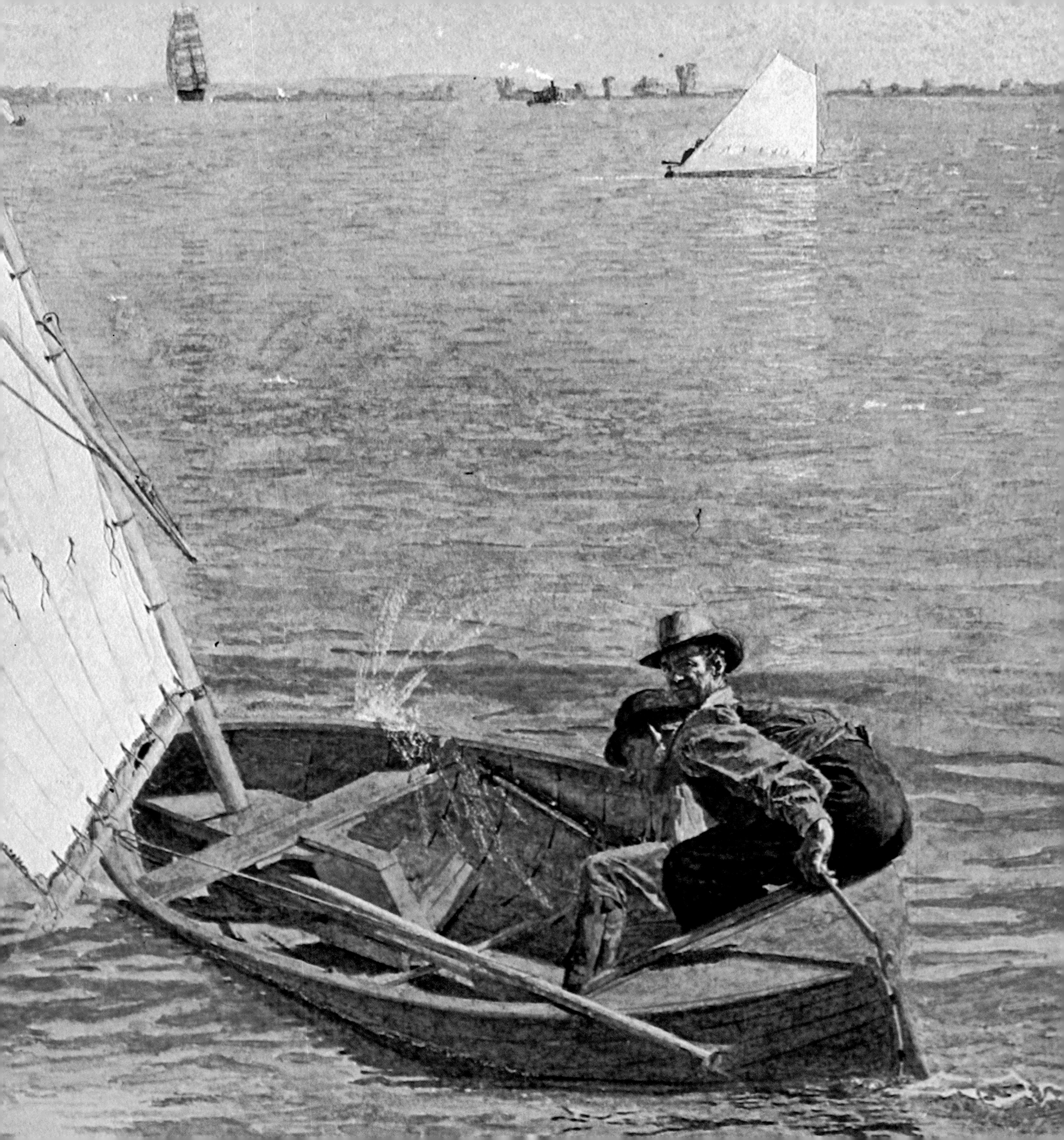

Plate 6
BASEBALL PLAYERS PRACTICING
1875
9⅜″ x 10½″ (23.8 cm. x 26.6 cm.)
Museum of Art, Rhode Island School of Design

In his letter of January, 1875, to his friend Shinn, Eakins commented further on his watercolors. About the baseball players practicing, he wrote: "The moment is just after the batter has taken his bat, before the ball leaves the pitcher's hand. They are portraits of athletic boys, a Philadelphia club. I can see that they are pretty well drawn. Ball players are very fine in their build. They are the same stuff as bullfighters only bullfighters are older and a trifle stronger perhaps. I think I will try to make a baseball picture someday in oil. It will admit a fine figure painting."

Here again, Eakins employs the same device we see in Plate 1 and Plate 3: the placement of the central figures' heads near a continuous line. In the other pictures this was a horizon line, but here it is the railing in front of the bleacher seats. There is evidence that Eakins may have conceived this picture as a smaller one and then enlarged it in the process of painting. This is evident from the discontinuous color which can be noted at the left and right of the central portion of the picture. Since this work was one of those shown in the Centennial Exhibition in Philadelphia in 1876, Eakins presumably regarded it as finished in spite of its uncompleted appearance.

The source of the sunlight that illuminates the scene is low in the sky, creating the same dramatic shadows on the figures as in the Biglin watercolor (Plate 1). As in *Whistling for Plover* (Plate 3), figures are anticipating an event which takes place outside the picture. Such pictures are not discontinuous, but carry the viewer's imagination well beyond the borders of the composition.

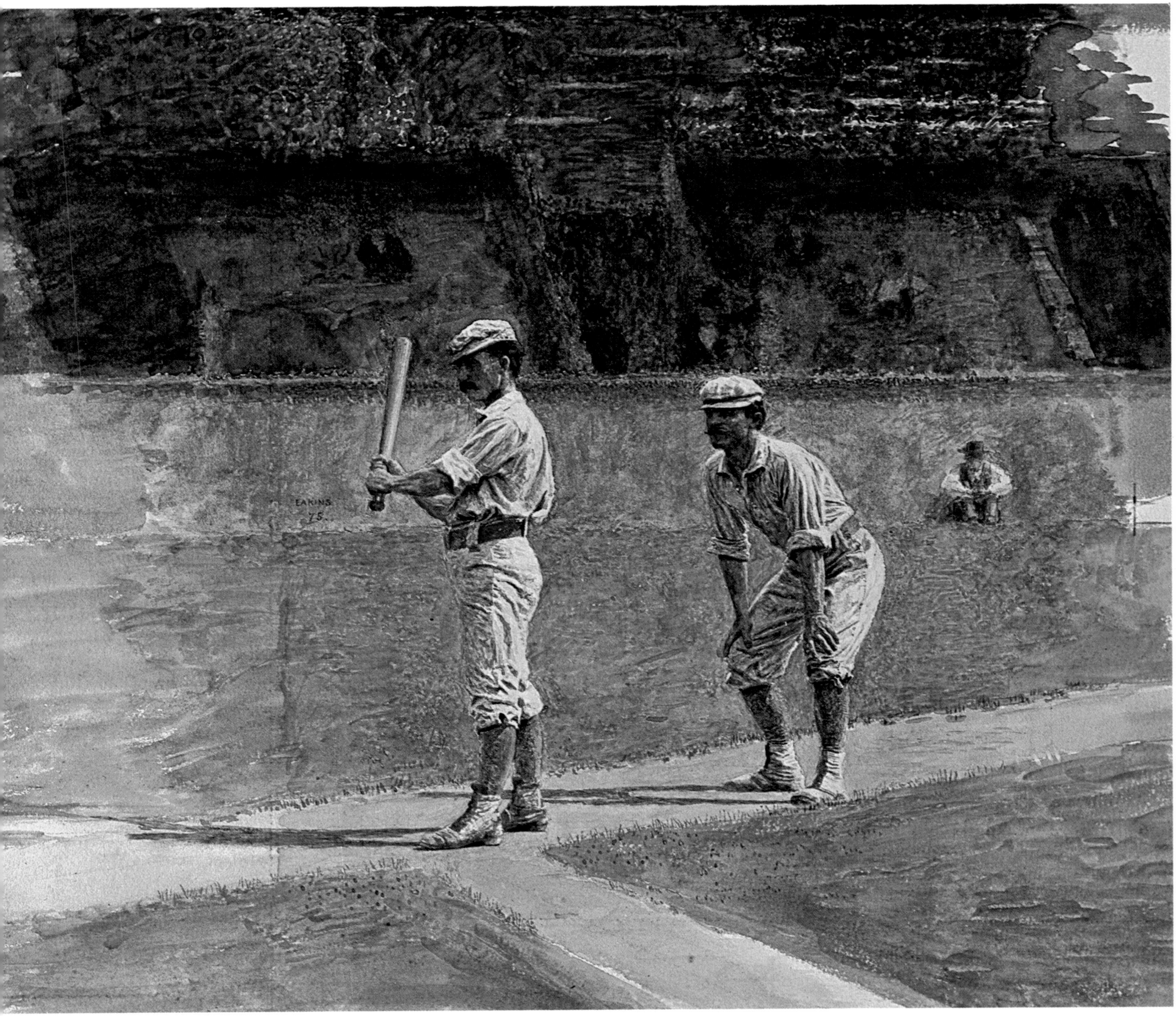
EAKINS
75.

Plate 7
DRIFTING
1875
10¾" x 16½" (27.3 cm. x 41.9 cm.)
Collection Mr. Thomas S. Pratt

Eakins painted at least three identical compositions in oil at the same time that he made this watercolor, but the watercolor is the only one with a record of exhibition; this was the third watercolor he exhibited in the American Society of Painters in Water Colors, February, 1875, in New York.

In his letter to Shinn, Eakins described it as "a drifting race." He wrote: "It is a still August morning, 11:00 o'clock. The race has started down from Tony Brown's at Gloucester [New Jersey] on the ebbtide. What wind there is from time to time is eastern and the big sails flop out some one side and some the other. You can see a least little breeze this side of the vessels at anchor. It turns up the water enough to reflect the blue sky of the zenith. The rowboats and the sailboats in the foreground are not the racers but starters and lookers on." When it was shown in 1874, the painting bore a more descriptive title: *No Wind— Race-boats Drifting*.

In the picture Eakins strives for the same diffused light and pearly tonality found in *Whistling for Plover* (Plate 3). He went on to remark to his friend Shinn that "the color was very true." This is one of the very few subjects Eakins painted as a pure landscape, without specific human references. The subject is really light and enveloping atmosphere; its hushed, poetic mood reminds one of Whistler. The picture must have had a special place in Eakins' intentions, for according to his own records, he contributed it to a sale in 1880 for the benefit of the family of his late friend and professor at the Academy, Christian Schussele.

Figure 4. *Becalmed on the Delaware*, 1874, oil on canvas, 10⅛" x 17¼" (25.7 cm. x 43.8 cm.). Philadelphia Museum of Art.

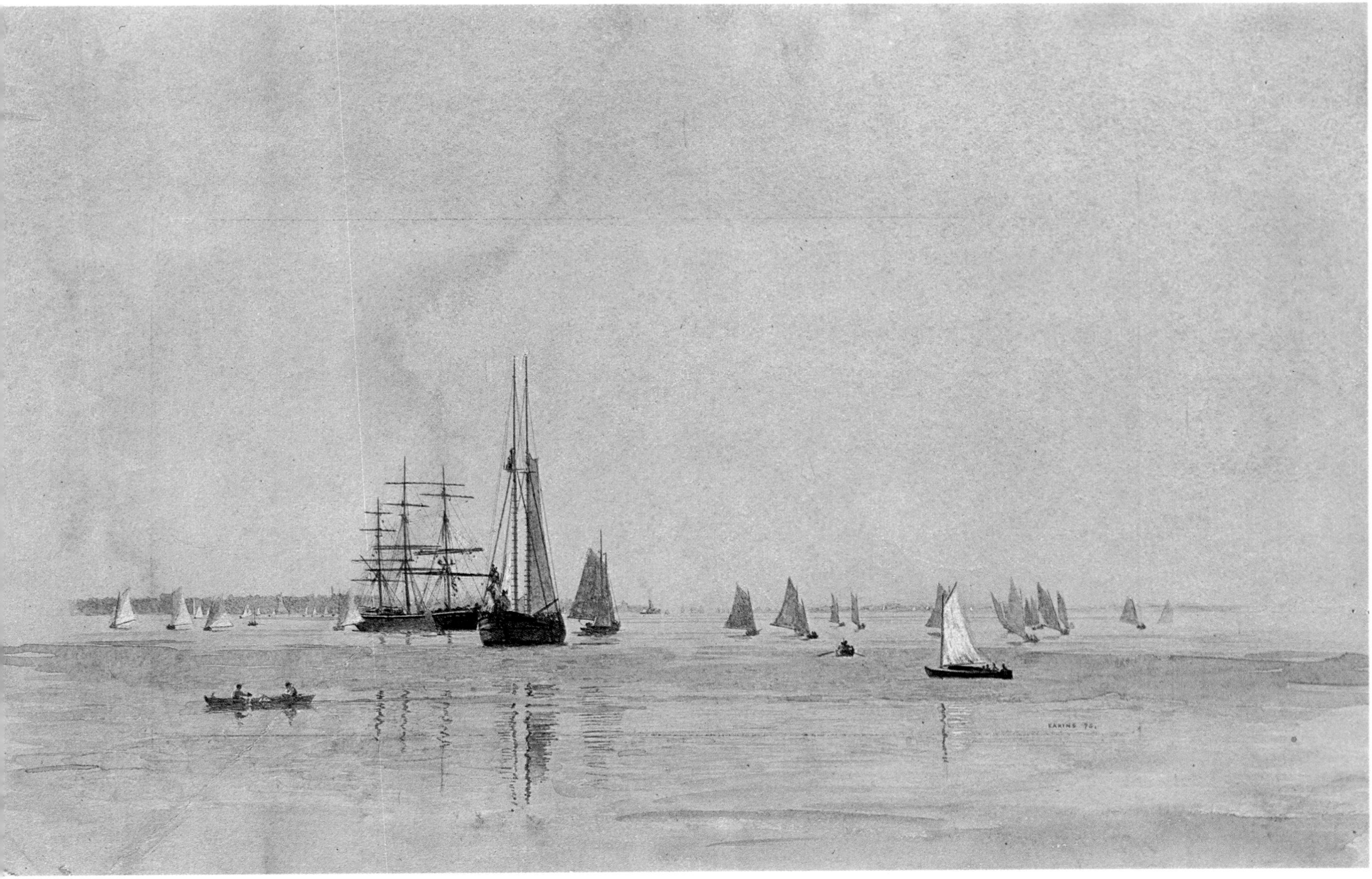
EAKINS 75.

Plate 8
DRIFTING
Detail of Plate 7, Actual Size

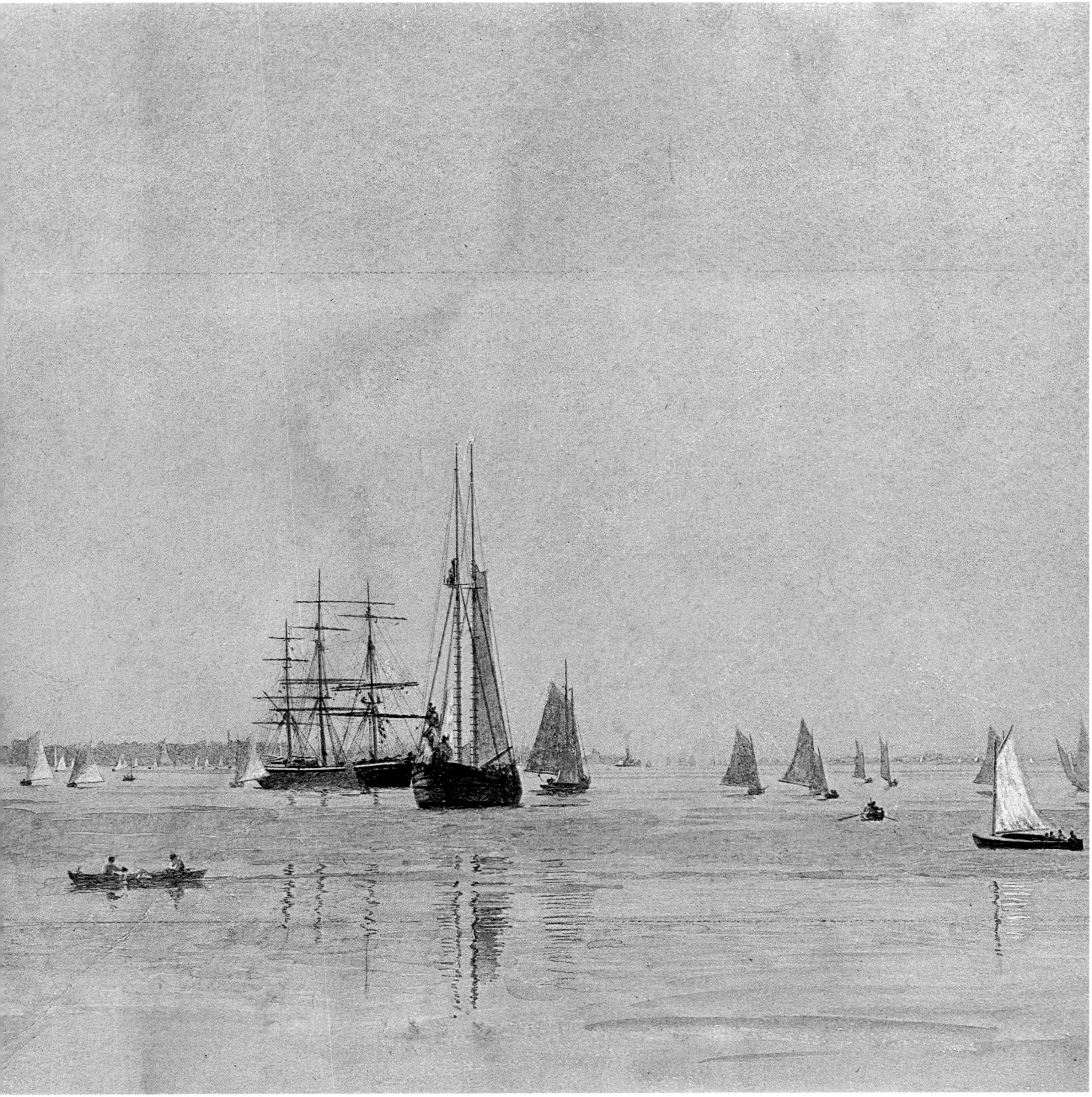

Plate 9
THE ZITHER PLAYER
1876
12⅛″ x 10½″ (30.8 cm. x 26.6 cm.)
Art Institute of Chicago

Both in subject matter and in treatment, the subject is related very closely to *The Chess Players* (Metropolitan Museum of Art), also of 1876. The two men represented in the watercolor are the artist's friends, Max Schmitt and the painter William Sartain, shown seated to the left. The room is plunged into deep shadow; toward the back is a silk hanging on the wall, partially draping over the chair in which Sartain is seated and lending a bright note of alizarin to the composition. The furniture was probably borrowed from the mixed assortment in the Eakins family parlor, a mixture of the fashionable eclectic styles. The armchair appears to be Jacobean revival and the side chair a high Victorian Rococo revival—with an 18th century Philadelphia tilt-top table. The same table appears in *Young Girl Meditating* (Plate 11), completed the following year.

The focus of interest in *The Zither Player* is the top of the table, with its bottles and glasses, its corkscrew, its zither tuning key, and the zither itself. Beyond the midpoint of the table, the focus becomes blurred, and one is reminded of Eakins' theories about perception and his interest in photographic studies. Eakins has signed the work in a typical way, with the script letters and the date laid out in perspective on the floor.

About seven years later, Eakins painted *Professionals at Rehearsal* (Figure 5), a reworking of the zither theme. While the central elements of the table and the zither remain the same, it is clear that Eakins has rethought this composition and has injected a much more dramatic note by bringing the heads of both subjects into a stronger chiaroscuro. The figure to the left has become a participant in the scene now, rather than a spectator as he was in the watercolor version. There is the suggestion, also, that Eakins may have been recalling the genre subject matter of the 17th century Spanish masters, particularly Velasquez.

Figure 5. *Professionals at Rehearsal*, ca. 1883, oil on canvas, 16″ x 12″ (40.6 cm. x 30.4 cm.). Philadelphia Museum of Art, John D. McIlhenny Collection.

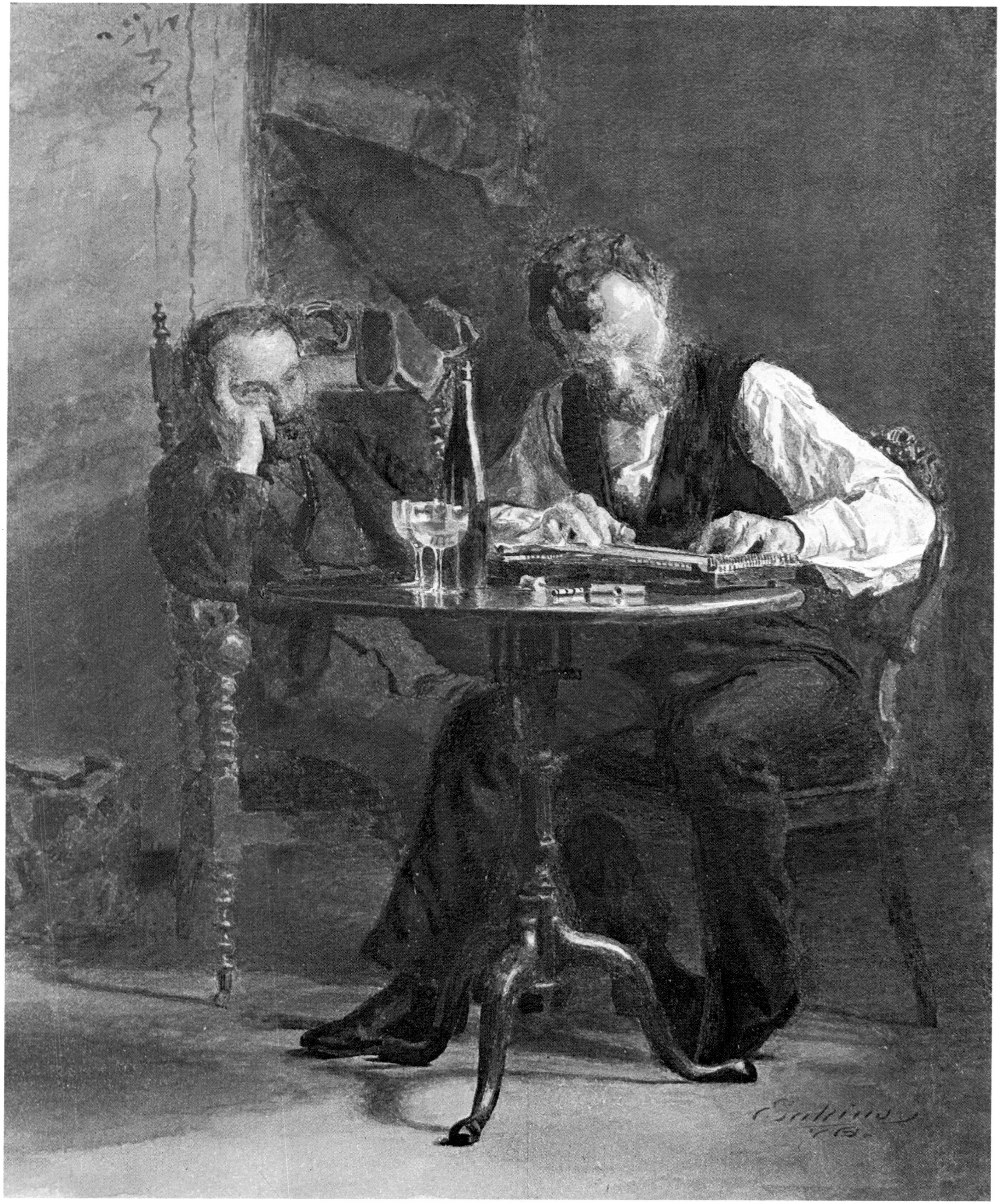

Plate 10
SEVENTY YEARS AGO
1877
15 ⅝" x 11" (39.7 cm. x 27.9 cm.)
The Art Museum, Princeton University

This watercolor, one of Eakins' most luminous and subtle color statements, appears in his work at the same time as the large oil, *William Rush Carving His Allegorical Figure of the Schuylkill River*. The subject of the watercolor, who also appears as a secondary character in the William Rush painting, is known to us only as Mrs. King. The watercolor may have been intended as a study for a portion of the large oil of the William Rush subject; however, there are significant differences between the watercolor and the portion of the oil in which Mrs. King is painted, and these suggest that the watercolor was an independent work.

The title of the watercolor clearly refers to the time of William Rush, the Philadelphia sculptor who flourished around the end of the preceding century and into the second quarter of the 1800's. Mrs. King's chair is a high style Philadelphia Chippendale side chair; to the left is an 18th century spinning wheel, while to the right may be seen a tilt-top table, perhaps the same one that Eakins used in *The Zither Player* (Plate 9). The simple, yet highly effective color composition of the picture is notable for its subtle use of pale blues and gray lavenders which are juxtaposed against umbers and dull reds. The almost impression-ist treatment of the carpet in the foreground, with its brilliant reds and blues against a tan ground, provides a very effective foil for the lustrous whites of the dress and the broad gray washes of the background.

Eakins has paid special attention to the lady's face and hands, investing them with character and dignity. Also notable is his attention to the differences in textures: the warm fleshiness of the hands and face, the glistening softness of the veil and hair, the smooth folds of the dress, and the burnished, cresting rail of the chair. Eakins also used the subject of the old lady knitting in a sculpture (dating from 1882 or early 1883) which was commissioned as a chimney piece decoration for a house in Philadelphia. Eakins' use of historical costume and furniture in his work—with a deliberately nostalgic title—is not the only instance of a return to the colonial past for subject matter. Between 1878 and 1881, he painted some dozen subjects in oil and watercolor which are deliberate evocations of the mood of early 19th century American genre painting. The Centennial Exhibition of 1876, which revived many furniture styles of the late 18th and early 19th centuries, may very well have inspired and provided material for this look into the past.

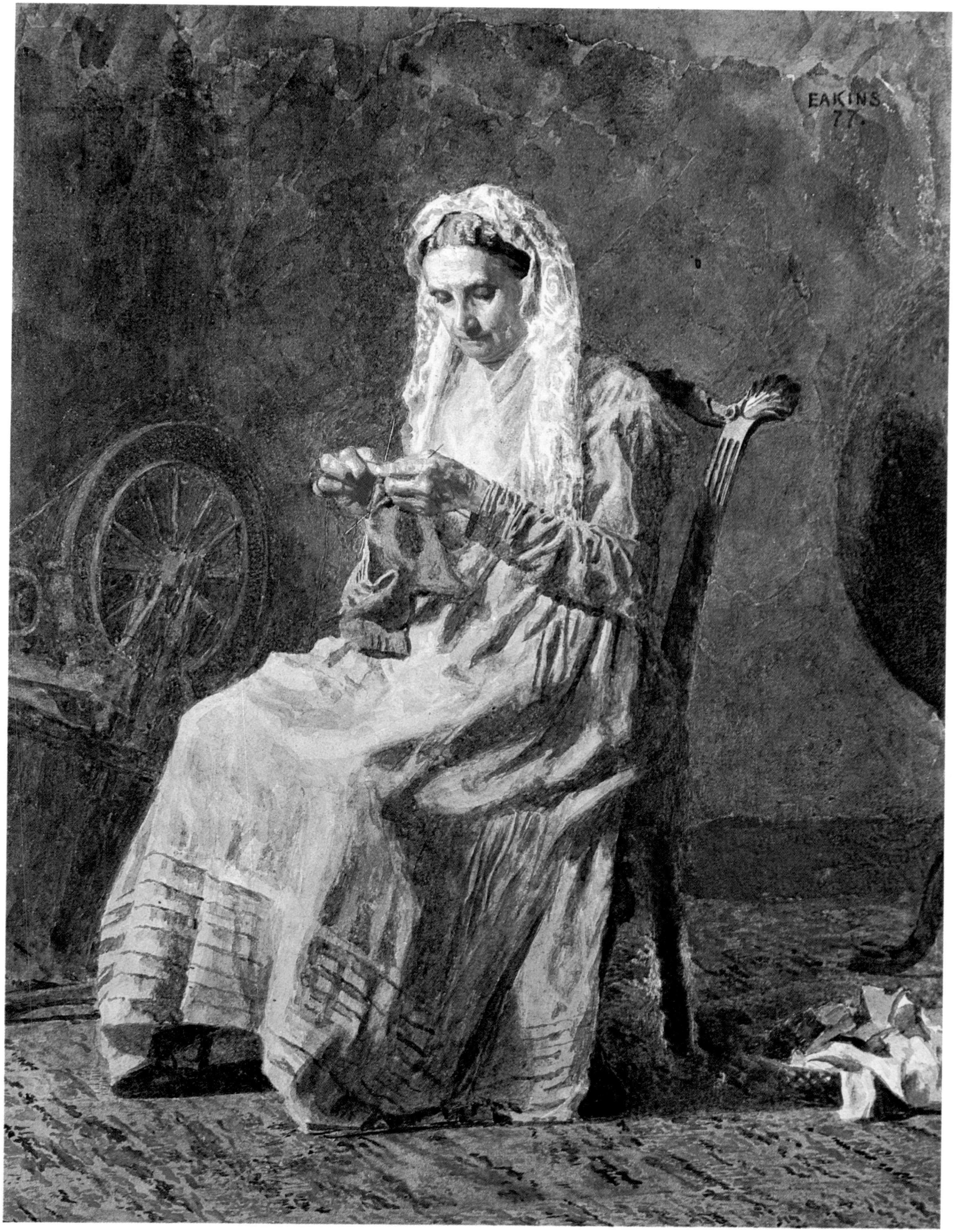
EAKINS
77.

Plate 11
YOUNG GIRL MEDITATING
1877
8¾" x 5½" (22.2 cm. x 13.9 cm.)
The Metropolitan Museum of Art, Fletcher Fund, 1925

It is a singular fact that Eakins, as an artist, had no interest in the industrialized society which was growing up around him in Philadelphia. Many of his pictures from this post Civil War period seem to look backward in time, toward a more agrarian age. Eakins did not retreat overtly into the past, but simply turned his eyes to scenes which pleased him. The subjects which he chose to paint on the rivers around Philadelphia or in the New Jersey marshes include no hint of the industrialism that was growing in the Delaware River Valley. Eakins led a quiet, contemplative existence, perhaps reinforced in his isolation by the fiasco of *The Gross Clinic* and the bitter criticism of his art which followed the exhibition of the picture in 1876.

Both in its small size and in its intensely introspective mood, this little interior—with its solemn figure dressed in an old-fashioned yellow silk dress—is an intensely personal statement. The watercolor bore other titles, given it by Eakins, such as *Fifty Years Ago* and *A Young Lady Admiring a Plant*. Eakins has been criticized for retreating from the world which met his *Gross Clinic* with such hostility; it has been pointed out that such work as this watercolor does not truly represent him as an artist. Perhaps this picture, like some of the other small watercolors, does appeal to a more genteel sensibility than Eakins was accustomed to address. But there is undeniable charm in this small figure of one of his pupils, and in spite of the self-conscious arrangement of studio props, Eakins achieved an undeniably poetic statement concerning light and color.

This charming emissary was sent to an exhibition in Boston in 1878, where it was awarded the silver medal under the unlikely auspices of the Massachusetts Charitable Mechanics Association Exhibition.

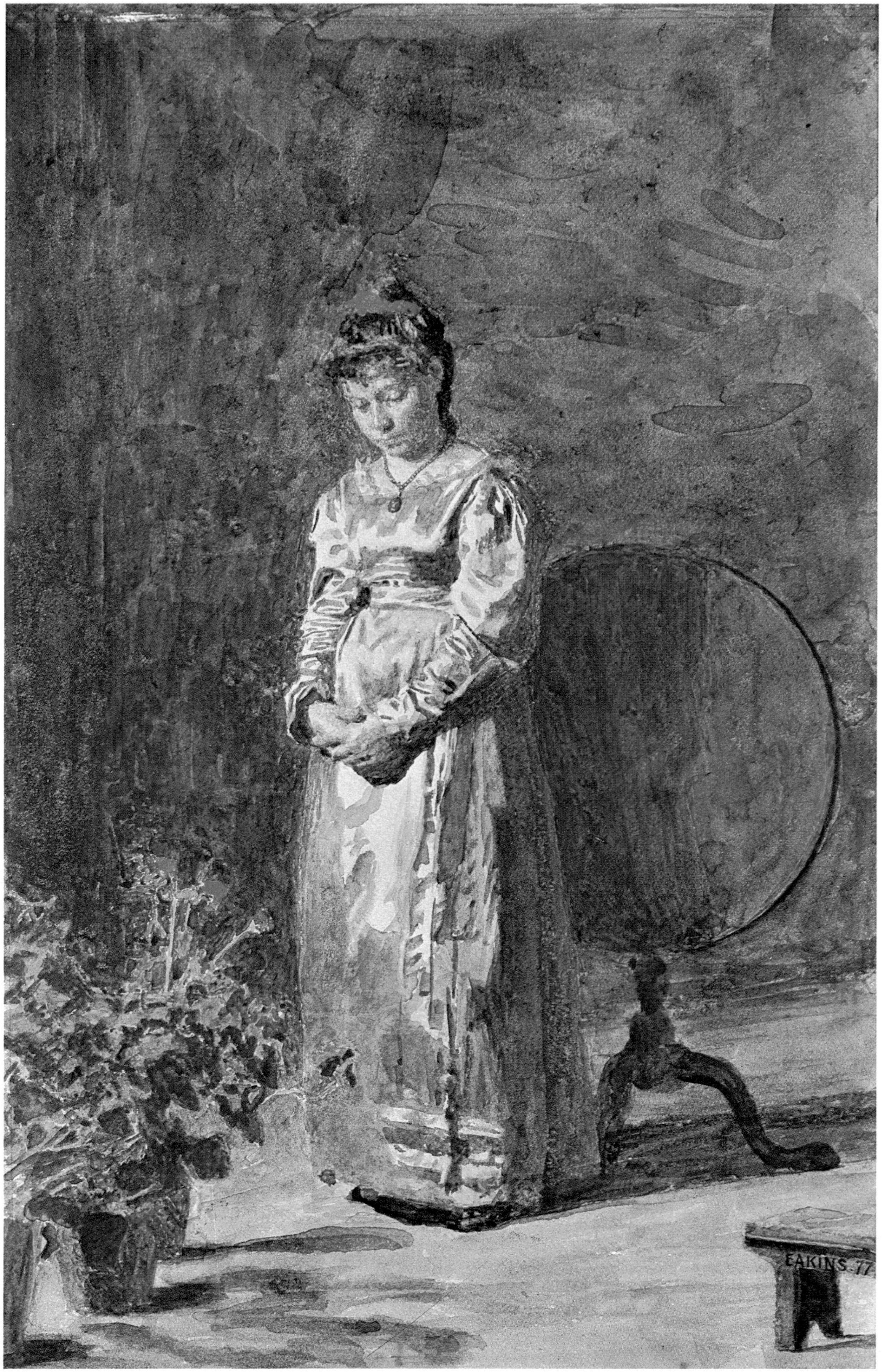
EAKINS.77

Plate 12
NEGRO BOY DANCING
1878
18⅛" x 22⅝" (46 cm. x 57.5 cm.)
The Metropolitan Museum of Art, Fletcher Fund, 1925

The 19th century white American painter usually portrayed the black man as a happy, singing, carefree stereotype. Even the most sympathetic portraits by an artist such as William Sidney Mount (1807-1868) reveal a patronizing attitude toward the subject. Eakins, with his insistent need for truthful representation about life, looked for those particular qualities in men, black and white, that revealed their individuality. One of America's important black artists, Henry O. Tanner (1859-1937), had been a pupil of Eakins at the Pennsylvania Academy. Eakins painted a very moving portrait of Tanner around 1900, in which he mirrored his friend's frustrations and deep personal struggles.

Nothing is known of the identities of the three persons represented in this watercolor. However, the wooden bench to the right, which appears in other pictures by Eakins, indicates that this scene may have been posed in the studio on Mt. Vernon Street. Its three protagonists symbolize three ages of man: childhood, early manhood, and old age. Both in the way the figures are posed and in their facial expressions, one can read different states of consciousness. The child with his chubby face and buoyant energy, dancing artlessly and intuitively to the rhythm of the banjo; the banjo player himself, seated easily and assuredly on the chair, bending rhythmically in time with his own music; the old man keeping time to that music with his foot and leaning on the chair, while he gazes down fondly at the child—they are all closely bound by strong cultural and personal ties. This is a mystical circle, a continuity of life which never ceases. Above them to the left, Eakins has included a small portrait of Abraham Lincoln and his son in an oval frame hanging on the wall. This is a gratuitous and hardly necessary element in the composition, although it is a visual reminder that the subjects of the picture are free men.

Again, Eakins worked from the large oil sketch toward the smaller, finished watercolor. The boy dancing and the banjo player seem quite independent from one another in feeling. Eakins may have observed and sketched them separately, joining the two together in a composition at a later time.

44

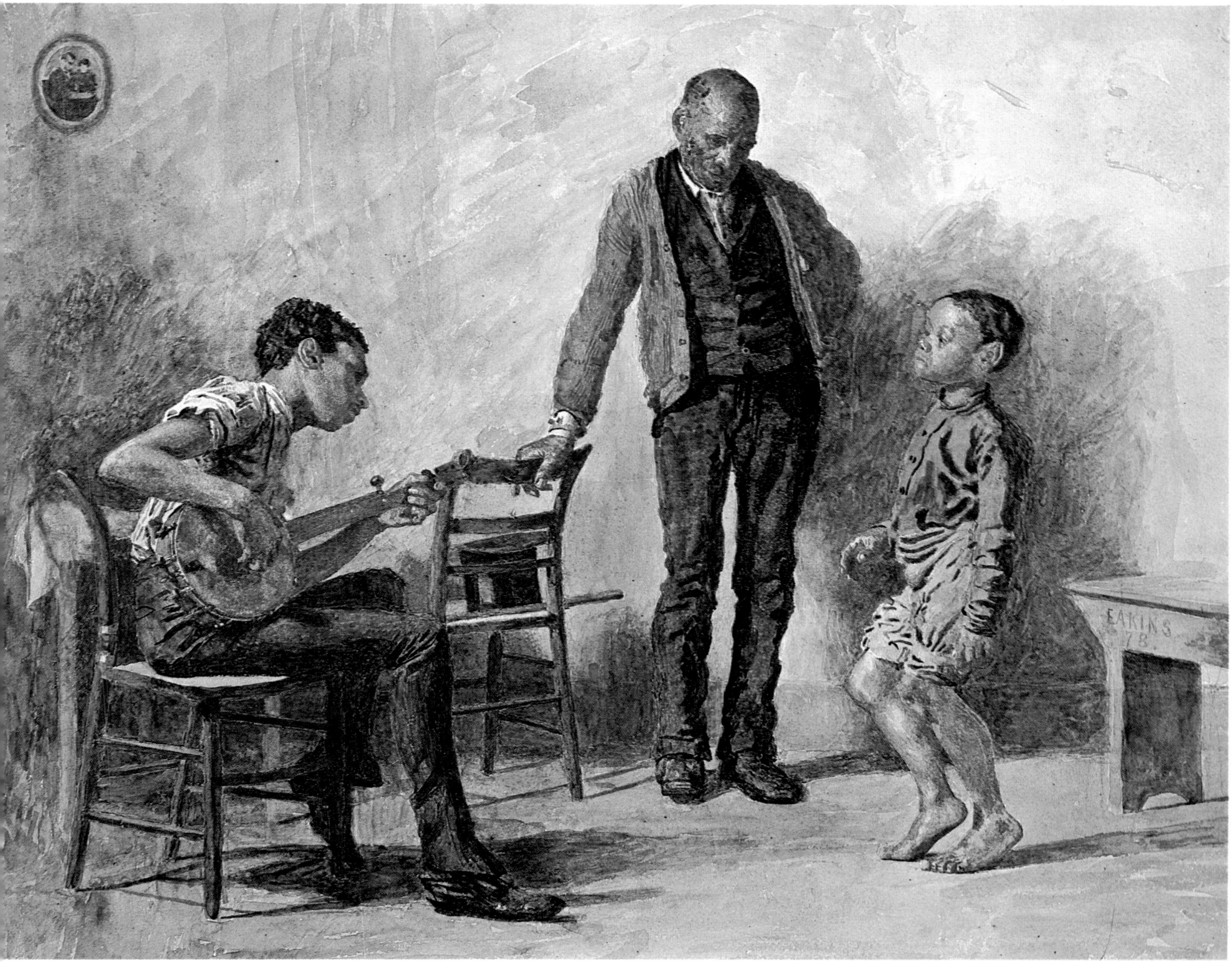
EAKINS
78.

Plate 13
BANJO PLAYER FROM NEGRO BOY DANCING
Detail of Plate 12, Actual Size

Figure 6. *The Banjo Player*, 1878, oil on canvas, 19″ x 14⅜″
(48.2 cm. x 36.5 cm.). Collection Mr. and Mrs. Paul Mellon.

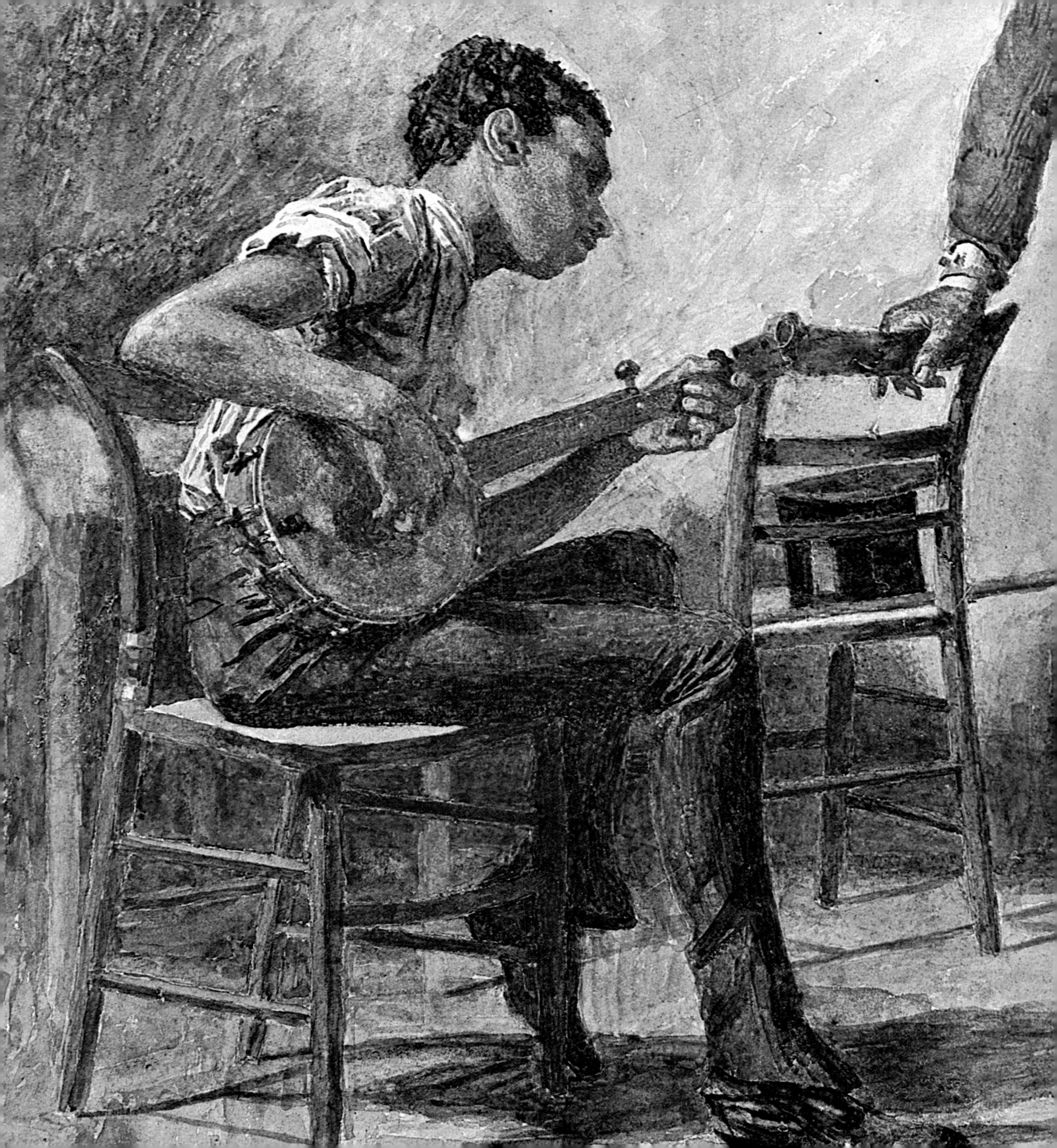

Plate 14
NEGRO BOY DANCING
Detail of Plate 12, Actual Size

Figure 7. *Study for Negro Boy Dancing*, 1878, oil on canvas, 21″ x 9″ (53.3 cm. x 22.8 cm.). Collection Mr. and Mrs. Paul Mellon.

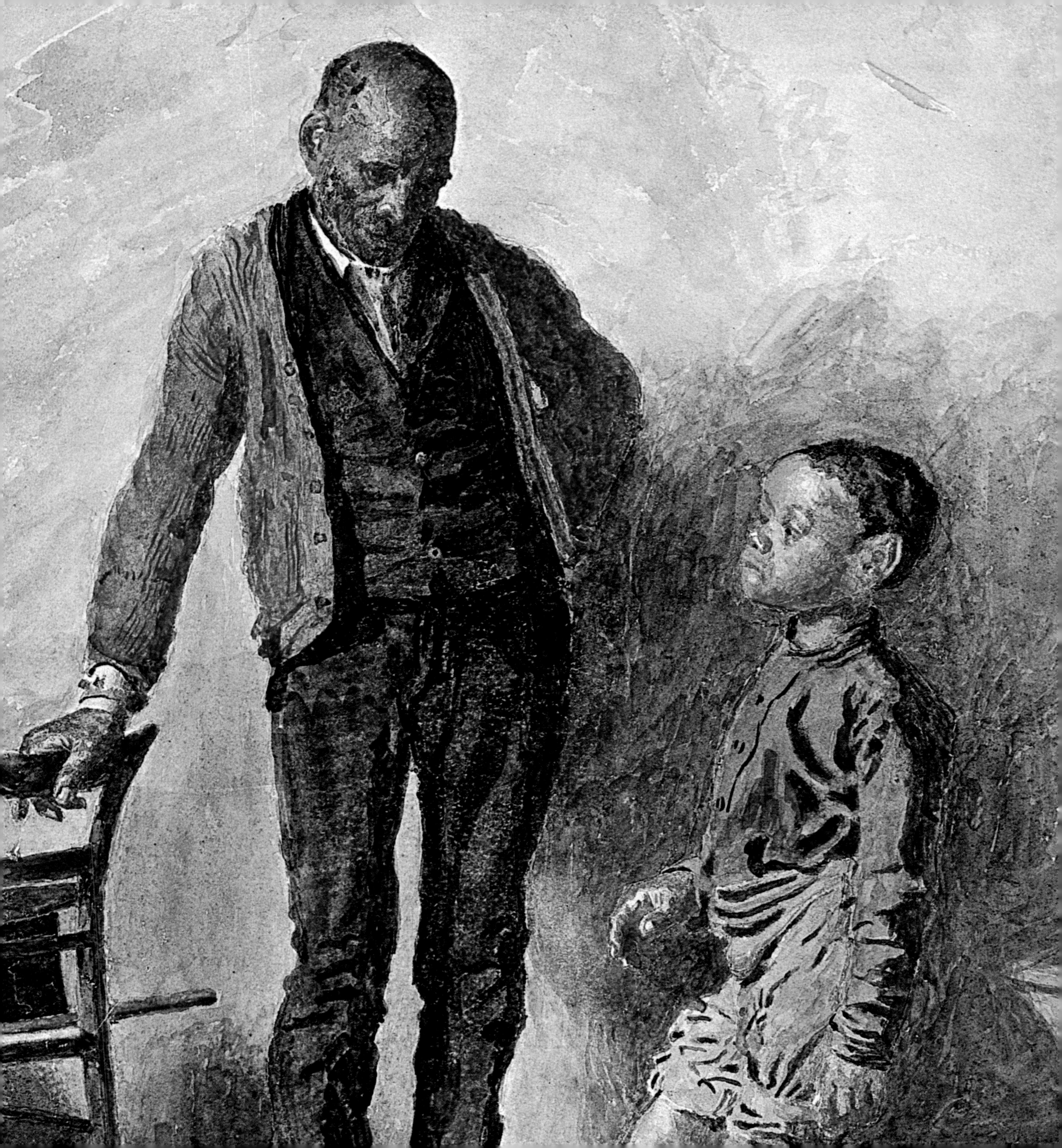

Plate 15
FEMALE NUDE
Early 1880's
17″ x 9″; image 11″ x 3½″ (43.2 x 22.8 cm.; image 27.9 x 8.9 cm.)
Philadelphia Museum of Art

As a student in Paris, Eakins had seen the exhibitions of the offi-cial Salon and observed how the French painters (so acclaimed by the public taste of the day) painted nudes. Probably in 1867, he wrote to his father: "I send by mail a catalog of the Exhibition of Fine Arts. The great painters don't care to exhibit there at all; about twenty pictures in the whole lot interest me. The rest of the pictures are of naked women, standing, sitting, lying down, flying, dancing, doing nothing, which they call Phrynes, Venuses, Nymphs, Hermaphrodites, Houris, and Greek proper names. The French court has become very decent since Eugénie had fig leaves put on all of the naked statues in the Garden of the Tuileries. When a man paints a naked woman he gives her less than poor Nature did. I can conceive of few circumstances wherein I would have to paint a woman naked, but if I did I would not mutilate her for double the money. She is the most beautiful thing there is—except a naked man, but I never yet saw a study of one exhibited. It would be a godsend to see a fine man painted in the studio with bare walls, alongside the smiling, smirking goddesses of many complexions, amidst the delicious arsenic green trees and gentle wax flowers and pearling streams a'running up and down the hills, especially up: I hate affecta-tion."

His hatred of affectation extended into his art long after his student days were over. When he returned to the Pennsylvania Academy in Philadelphia in 1876, this time to teach, Eakins gave greater emphasis to figure painting than had ever been known at the Academy before his time. But outside the studio classes, there were few "circumstances" in which Eakins could paint the nude human figure. A year later, in 1877, Eakins invented such a circumstance in *William Rush Carving His Allegorical Figure of the Schuylkill River*. The painting is an elaborate theatrical setting for the nude figure, although the picture does not repre-sent a historical fact. William Rush actually carved from a clothed figure, but Eakins invented the situation in order to provide an excuse for painting a nude. And excuses were neces-sary if he were to exhibit the painting publicly, for the public had been conditioned to accept the idea of the nude in painting only when it was disguised in the form of allegory or mythol-ogy. The idea of representing a realistic nude—a palpable, objec-tive statement of the truth—would have earned Eakins the same

Figure 8. *Study for Female Nude*, 1882, oil on canvas, 24¼″ x 14½″ (61.6 cm. x 36.8 cm.). Collection Mrs. and Mrs. C. Hum-bert Tinsman.

Unfinished Water Color
T. Eakins

Plate 16
FEMALE NUDE
Detail of Plate 15, Actual Size

kind of hostility as he received for his realistic statement of a surgical operation in *The Gross Clinic*.

There are at least three studies in oil for *Female Nude*, one of them illustrated in Figure 8. The figure has the same general posture as the nude in the William Rush subject, but the quality of the raking light, which comes from directly above the figure, is different. These studies suggest a studio pose, and are much more objective, tending toward a literal statement in contrast with the more idealized one found in the William Rush painting.

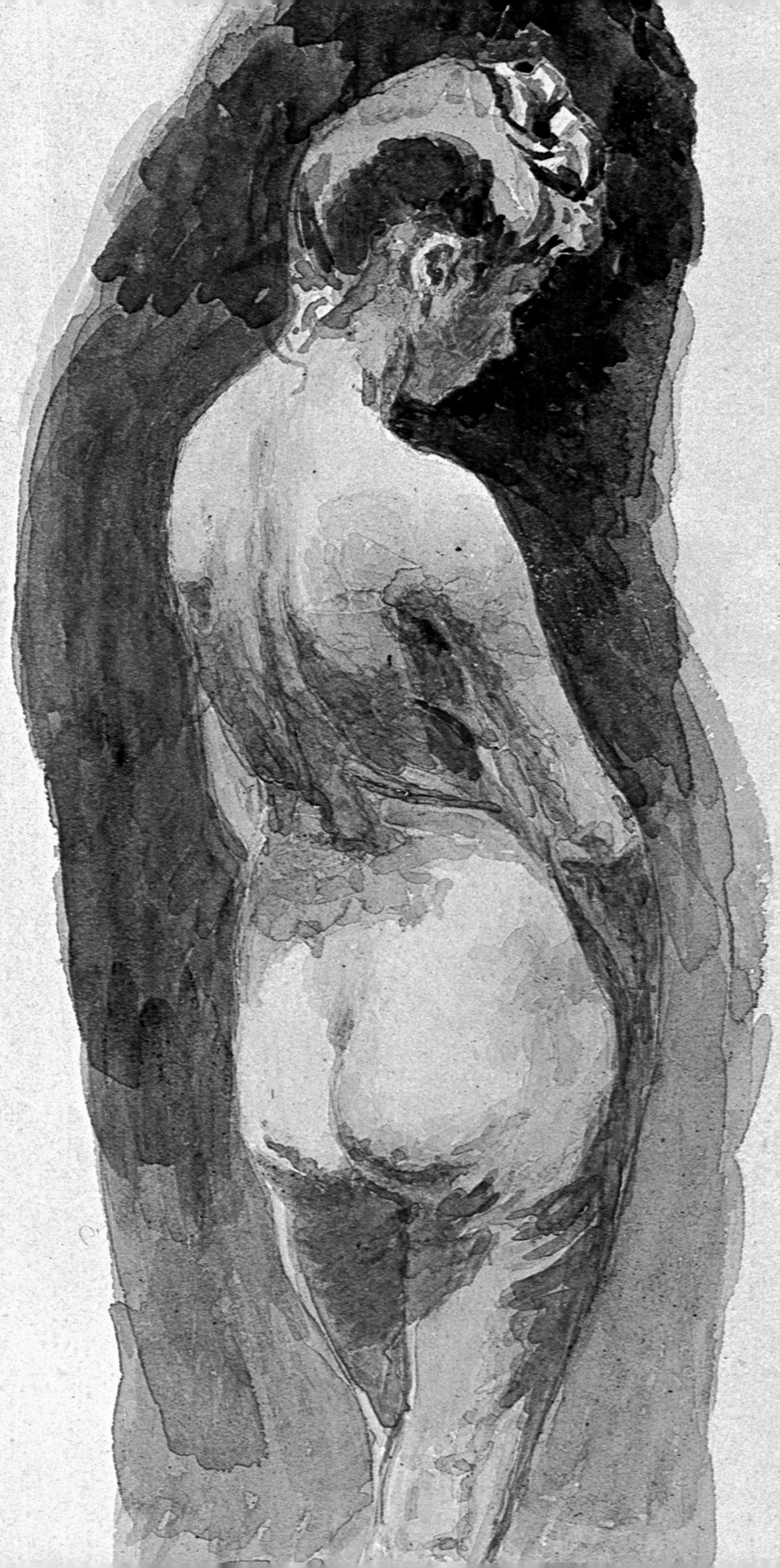

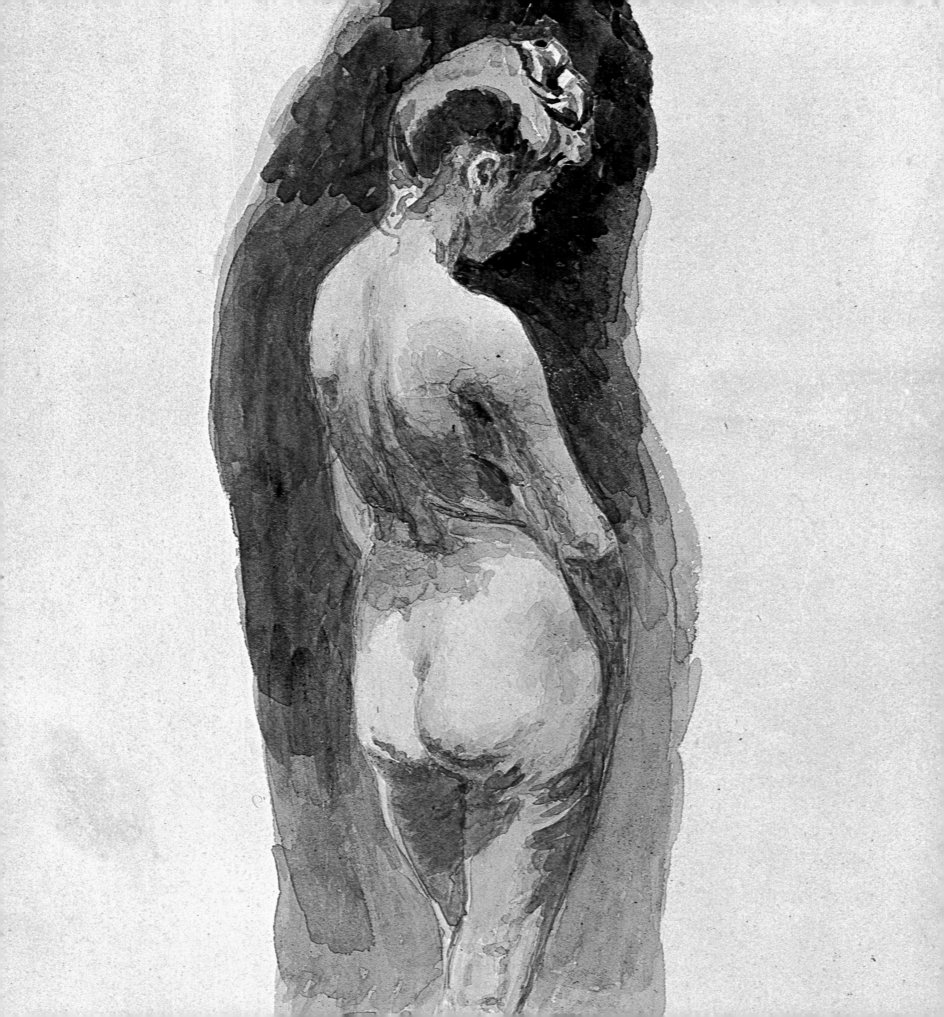

Plate 17
RETROSPECTION
ca. 1880
14⅝" x 10⅝" (37.1 cm. x 27 cm.)
Philadelphia Museum of Art

The subject of this study is known only as Mrs. Perkins, and the circumstances of the picture are unknown. The composition is one of Eakins' most somber; the subject is shown in a mood of dejection, with folded hands, head slightly bowed, and the face in shadow. Eakins has dressed the subject in an Empire gown and posed her in the same 18th century Chippendale that he used for *Seventy Years Ago* (Plate 10). It is another example of Eakins' interest in the past, and an attempt to make a statement about his feelings of nostalgia for that time. About 1885, a year after he married Susan Macdowell, he painted her in nearly an identical pose; except for minor details, the 1885 portrait is a reworking of the *Retrospection* theme.

This watercolor version of *Retrospection* was painted after the oil (Figure 9). The canvas and the paper are nearly identical in size, but Eakins has reduced the figure in the watercolor. The relationship of the figure to the area of the composition seems more comfortable in the oil. Note the discrepancies in the technique used in the watercolor, particularly in the background, where broad washes are employed on the left, while on the right the color appears to have been applied with mechanical, horizontal strokes. The general effect of dark interior space, too, appears to be more suitable to the oil technique. The treatment of the figure especially seems to have been a problem for Eakins. In the watercolor, only the details which are modeled from light to dark are realized with any degree of success. Eakins seems to have concentrated on the side of the girl's head, the folds of the puffed sleeves, and the shell motif on the cresting rail of the chair. Having done with the most interesting details, perhaps Eakins realized that he had reduced the size of the figure too much, and that it no longer related satisfactorily to the composition he originally intended.

Figure 9. *Retrospection*, 1880, oil on canvas, 14½" x 10⅛" (36.8 cm. x 25.7 cm.). Yale University Art Gallery.

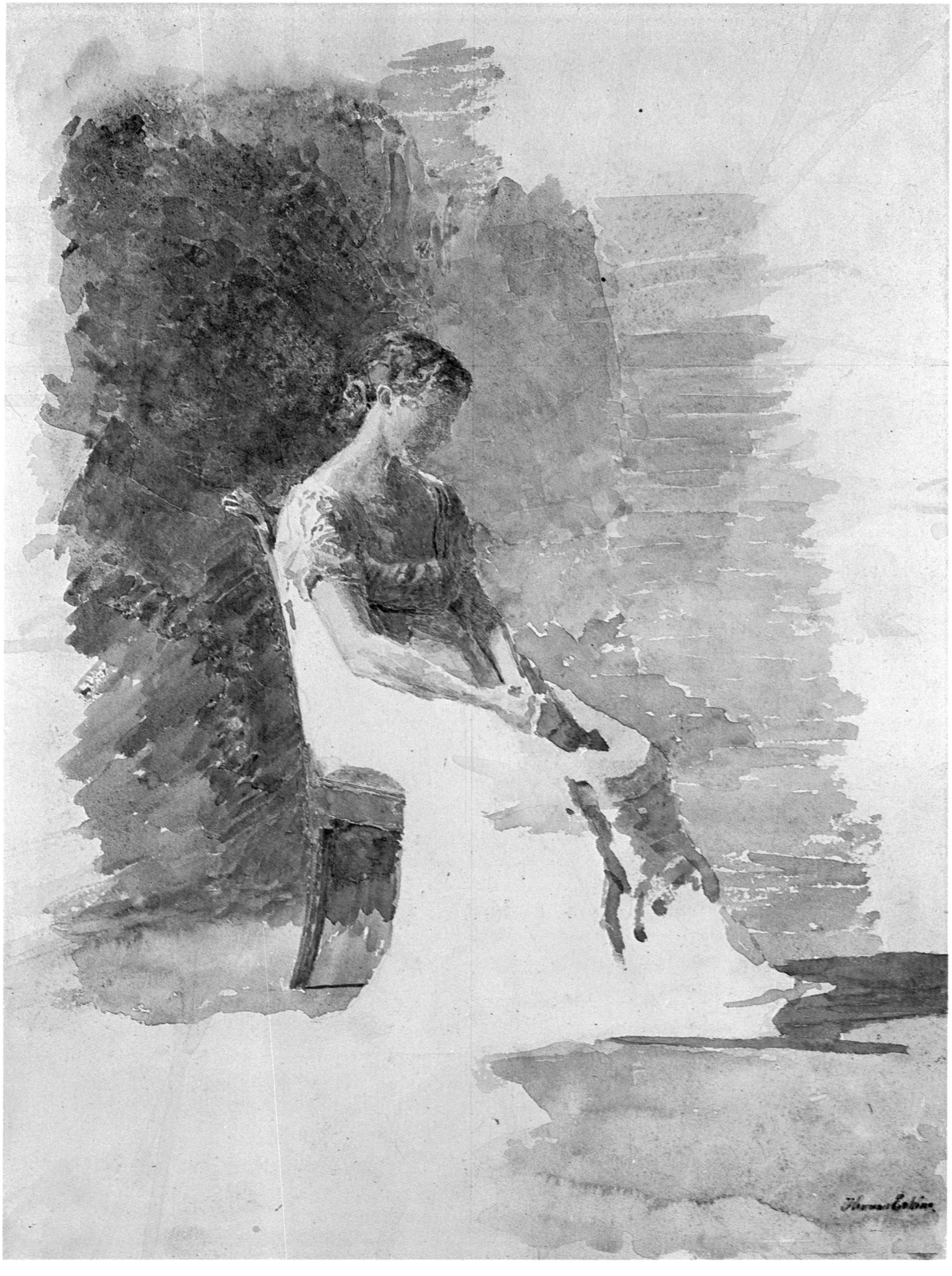
Thomas Eakins

Plate 18
RETROSPECTION
Detail of Plate 17, Actual Size

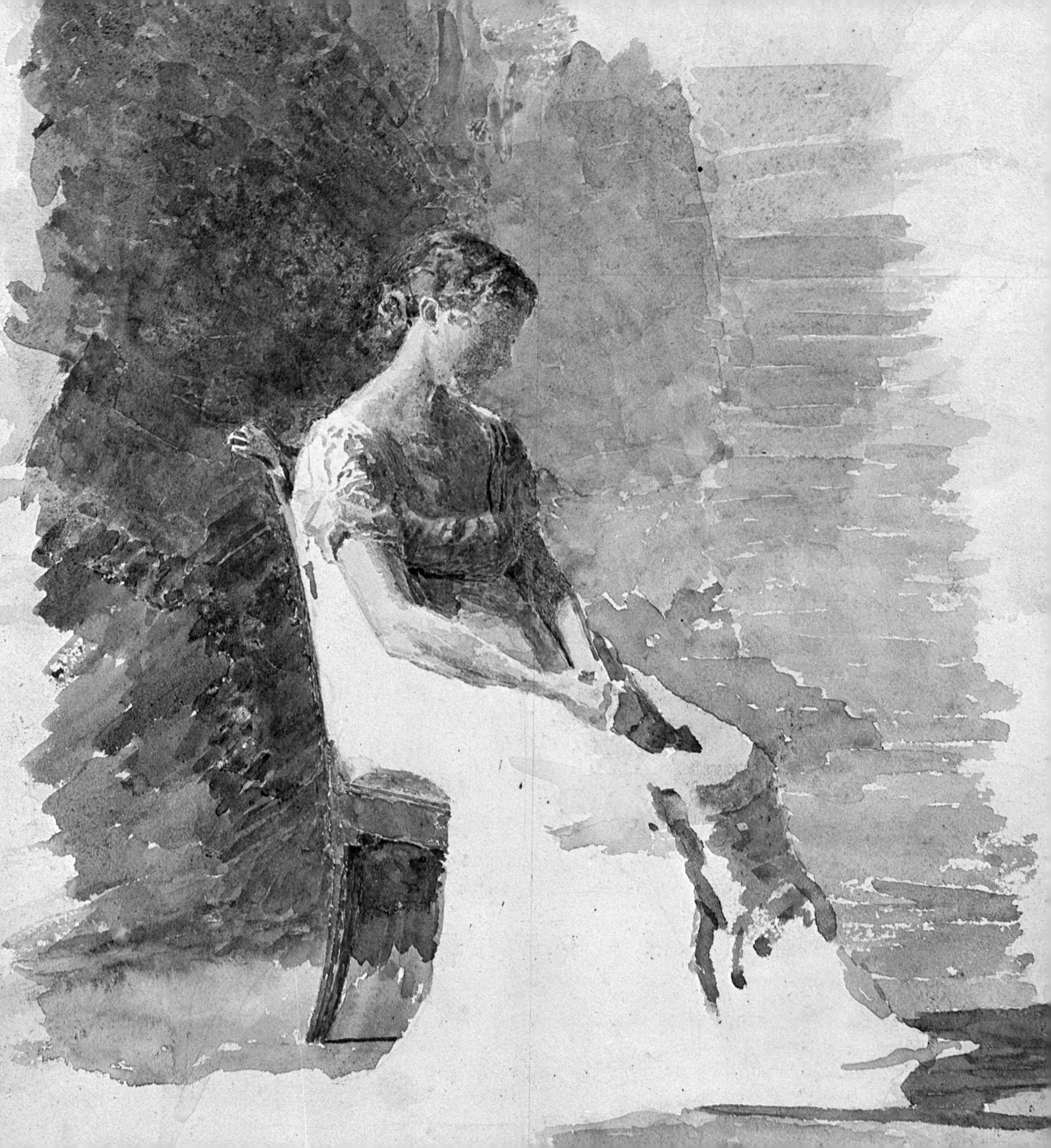

Plate 19
SPINNING
1881
14″ x 10⅞″ (35.5 cm. x 27.6 cm.)
The Metropolitan Museum of Art, Fletcher Fund, 1925

When Eakins returned from Paris in the spring of 1870, his happiness at the reunion with his family was evident in the number of portraits he painted of them. With the exception of *Max Schmitt in a Single Scull* and one imaginary subject, his family was the exclusive source of his inspiration until 1872. Of his three sisters—Frances, Margaret, and Caroline—the favorite was his middle sister, Margaret, who appears in *Spinning*. She frequently posed for him until her untimely death in 1882, a year after the creation of this watercolor. Two of Eakins' most affecting and accomplished genre scenes, *At The Piano* (University Art Museum, University of Texas) and *Home Scene* (The Brooklyn Museum), center on portraits of Margaret, seated or standing by the piano in the family parlor on Mt. Vernon Street. They are sympathetic but forthright portraits, describing her not too pretty, flat face with feeling and power.

The period of the mid-70's was one of enormous productive activity for Eakins. He spent it largely outside his Mt. Vernon Street studio, painting scenes of rowing on the rivers, shooting birds in the New Jersey marshes, and racing sailboats on the Delaware River. The chronology suggests that Eakins tended to return to interior scenes after the unpleasant incident with *The Gross Clinic*. Between 1876 and 1881, he painted only

two landscapes and one other outdoor scene, *The Fairman Rogers Four-in-Hand*. The balance of his work was made up of portraiture and figure studies representing his nostalgic interest in the past. Also from this troubled period of his life came *The Crucifixion* (Philadelphia Museum of Art), painted a year after the death of his fiancée, Katherine Crowell. But by 1881, the date of *Spinning*, Eakins had met his future wife, Susan Macdowell, and his mood was changing.

This watercolor was the first subject that Eakins painted following the completion of *The Crucifixion*. Margaret posed for him in the same Empire gown he used in painting *Retrospection* (Plate 11). The setting is deliberately antiquarian; in the background, an open cabinet displays various objects, including a monteith and a shelf containing Canton ware. Margaret works at the same spinning wheel that appeared in *Seventy Years Ago* (Plate 10), seated on a turned wooden stool painted a bright viridian green. As her foot works the treadle of the spinning wheel, Eakins has represented the wheel in motion, its spokes blurred. The focal point of the composition seems to be Margaret's head, especially her ear, which is seen to glow as the light strikes it and partially passes through. The strong pattern of light and shadow clearly defines the direction of the light.

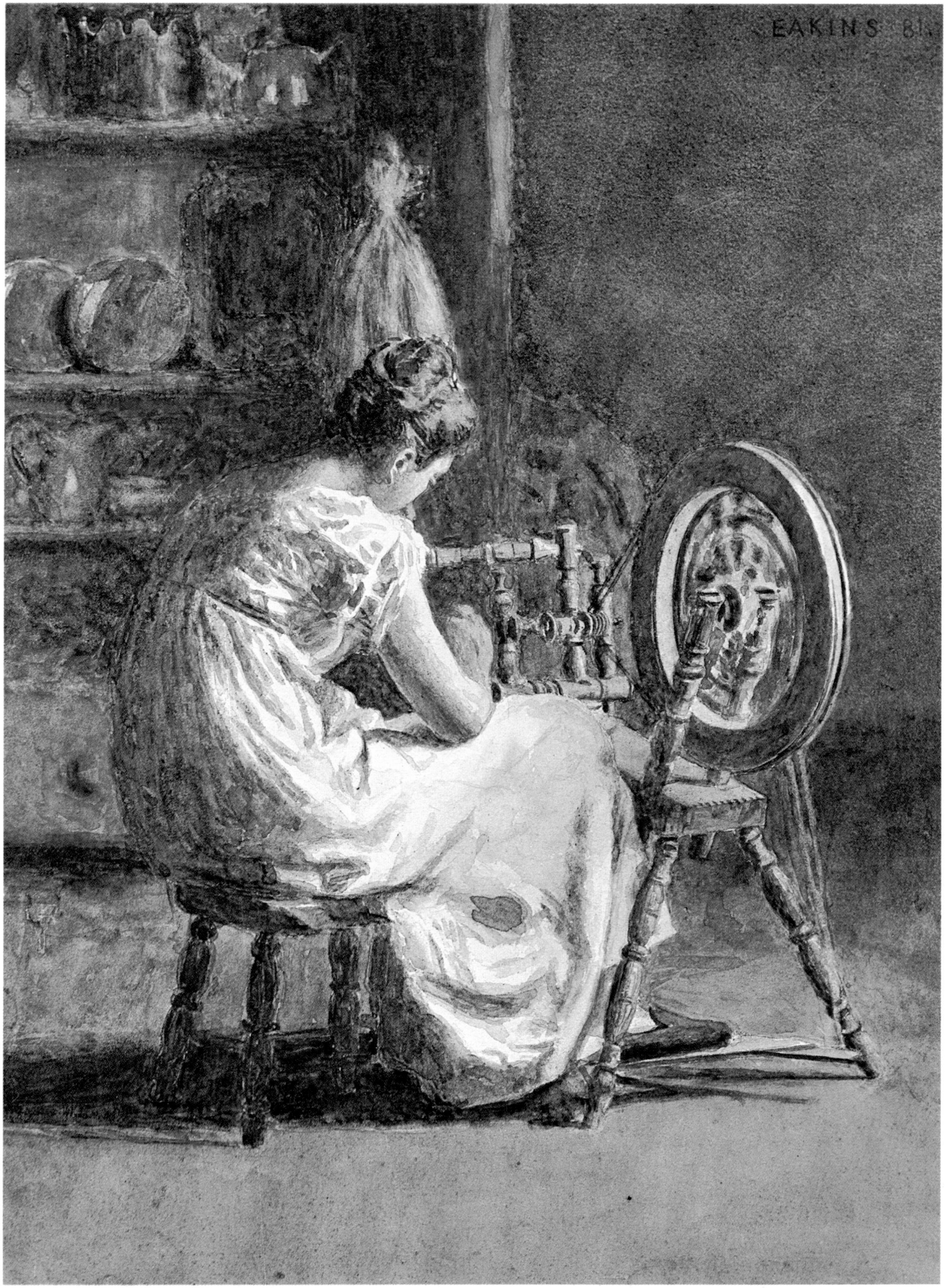
EAKINS 81

Plate 20
SPINNING
Detail of Plate 19, Actual Size

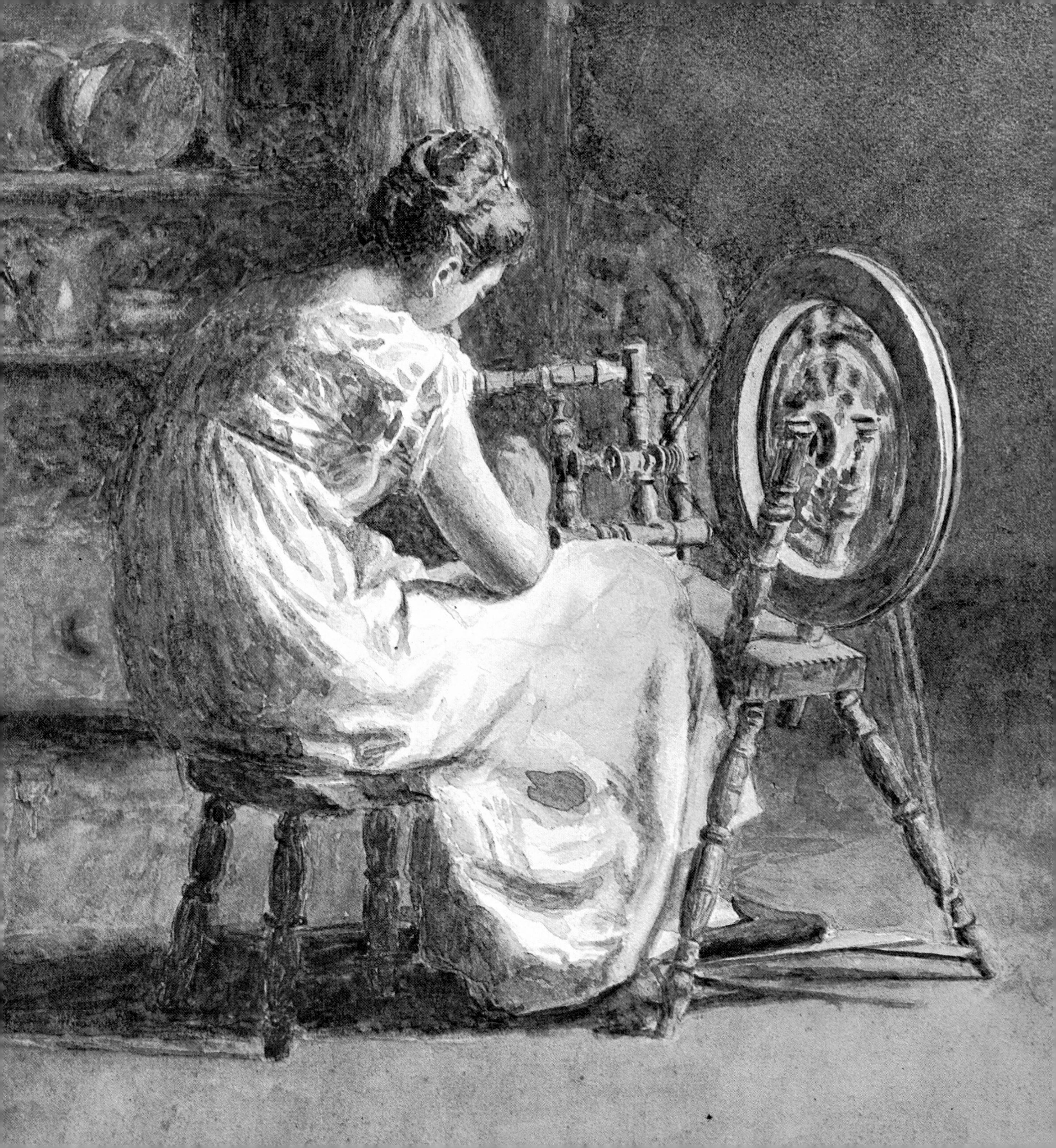

Plate 21
SPINNING
1881
11″ x 8″ (27.9 cm. x 20.3 cm.)
Collection Mrs. John Randolph Garrett, Sr.

This watercolor, a variation of the preceding plate and painted the same year, may have been created shortly before or after the other example.

Eakins thought out his various compositions in sculptural terms to understand more fully the volume of any given subject. In fact, the spinning subject was intended to be a bas-relief plaque. In 1882, he was commissioned by a Philadelphia art patron, James P. Scott, to provide designs for two mantelpiece sculptures. These were to be two small, oval reliefs. One was similar in subject matter to the watercolor, *Seventy Years Ago* (Plate 10), and the second was taken from the spinning theme. Goodrich records that the architect for the house persuaded Eakins to undertake the commission; Eakins remarked that the architect "easily induced me, for the work was much to my taste." Eakins apparently had Margaret take spinning lessons in order to assure the accuracy of the picture. Evidently, Margaret's ability with the spinning wheel increased perceptibly as the pose went on. Eakins remarked in a letter to Scott: "After I had worked some weeks, the girl in learning to spin well became so much more graceful than when she had learned to spin only passably, that I tore down all my work and recommenced." Eakins had obviously translated the watercolor studies into clay. By observing Margaret in two distinctly different positions in the two watercolors, Eakins established a thorough understanding of the plasticity of form involved.

The clay models for the plaques were submitted to Scott for his approval. Eakins wrote a letter to accompany them: "Relief work . . . has always been considered the most difficult composition and the one requiring the most learning. The mere geometrical construction of the accessories in a perspective which is not projected on a single plane but in a variable third dimension is a puzzle beyond the sculptors whom I know."

There was a disagreement over the project, and the bas-relief plaques were never translated into stone, as had been envisioned.

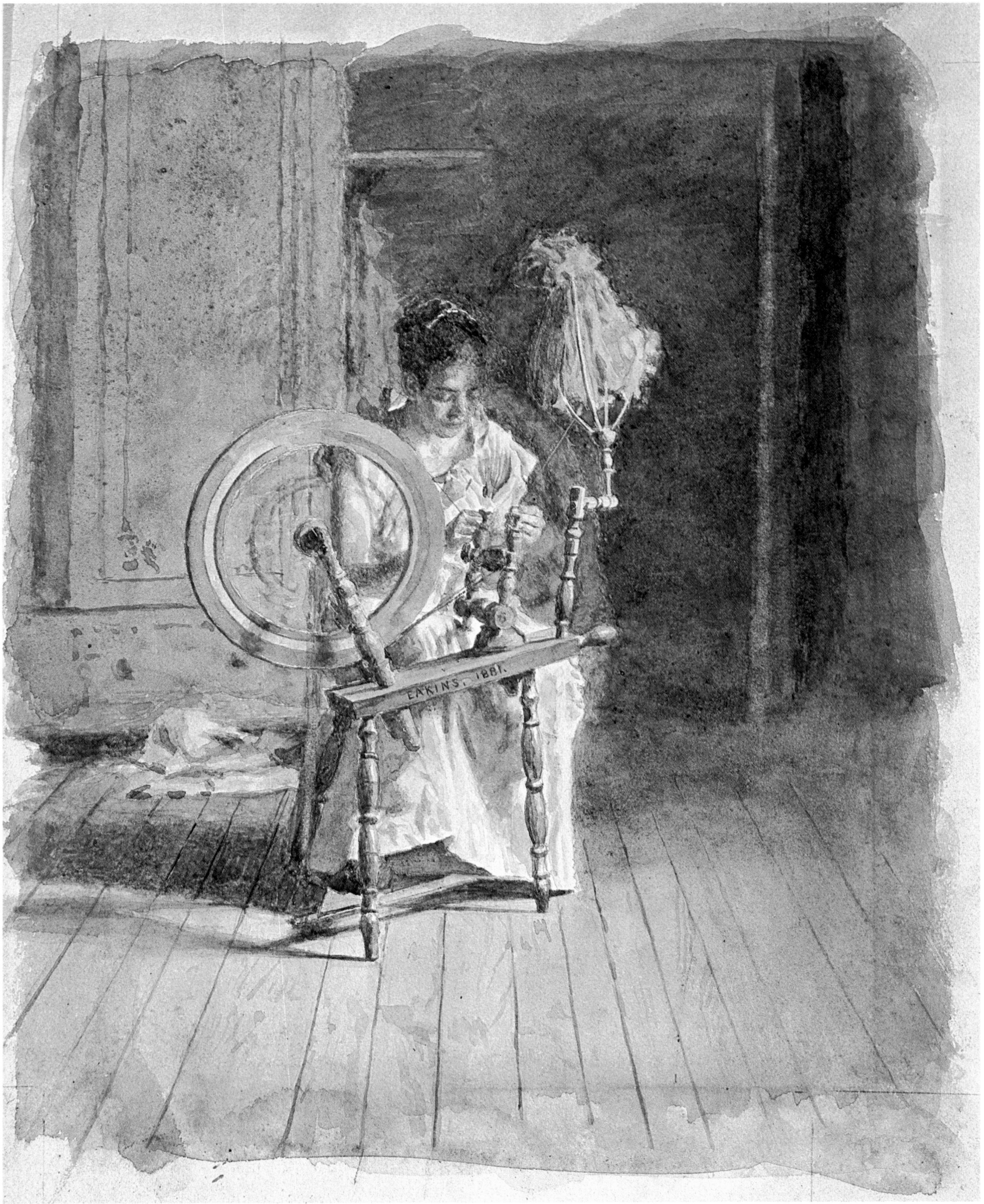
EAKINS. 1881.

Plate 22
TAKING UP THE NET
1881
9½″ x 14⅛″ (24.1 cm. x 25.9 cm.)
The Metropolitan Museum of Art, Fletcher Fund, 1925

In the 19th century, shad were plentiful in the Delaware River. In the spring of each year, as the fish returned to their spawning grounds, commercial fishermen would cast their nets. During the spring of 1882, Eakins went to Gloucester, a small town on the New Jersey side of the Delaware river, to watch the operations. This was a family outing, for *Shad Fishing at Gloucester on the Delaware River* (Figure 10) shows the artist's father, Benjamin Eakins, as well as one sister and the family dog, Harry.

In the watercolor version, *Taking Up the Net*, the composition is narrowed to focus on the scene of the fishermen in their blue denim work shirts and colorful yellow oilskins. The watercolor strongly suggests that Eakins based this work on a photograph, rather than on actual observation of the scene itself. The poses of the fishermen are frozen in attitude, indicative of the camera's instant recording of a scene.

Figure 10. *Shad Fishing at Gloucester on the Delaware*, 1881, oil on canvas, 12½″ x 18¼″ (31.7 cm. x 46.3 cm.). Philadelphia Museum of Art.

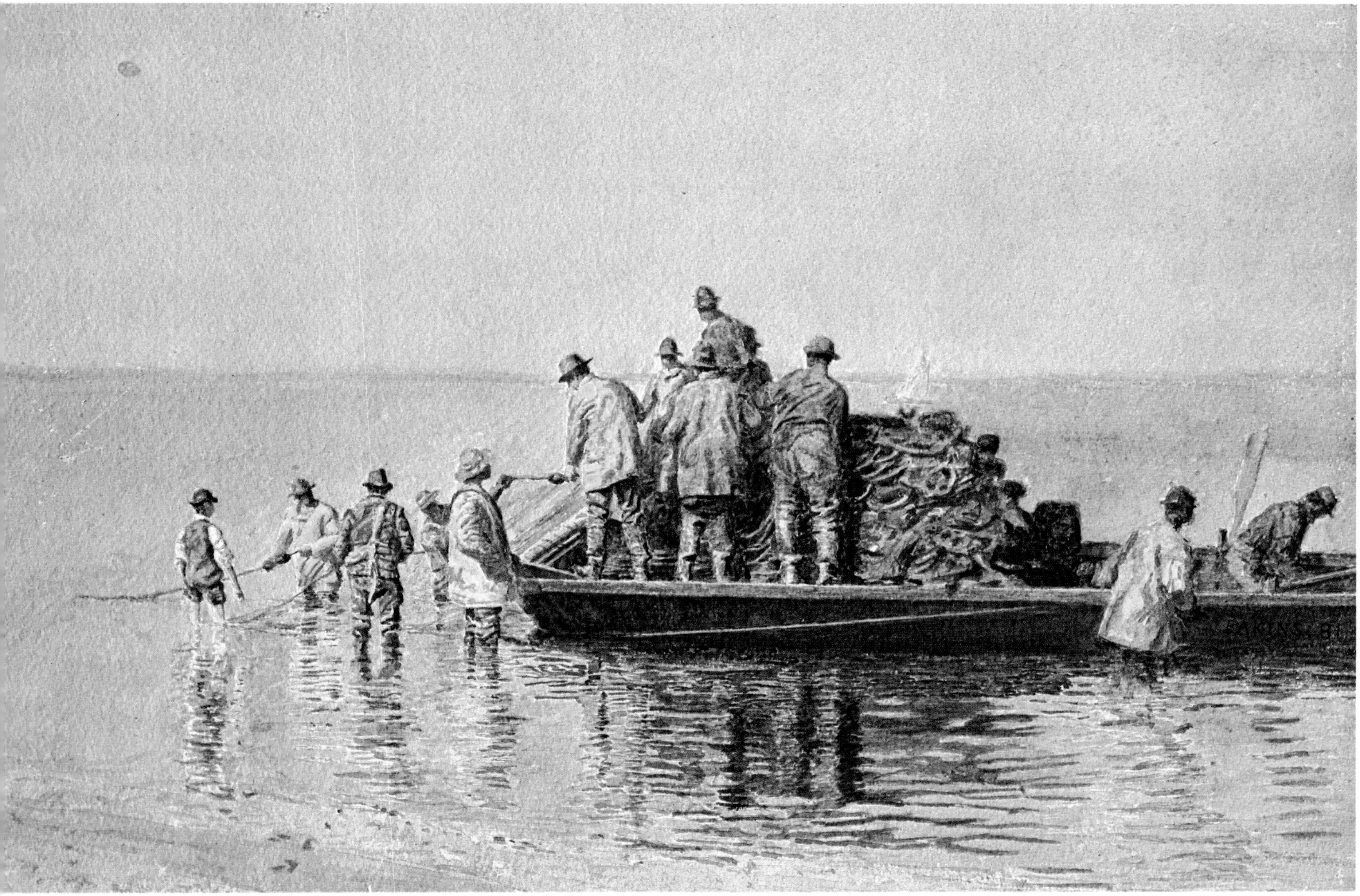
EAKINS 81

Plate 23
TAKING UP THE NET
Detail of Plate 22, Actual Size

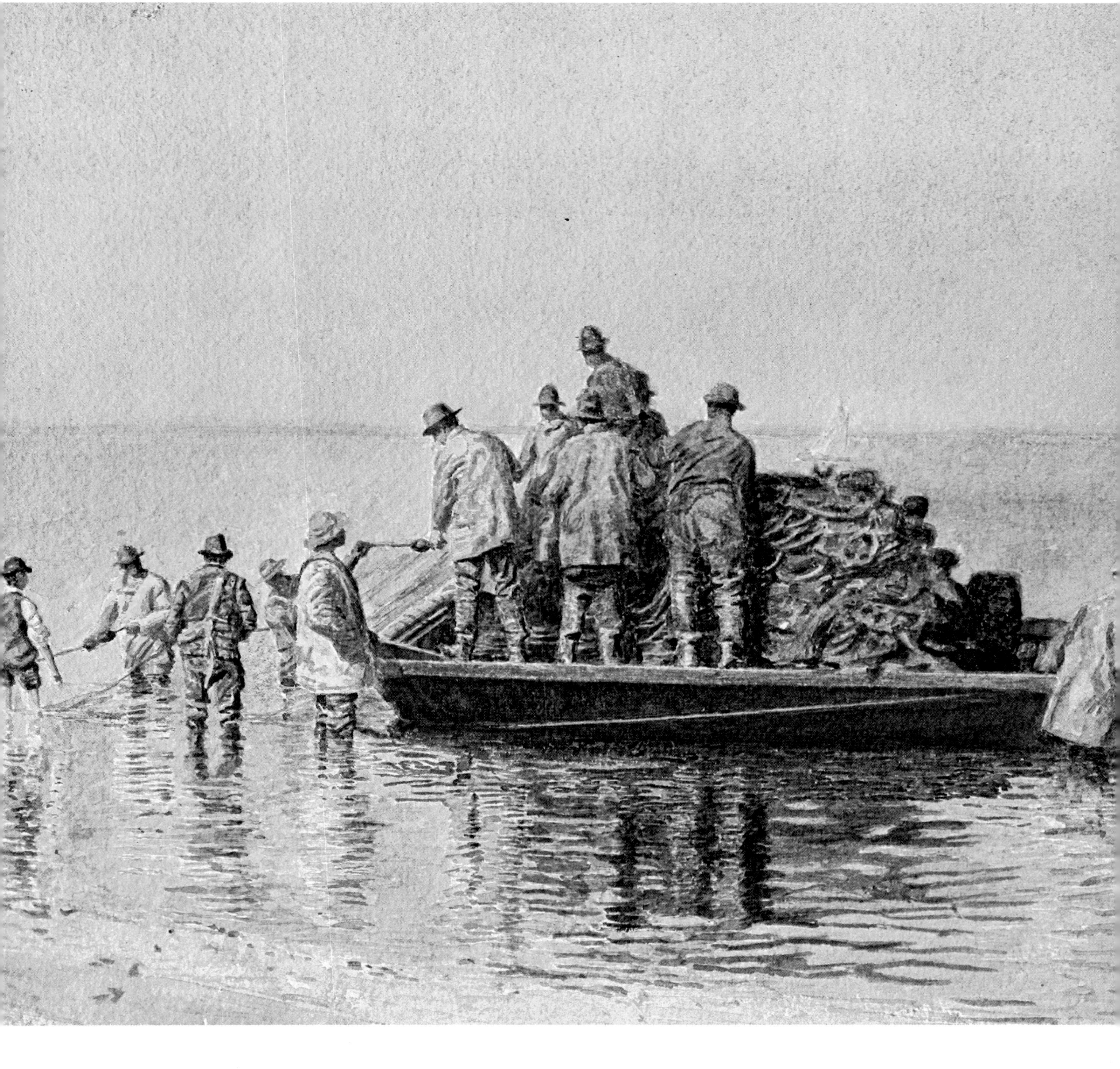

Plate 24
THE PATHETIC SONG
ca. 1881
15″ x 12″ (38.1 cm. x 30.4 cm.)
Hirschl and Adler Galleries

Eakins had been working up to the creation of this, his most successful genre painting, through that whole series of nostalgic backward looks that included *Seventy Years Ago* (Plate 10) and the *Spinning* subjects (Plates 19 and 21). *The Pathetic Song* is a culmination of all his ideas concerning the beauty and expressiveness of women in interiors. Although Eakins has distilled the essence of an affecting moment, he deals with time at hand, not the past. Again, as in so many of his pictures, he has selected a particular moment and has rendered it precisely. Eakins was fascinated by the movement of muscles in a singer's throat (eleven years later, he returned to this same subject in *The Concert Singer*) and has chosen a moment in the music when the singer has reached a sustained note, perhaps the concluding chord of the song. As she holds the note, her hands lower the score and she fixes her gaze sadly across the room. Her accompanists, the cellist and the pianist, sustain the note also, and the song comes to an end.

The principal subject in this picture was Margaret Alexina Harrison, then thirty years old and a pupil of Thomas Eakins at the Academy; her two brothers were the painters, Alexander Harrison (1853-1930) and Birge Harrison (1854-1929). The elderly man playing the cello was a Mr. Stolte, a member of the Philadelphia Orchestra. (Fifteen years later, Eakins made the subject of a man playing a cello one of his most famous works.) The woman at the piano was Susan Macdowell, then a student at the Academy under Eakins. They had met for the first time at the Haseltine Galleries in Philadelphia, where *The Gross Clinic* had been exhibited. Susan was exactly the age of Eakins' dead fiancée, and her appearance in one of Eakins' most important pictures at this time probably indicates that their romance had already begun. Three years later, in 1884, Eakins married Susan Macdowell.

Figure 11. *The Pathetic Song*, 1881, oil on canvas, 45½″ x 32½″ (115.5 cm. x 82.5 cm.). The Corcoran Gallery of Art.

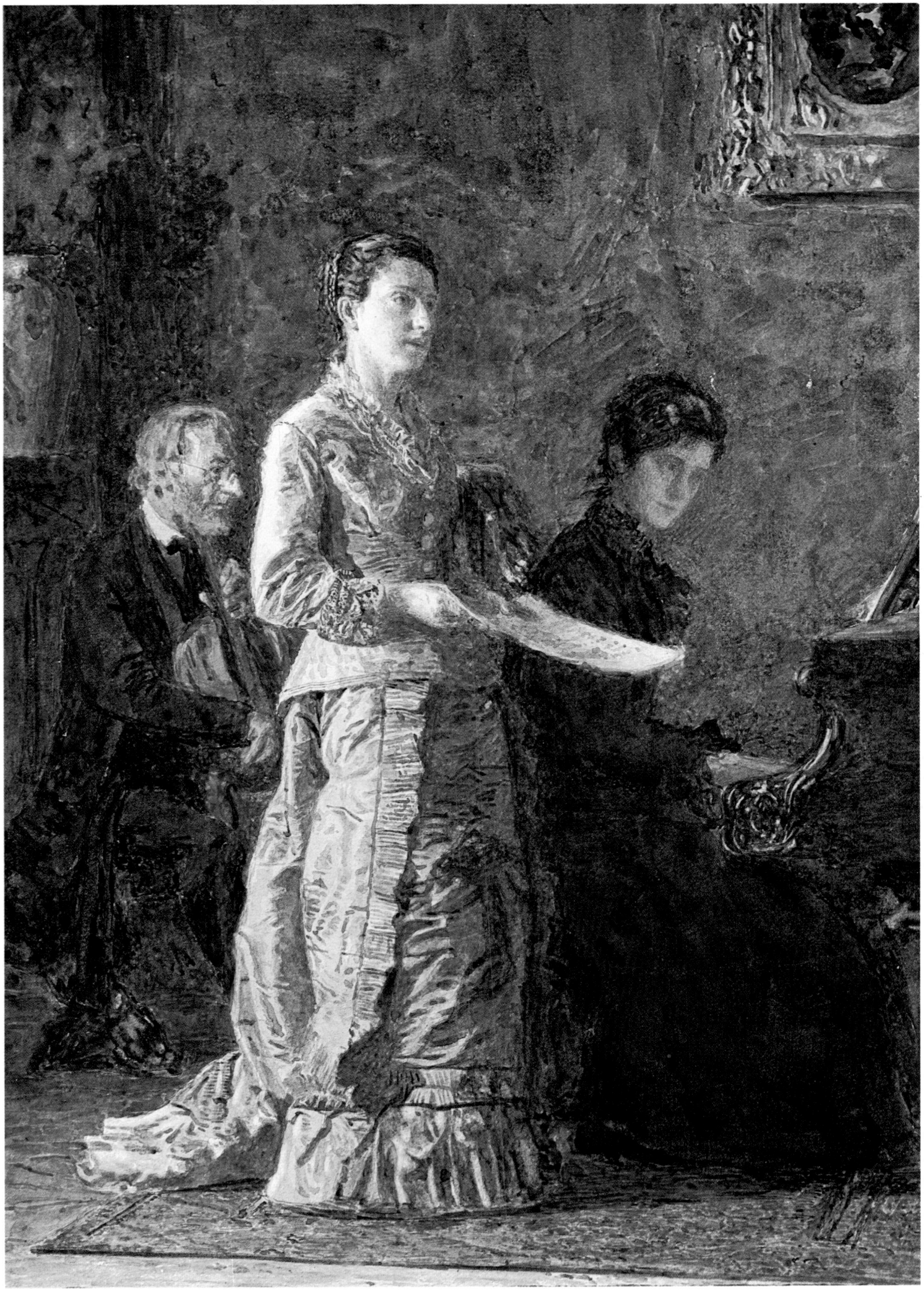

Plate 25
THE PATHETIC SONG
Detail of Plate 24, Actual Size

The watercolor version of *The Pathetic Song* was made after the oil painting (Figure 11) which Eakins gave to the principal subject, Margaret Harrison, in appreciation for her posing. While the watercolor is exactly one third the size of the oil painting, Eakins has rendered the details of the singer's dress with an undiminished power of observation. That grave and elusive color—an undefinable grayish lavender—is preserved, as is the intricately worked detail of the oriental rug in perspective on the floor. He has preserved the luminous skin tones and rendered the luminous, translucent folds of the ear with extreme care. He makes no attempt to represent the mottled effect of the wallpaper, with its sunflower motif, but simply indicates the background with umber washes. The supporting characters in the scene also receive a more cursory treatment. However, his portrait of Susan is milder and more serene in the watercolor.

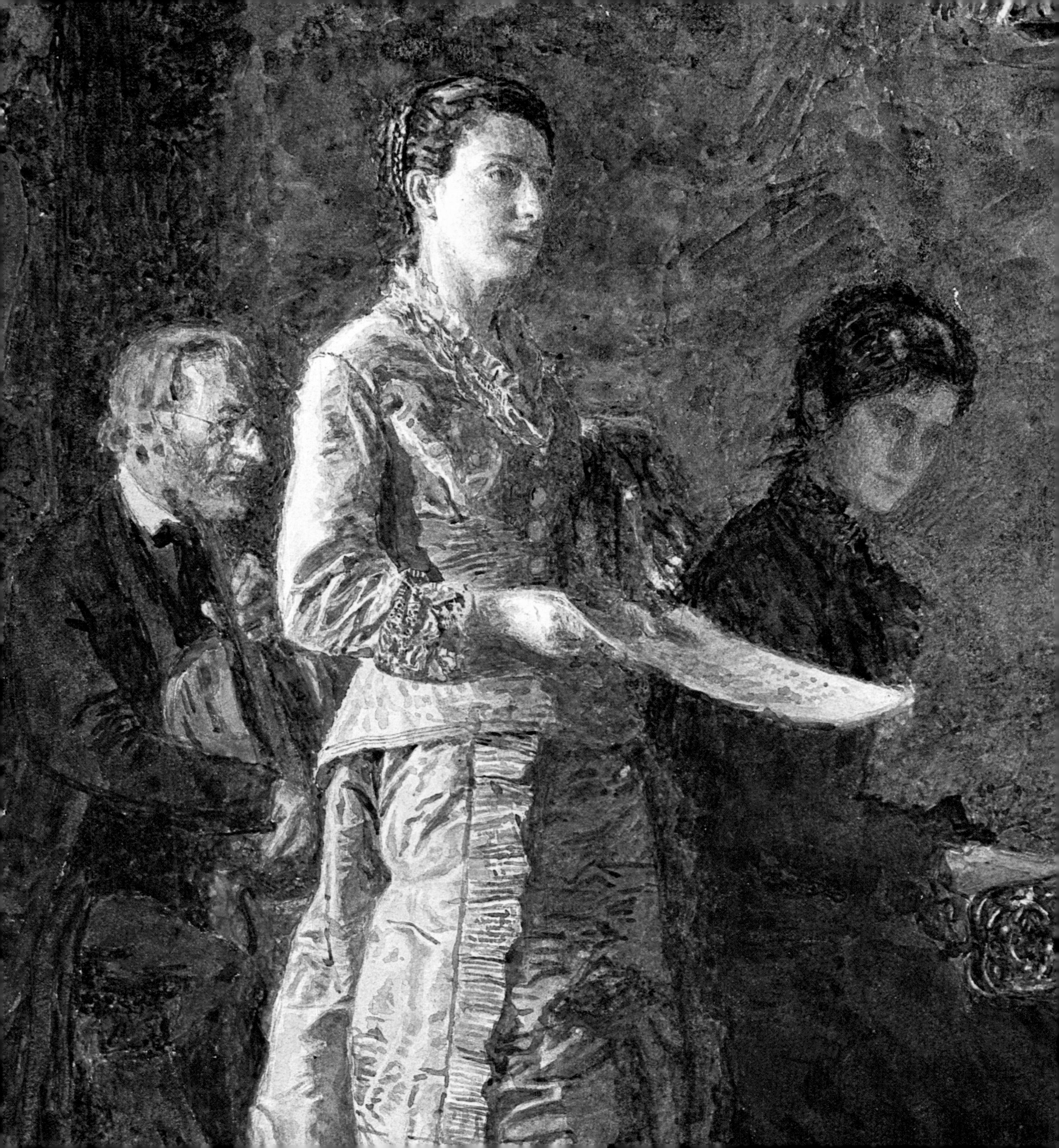

Plate 26
MENDING THE NET
1882
10¾″ x 16½″ (27.3 cm. x 41.9 cm.)
Collection Mrs. George E. Buchanan

The scene is a bank of the river at Gloucester, New Jersey, sometime during the spring of 1882. A fisherman is inspecting his net and mending the tears, while a friend looks on. They are in a plowed field on the banks of the Delaware, ideal for inspecting a large area of net. The time of day is noon, with the sun directly overhead, casting dramatic shadows. The sense of aloneness in nature is intensified by the scale of the figures in relation to their surrounding landscape. Once more, Eakins has worked in an almost miniaturist style, carefully delineating all the folds of the men's clothing. The standing figure is related in attitude to the oil, *Mending the Net* (Philadelphia Museum of Art), of the same year, in which Eakins has posed figures of men bending over their nets with their faces hidden from view.

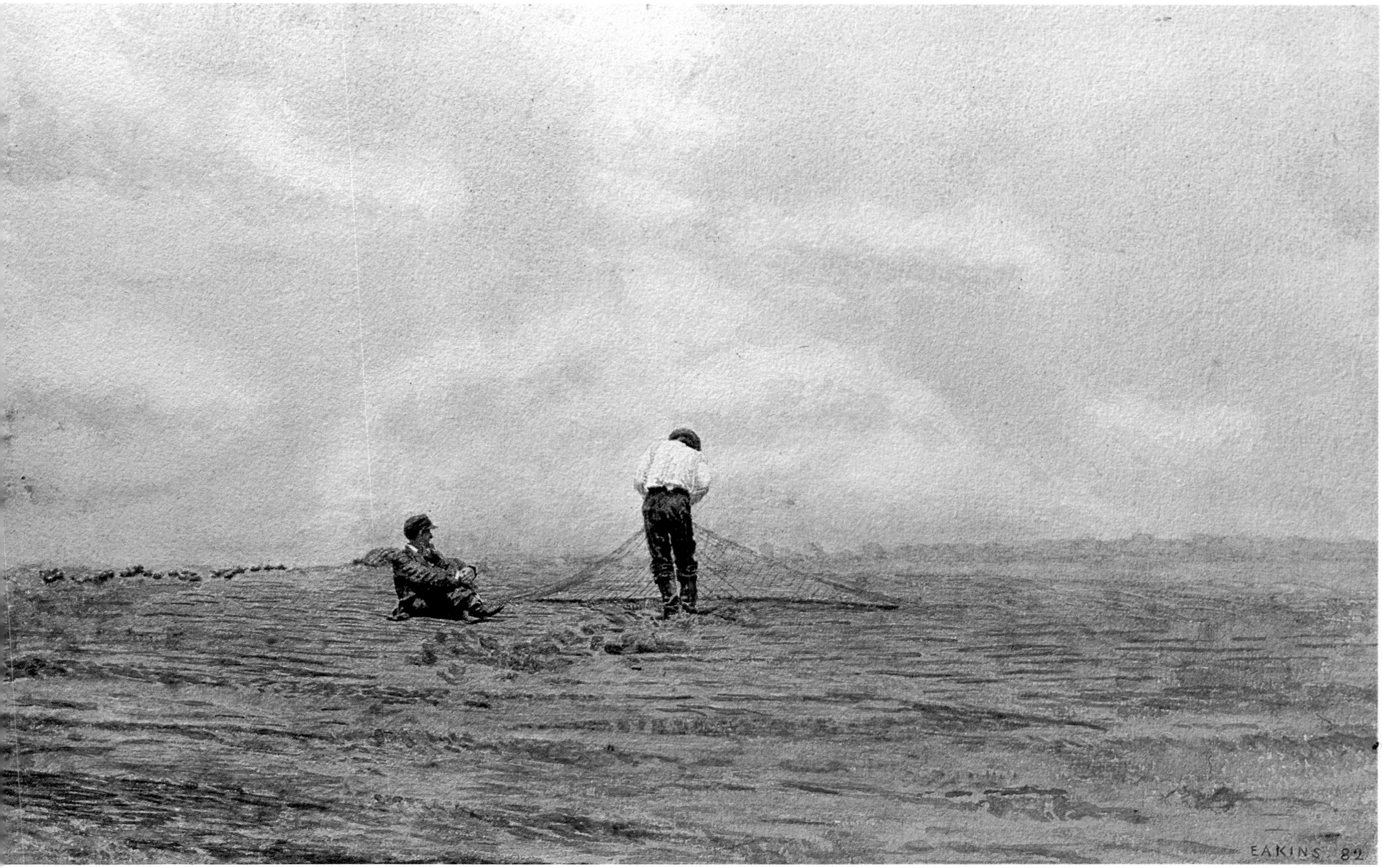
EAKINS 82

Plate 27
DRAWING THE SEINE
1882
8″ x 11″ (20.3 cm. x 27.9 cm.)
Philadelphia Museum of Art, John G. Johnson Collection

In *Drawing the Seine*, a smaller paper than *Mending the Net* (Plate 26), Eakins achieved a more pleasingly fluid style of painting. There is an easy handling of sky passages and peripheral detail, such as the sailboat at anchor in the river and the fishing shed to the left of the composition. This landscape, also at Gloucester, New Jersey, shows a seine being drawn from the river with a capstan turned by the fishermen with the aid of a horse. Eakins has employed a noticeably selective system of focus. The eye is led into the composition from the lower right, along the line of logs to the middle distance. However, the focus does not become sharp until halfway to that middle distance. Only the center of the composition remains consistently in focus.

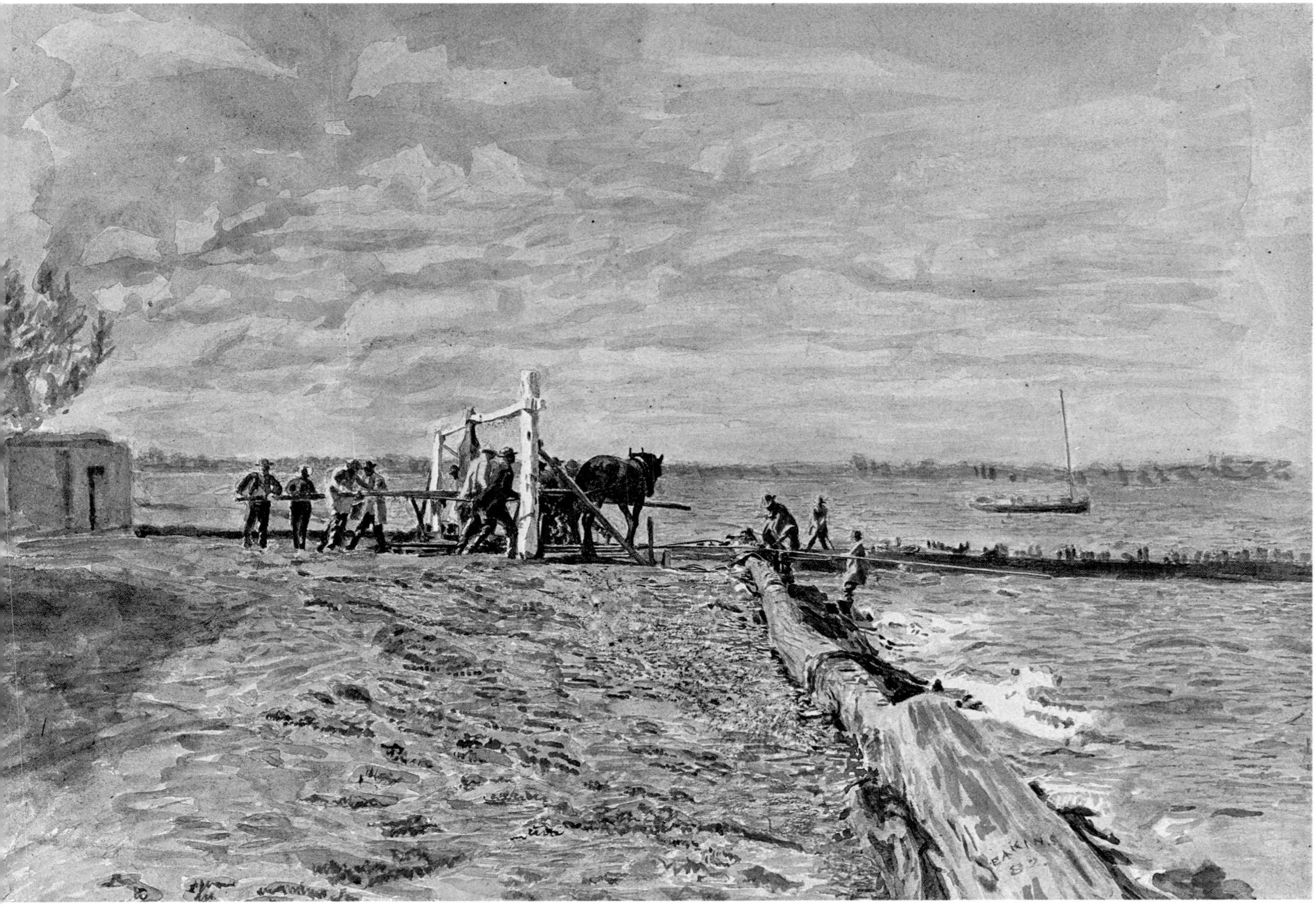
EAKINS
82

Plate 28
IN THE STUDIO
ca. 1884
21″ x 17″ (53.3 cm. x 43.2 cm.)
Philadelphia Museum of Art

The finished oil study (Figure 12) for the watercolor is dated 1884, and establishes the relationship of this composition to the portrait of Eakins' wife, *Portrait of a Lady with a Setter Dog*, painted about 1885. The similarity in costume and the use of Eakins' red setter dog, Harry—who is shown lying on the floor beside the subject of both paintings—reinforces that relationship. The identity of the girl in the composition *In the Studio* is unknown; however, it has been established that she was another of his students at the Academy. Although the watercolor version is one of Eakins' least finished works, the abstract division of the picture into nearly equal dark and light halves is visually engaging. The very subtle, but convincing notations which constitute all of the modeling in the figure do achieve a convincing shorthand for describing form. Although this subject is essentially a reworking of *Young Girl Meditating* (Plate 11) of 1877, a comparison between the two reveals Eakins' advancement in watercolor technique.

Figure 12. *In the Studio*, 1884, oil on canvas, 22¼″ x 18¼″ (56.5 cm. x 46.3 cm.). The Hyde Collection.

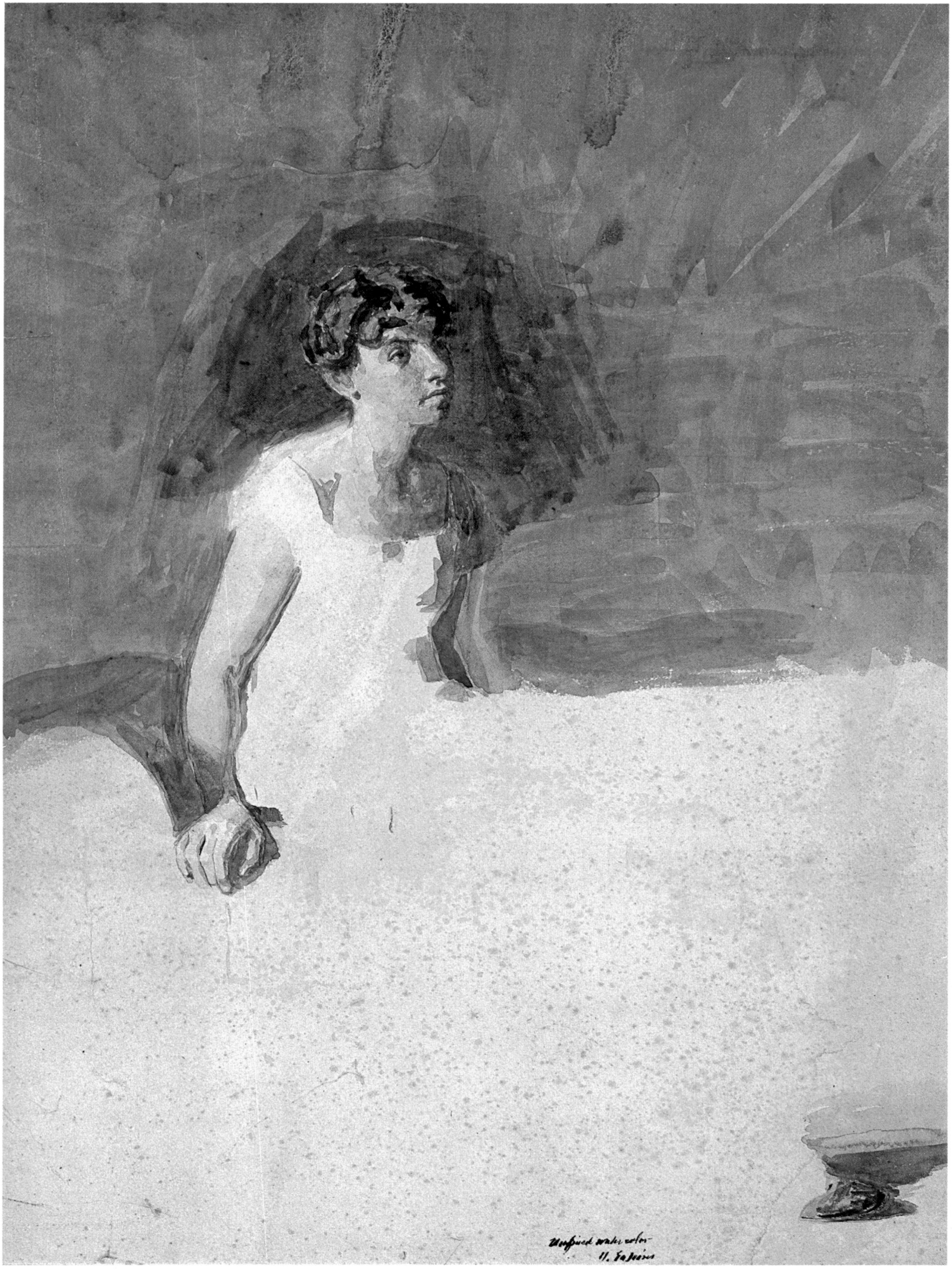
Unfinished water color
H. Eakins

Plate 29
IN THE STUDIO
Detail of Plate 28, Actual Size

Plate 30
COWBOY SINGING
ca. 1890
18″ x 14″ (45.7 cm. x 35.5 cm.)
The Metropolitan Museum of Art, Fletcher Fund, 1925

In the summer of 1887, Eakins made a trip to North Dakota. There he discovered what was, for him, an entirely new subject: the life of the American cowboy. During his stay in the west, he worked in oil on canvas mounted on cardboard, usually on a small scale. After his return to Philadelphia in the fall of 1887, he began translating these rapid sketches, both of landscape and figure subjects, into finished works.

While he was in the west, Eakins had not only bought several suits of buckskin clothing, but had acquired two western horses as well. *Cowboy Singing* was posed in the Mt. Vernon Street studio. Eakins dressed his friend, the painter, Franklin L. Schenck (1885-1926), in a suit of buckskin. Schenck had been a pupil of Eakins at the Art Students League of Philadelphia and was its second curator. Goodrich described him as having "a poetic, unworldly temperament, he afterwards lived like a hermit on Long Island, raising all his own food and painting romantic landscapes suggestive of Blakelock. He was fond of singing and playing the guitar."

There are two oil versions of this subject, both slightly larger than the watercolor. The first version, *Home Ranch* (Philadelphia Museum of Art), appears with supporting details: behind the cowboy, who is playing a guitar, there is another man in the right background, seated at a table and holding a fork, while a black cat rubs against the table leg. This would seem to be Eakins' attempt to create a naturalistic bunkhouse scene. In the second oil version (Figure 13), Schenck also appears, but is now playing a banjo, rather than a guitar (as in *Home Ranch*), and is turned half left.

Figure 13. *Cowboy Singing*, ca. 1890, oil on canvas, 24″ x 20″ (60.9 cm. x 50.8 cm.). Philadelphia Museum of Art.

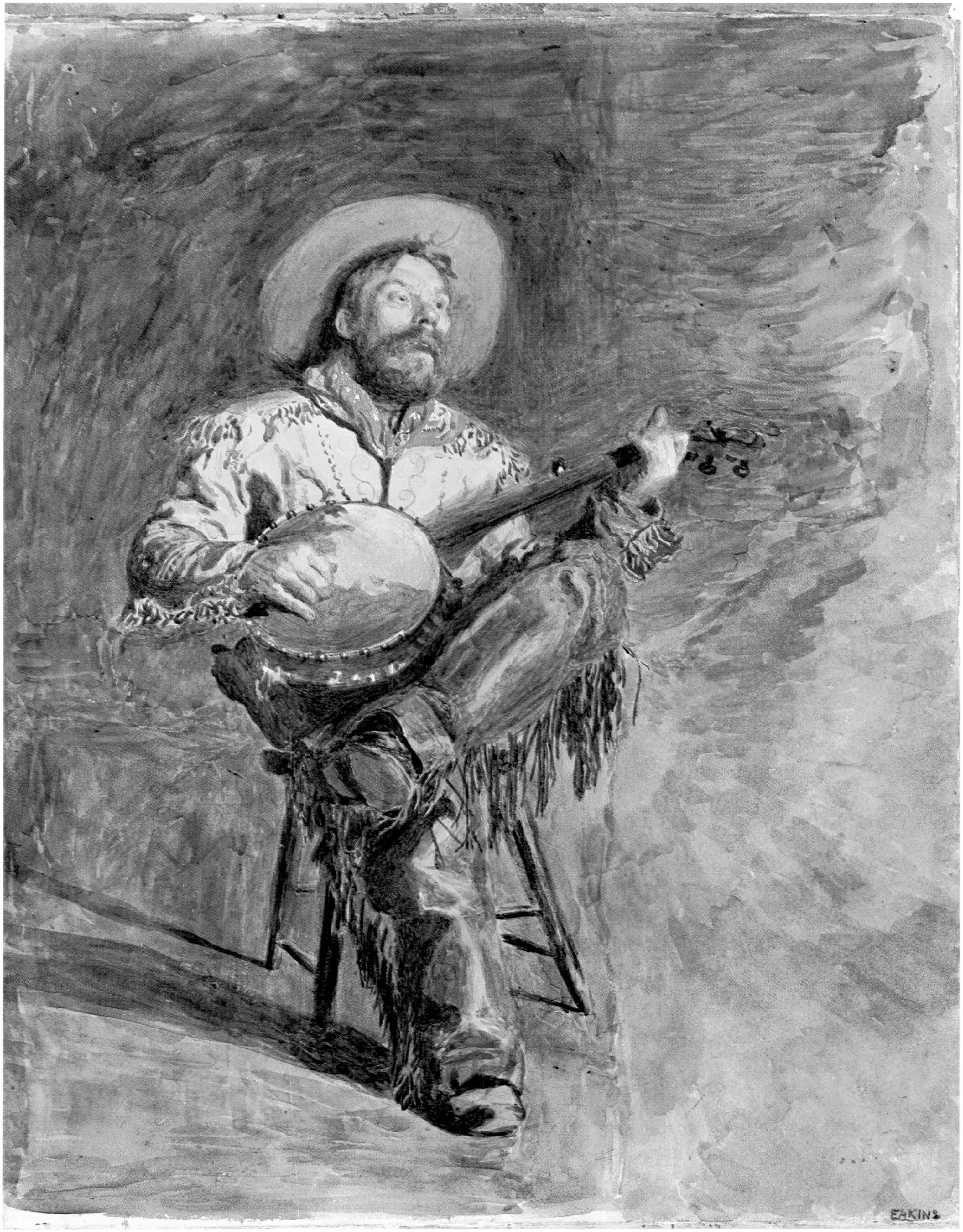
EAKINS

Plate 31
COWBOY SINGING
Detail of Plate 30, Actual Size

The watercolor appears somewhat unfinished, especially at the right edge of the composition, indicating perhaps that Eakins intended to finish the work in keeping with Figure 13. The watercolor contains a solitary figure who seems to be illuminated by a fire, suggesting a bunkhouse interior. While the subject matter is full of potential for a highly romantic sentimental treatment, Eakins gives us nothing of the sort. Schenck is made to appear natural in his clothes—so strange to his real personality—and the scene is entirely believable.

When *Home Ranch*, the oil painting of this subject, was submitted to the Carnegie International Exhibition in 1896, it was rejected. Today, it is difficult to understand why such a forthright and honest work would find rejection at the hands of a jury as late as 1896. Perhaps the answer is that the west had been thoroughly romanticized by artists like Frederic Remington (1861-1909), who provided an acceptable romantic mirror for a false image.

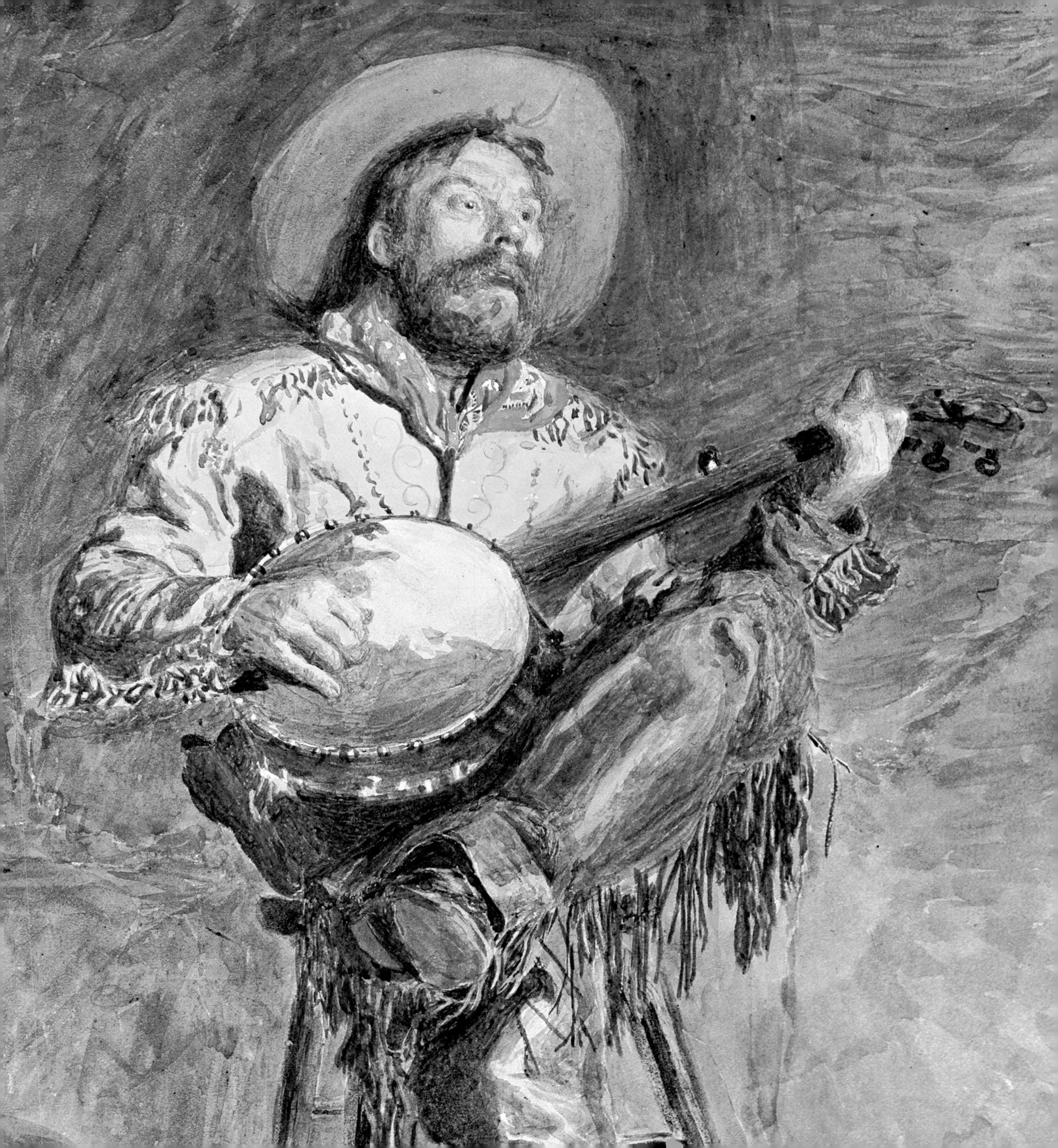

Plate 32
PORTRAIT OF WILLIAM H. MACDOWELL
ca. 1891
27" x 21½" (68.6 cm. x 54.6 cm.)
The Baltimore Museum of Art

When Eakins married Susan Macdowell in January, 1884, he acquired a father-in-law of unusual character, with whom he formed a lifelong friendship. Like Eakins' own father, Macdowell had been a craftsman, working in the art of engraving. On occasion, Macdowell and the elder Eakins collaborated, the former providing the engraved plate, while the latter added the engrossing to the blank spaces in the printed engraving. Macdowell was regarded as a freethinker; his favorite personality in American history was the Revolutionary writer, Thomas Paine. Macdowell was, as Goodrich remarked, "fond of new ideas and lively argument." The atmosphere of the Macdowell home in Philadelphia must have even been freer than that at the Eakins home. Susan had been reared in an environment which was, therefore, very close to the character of the Eakins home.

Over a period of about fourteen years, Eakins painted six portraits of his father-in-law. The oil study illustrated here (Figure 14) is the second of two portraits painted in 1891 in preparation for the watercolor scaled to the same size. The oil portrait is painted in a noticeably heavy impasto technique and is squared off for transfer to the watercolor paper. Eakins never completed the watercolor, and it remains a tentative exercise in his use of the medium. In both versions, the characterization of William Macdowell is penetrating and poignant. The angular face and piercing eyes which gaze out querulously, the fingers of the left hand, gnarled by years of work, comprise one of Eakins' most moving statements in the art of portraiture.

Figure 14. *Portrait of William H. Macdowell*, ca. 1891, oil on canvas, 28" x 22" (71.1 cm. x 55.8 cm.). Randolph-Macon Woman's College.

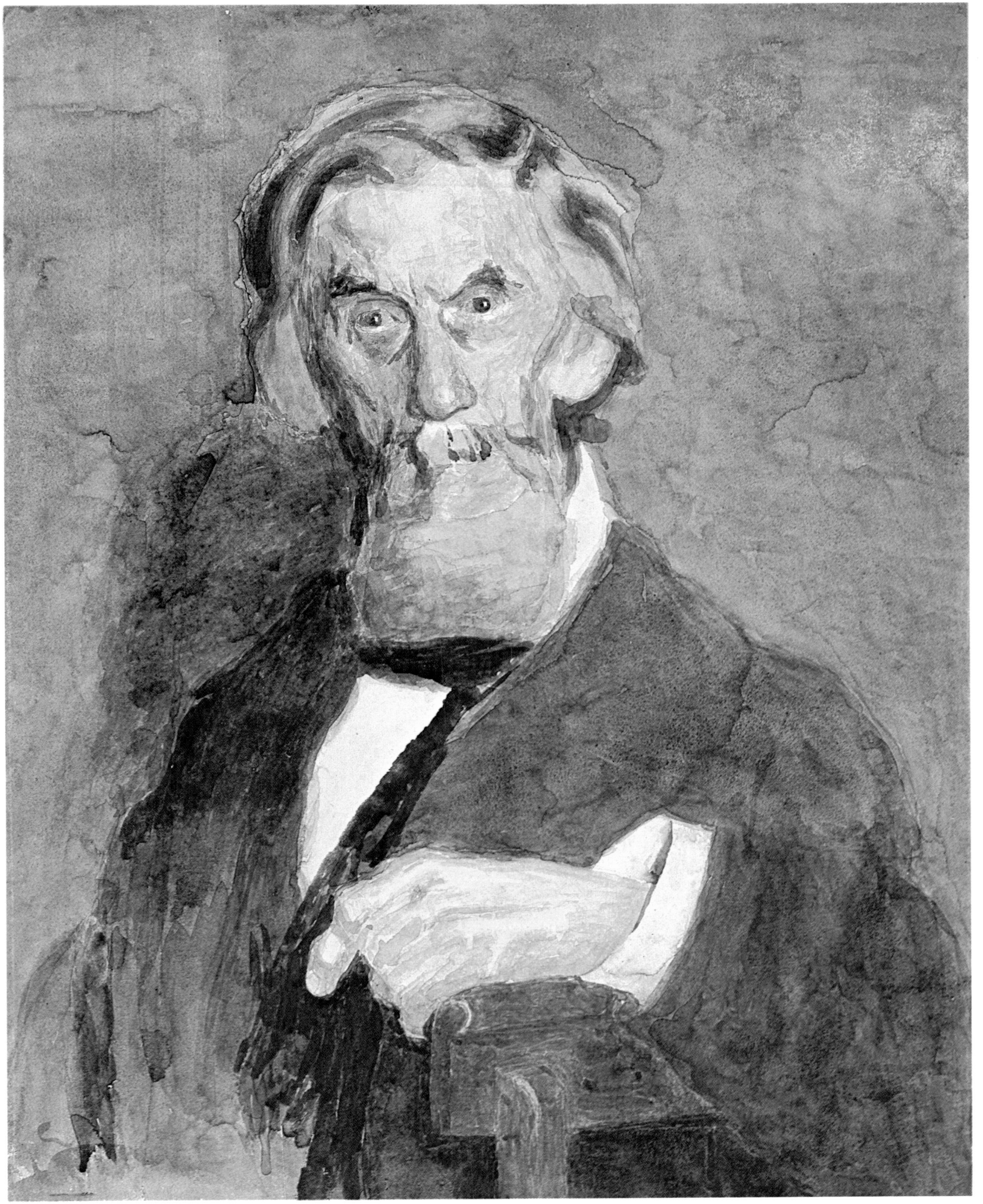

INDEX

Edited by Donald Holden and Margit Malmstrom
Designed by James Craig and Robert Fillie
Graphic Coordination by Frank DeLuca
Set in 10 point Janson by York Typesetting Co., Inc.
Printed in Japan by Toppan Printing Company, Ltd.